Early praise for *Rails 4 Test Prescriptions*

Rails 4 Test Prescriptions is quite simply the best book on the market on the topic of testing Rails applications. It's full of distilled wisdom from Noel's many years of experience. I especially love the emphasis on thinking through the tradeoffs involved in picking a test strategy; in my experience, thinking intentionally about those tradeoffs is one of the most important steps you can take toward building an effective test suite.

➤ **Myron Marston**
    Lead maintainer of RSpec and creator of the VCR gem

Rails 4 Test Prescriptions will benefit both developers new to test-driven development and those who are more experienced with it. Noel Rappin presents concepts like mocking and stubbing in a very detailed but also approachable and entertaining way. I loved the first edition of this book, and the second is even better. I highly recommend it!

➤ **Nell Shamrell-Harrington**
    Senior developer, PhishMe

If anyone asks me how to master testing in Rails applications, I will tell them to read this book first.

➤ **Avdi Grimm**
    Head chef, RubyTapas

Sometimes testing sucks. This book magically makes testing not suck; it makes it easy and rewarding with well-written explanations. It is the essential resource for any developer testing Rails applications. It's more than just a testing primer; developers will learn how to create optimal and efficient test suites for Rails. A must-read for beginners and seasoned programmers alike.

➤ **Liz Abinante**
    Software engineer, New Relic

Rails 4 Test Prescriptions

Build a Healthy Codebase

Noel Rappin

The Pragmatic Bookshelf

Dallas, Texas • Raleigh, North Carolina

Many of the designations used by manufacturers and sellers to distinguish their products are claimed as trademarks. Where those designations appear in this book, and The Pragmatic Programmers, LLC was aware of a trademark claim, the designations have been printed in initial capital letters or in all capitals. The Pragmatic Starter Kit, The Pragmatic Programmer, Pragmatic Programming, Pragmatic Bookshelf, PragProg and the linking g device are trademarks of The Pragmatic Programmers, LLC.

Every precaution was taken in the preparation of this book. However, the publisher assumes no responsibility for errors or omissions, or for damages that may result from the use of information (including program listings) contained herein.

Our Pragmatic courses, workshops, and other products can help you and your team create better software and have more fun. For more information, as well as the latest Pragmatic titles, please visit us at *https://pragprog.com*.

The team that produced this book includes:

Lynn Beighley (editor)
Potomac Indexing, LLC (indexer)
Candace Cunningham (copyeditor)
Dave Thomas (typesetter)
Janet Furlow (producer)
Ellie Callahan (support)

For international rights, please contact *rights@pragprog.com*.

Printed in the United States of America.
ISBN-13: 978-1-941222-19-5
Printed on acid-free paper.
Book version: P1.0—December 2014

Contents

Acknowledgments

It's been six years since I first started working on a book called *Rails Test Prescriptions*. In that time, many people have helped me make this book better than I could have made it on my own. This includes but is by no means limited to the following people.

Without the encouragement of Brian Hogan and Gregg Pollack, this might still be a self-published book. Brian also provided a valuable review of this edition.

Lynn Beighley has been my editor on this version of the project and has shaped the material this time around. I've worked with Susannah Pfalzer on all my Pragmatic projects, and she's always been helpful and great to work with.

Many technical people reviewed this book and had their comments incorporated. They include Liz Abinante, Ashish Dixit, Mike Gehard, Derek Graham, Avdi Grimm, Sean Hussey, John Ivanoff, Evan Light, Myron Marston, Kerri Miller, Tim Morton, Matt Rohrer, Nell Shamrell, Brian Van Loo, and Andy Waite.

I've been very fortunate to be working at Table XI while writing this book. Not only have they been very supportive of the project; I've also had the chance to get insights and corrections from my very skilled coworkers.

This book is a commercial product built on the time and generosity of developers who create amazing tools and release them to the world for free. Thanks to all of you.

My family has always been encouraging. Thanks to my children, Emma and Elliot, who are more amazing and awesome than I ever could have hoped. And thanks to my wife Erin, the best part of my life and my favorite person. I love you very much.

## CHAPTER 1

Introduction

Test-driven development, or TDD, is the counterintuitive idea that developers will improve both the design and the accuracy of their code by writing the code test-first. When adding new logic to a program, the TDD process starts by writing an automated test describing the behavior of code that does not yet exist. In a strict TDD process, new logic is added to the program only after a failing test is written to prompt the creation of the logic.

Writing tests before code, rather than after, allows your tests to help guide the design of your code in small, incremental steps. Over time this creates a well-factored codebase that is easy to change.

We'll apply the TDD process to the creation of applications using Ruby and Rails. We'll talk about how to apply TDD to your daily coding and about the tools and libraries that make testing in Rails easier.

But first let me tell you a story.

A Test-Driven Fable

Imagine two programmers working on the same task. Both are equally skilled, charming, and delightful people, motivated to do a high-quality job as quickly as possible. The task is not trivial but not wildly complex either; for the sake of discussion, let's say it's a new user logging in to a website and entering some detailed pertinent information.

The first developer, who we'll call Sam, says, "This is pretty easy, and I've done it before. I don't need to write tests." And in five minutes Sam has a working method ready to verify.

Our second developer is named Jamie. Jamie says, "I need to write some tests." Jamie starts writing a test describing the desired behavior. The test is executable and passes if the corresponding code matches the test. Writing the test takes about five minutes. Five additional minutes later, Jamie also has a working method, which passes the test and is ready to verify. Because this is a fable, we are going to assume that Sam is allergic to automated testing, while Jamie is similarly averse to manually verifying against the app in the browser.

At this point you might expect me to say that even though it has taken Jamie more time to write the method, Jamie has written code that is more likely to be correct, robust, and easy to maintain. That's true. I am going to say that. But I'm also going to say that there's a good chance Jamie will be done before Sam even though Jamie is taking on the additional overhead of writing tests.

Let's watch our programmers as they keep working. Sam has a five-minute lead, but both of them need to verify their work. Sam needs to test in a browser; we said the task requires a user to log in. Let's say it takes Sam one minute to log in and perform the task to verify the code in a development environment. Jamie verifies by running the test—that takes about ten seconds. (At this point Jamie has to run only one test, not the entire suite.)

Perhaps it takes each developer three tries to get it right. Since running the test is faster than verifying in the browser, Jamie gains a little bit each try. After verifying the code three times, Jamie is only two and a half minutes behind Sam. (In a slight nod to reality, let's assume that both of them need to verify one last time in the browser once they think they are done. Since they both need to do this, it's not an advantage for either one.)

At this point, with the task complete, both break for lunch (a burrito for Jamie, an egg salad sandwich for Sam). After lunch they start on the next task, which is a special case of the first task. Jamie has most of the test setup in place, so writing the test takes only two minutes. Still, it's not looking good for Jamie, even after another three rounds trying to get the code right. Jamie remains a solid two minutes behind Sam.

Let's get to the punch line. Sam and Jamie are both conscientious programmers, and they want to clean up their code with a little *refactoring*, meaning that they are improving the code's structure without changing its behavior. Now Sam is in trouble. Each time Sam tries the refactoring, it takes two minutes to verify both tasks, but Jamie's test suite still takes only about ten seconds. After three more tries to get the refactoring right, Jamie finishes the whole thing and checks it in three and a half minutes ahead of Sam. (Jamie then catches a train home and has a pleasant evening. Sam just misses the train and gets caught in a sudden rainstorm. If only Sam had run tests.)

My story is simplified, but look at all the things I didn't assume. I didn't assume that Jamie spent less actual time on task, and I didn't assume that the tests would help Jamie find errors more easily—although I think Jamie would, in fact, find errors more easily. (Of course, I also didn't assume that Jamie would have to track down a broken test in some other part of the application.)

It is frequently faster to run multiple verifications of your code as an automated test than to always check manually. And that advantage only increases as the code gets more complex. And the automated check will do a better job of ensuring steps aren't forgotten.

There are many beneficial side effects of having accurate tests. You'll have better-designed code in which you'll have more confidence. But the most important benefit is that if you do testing well, your work will go faster. You may not see it at first, but at some point in a well-run test-driven project, you'll notice that you have fewer bugs and that the bugs that do exist are easier to find. It will be easier to add new features and modify existing ones. You'll be doing better on the only code-quality metric that has any validity: how easy it is to find incorrect behavior and add new behavior. One reason why it is sometimes hard to pin down the benefit of testing is that good testing often just feels like you are doing a really good job programming.

Of course, it doesn't always work out that way. The tests might have bugs. They might be slow. Environmental issues may mean things that work in a test environment won't work in a development environment. Code changes will break tests. Adding tests to existing code is a pain. As with any other programming tool, there are a lot of ways to cause yourself pain with testing.

Who You Are

This book's goal is to show you how to apply a test-driven process and automated testing as you build your Rails application. Being test-driven allows you to use testing to explore your code's design. We will see what tools are available and discuss when those tools are best used. Tools come and tools go, so I'm really hoping you come away from this book committed to the idea of writing better code through the small steps of a test-driven or behavior-driven development process.

I'm assuming some things about you.

I'm assuming you are already comfortable with Ruby and Rails and that you don't need this book to explain how to get started creating a Rails application in and of itself. I am *not* assuming you have any particular familiarity with testing frameworks or testing tools used within Rails.

Over the course of this book, we'll go through the tools that are available for writing tests, and we'll talk about them with an eye toward making them useful in building your application. This is Rails, so naturally I have my own opinions, but the goal with all the tools and all the advice is the same: to help you to write great applications that do cool things and still catch the train home.

Testing First Drives Design

Success with test-driven development starts with trusting the process. The classic process goes like this:

1. Create a test. The test should be short and test for one thing in your code. The test should run automatically.

2. Make sure the test fails. Verifying the test failure before you write code helps ensure that the test really does what you expect.

3. Write the simplest code that could possibly make the test pass. Don't worry about good code yet. Don't look ahead. Sometimes, write just enough code to clear the current error.

4. After the test passes, refactor to improve the code. Clean up duplication. Optimize. Create new abstractions. Refactoring is a key part of design, so don't skip this. Remember to run the tests again to make sure you haven't changed any behavior.

Repeat until done. This will, in theory, ensure that your code is always as simple as possible and is always completely covered by tests. We'll spend most of this book talking about how to best manage this process using the tools of the Rails ecosystem and solving the kinds of problems that you get in a modern web application. And we'll talk about the difference between "in theory" and "in practice."

If you use this process, you will find that it changes the design of your code.

Software design is a tricky thing to pin down. We use the term all the time without really defining it. For our purposes, *design* is anything in the way the code is structured that goes beyond the logical correctness of the code. You can design software for many different reasons—optimization for speed, clarity of naming, robustness against errors, resistance to change, ease of maintenance....

Test-driven development enables you to design your software continuously and in small steps, allowing the design to respond to the changes in the code.

Specifically, design happens at three different points in the test-driven process:

- When you decide which test to write next, you are making a claim about what functionality your code should have. This frequently involves thinking about how to add that functionality to the existing code, which is a design question.
- As you write a test, you are designing the interaction between the test and the code, which is also the interaction between the part of the code under test and the rest of the application. This part of the process is used to create the API you want the code to have.
- After the test passes, you refactor, identifying duplication, missing abstractions, and other places where the code's design can be improved.

Prescription 1	Use the TDD process to create and adjust your code's design in small, incremental steps.

Continually aligning your code to the tests tends to result in code that is made up of small methods, each of which does one thing. These methods tend to be loosely coupled and have minimal side effects. As it happens, the hallmark of easy-to-change code is small methods that do one thing, are loosely coupled, and have minimal side effects.

I used to think it was a coincidence that tested code and easy-to-change code have similar structures, but I've realized the commonality is a direct side effect of building the code in tandem with the tests. In essence, the tests act as a universal client for the entire codebase, guiding all the code to have clean interactions between parts because the tests, acting as a third-party interloper, have to get in between all the parts of the code to work. Metaphorically, compared to code written without tests, your code has more surface area and less work happening behind the scenes where it is hard to observe.

This theory explains why testing works so much better when the tests come first. Even waiting a little bit to write tests is significantly more painful. When the tests are written first, in very close intertwined proximity to the code, they encourage a good structure with low coupling (meaning different parts of the code have minimal dependencies on each other) and high cohesion (meaning code that is in the same unit is all related).

When the tests come later, they have to conform to the existing code, and it's amazing how quickly code written without tests will move toward low-cohesion and high-coupling forms that are much harder to cover with tests. If your only experience is with writing automated tests long after the initial code was written, the experience was likely quite painful. Don't let that turn you away from a TDD approach; the tests and code you will write with TDD are much different.

When you are writing truly test-driven code, the tests are the final source of truth in your application. This means that when there is a discrepancy between the code and the tests, your first assumption is that the test is correct and the code is wrong. If you're writing tests after the code, then your assumption must be that the code is the source of truth. As you write your code using test-driven development, keep in mind the idea that the tests are the source of truth and are guiding the code's structure.

> **Prescription 2** In a test-driven process, if it is difficult to write tests for a feature, strongly consider the possibility that the underlying code needs to be changed.

What Is TDD Good For?

The primary purpose of test-driven development is to go beyond mere verification and use the tests to improve the code's structure. That is, TDD is a software-development technique masquerading as a code-verification tool.

Automated tests are a wonderful way of showing that the program does what the developer thinks it does, but they are a lousy way of showing that what the developer thinks is what the program actually should do. "But the tests pass!" is not likely to be comforting to a customer when the developer's assumptions are just flat-out wrong. I speak from painful experience.

The kinds of tests written in a TDD process are not a substitute for acceptance testing, where users or customers verify that the code does what the user or customer expects. TDD also does not replace some kind of quality-assurance phase where users or testers pound away at the actual program trying to break something.

Further, TDD does not replace the role of a traditional software tester. It is a development process that produces better and more accurate code. A separate verification phase run by people who are not the original developers is still a good idea. For a thorough overview of more traditional exploratory testing, read *Explore It! [Hen13]*.

Verification is valuable, but the idea of verification can be taken too far. You sometimes see an argument against test-driven development that says, "The purpose of testing is to verify that my program is correct. I can never prove correctness with 100 percent certainty. Therefore, testing has no value." (Behavior-driven development and RSpec were created, in part, to combat this attitude.) Ultimately, though, testing has a lot of positive benefits to offer for coding, even beyond verification.

Preventing regression is often presented as one of the paramount benefits of a test-driven development process. And if you are expecting me to disagree out of spite, you're out of luck. Being able to squash regressions before anybody else sees them is one of the key ways in which strict testing will speed up your development over time.

You may have heard that automated tests provide an alternate method of documenting your program—that the tests, in essence, provide a detailed functional specification of the program's behavior. That's the theory. My experience with tests acting as documentation is mixed, to say the least. Still, it's useful to keep this in mind as a goal, and most of the things that make tests work better as documentation will also make the tests work better, period.

To make your tests effective as documentation, focus on giving them names that describe the reason for their existence, keeping tests short, and refactoring out common features such as test setup. The documentation advantage of refactoring includes removing clutter from the test itself—when a test has a lot of raggedy setup and assertions, it can be hard for a reader to focus on the important features. As you'll see, a test that requires a bunch of tricky setup often indicates a problem in the underlying code. Also, with common features factored out it's easier to focus on what's different in each individual test.

In a testing environment, blank-page problems are almost completely nonexistent. I can always think of something that the program needs to do, so I write a test for that. When you're working test-first, the order in which pieces are written is not so important. Once a test is written, the path to the next one is usually more clear: find some way to specify something the code doesn't do yet.

When TDD Needs Some Help

Test-driven development is very helpful, but it won't solve all of your development problems by itself. There are areas where developer testing doesn't apply or doesn't work very well.

I mentioned one case already: developer tests are not very good at determining whether the application is behaving correctly according to requirements. Strict TDD is not great at acceptance testing. There are, however, automated tools that do try to tackle acceptance testing. Within the Rails community, the most prominent of these is Cucumber; see Chapter 10, *Integration Testing with Capybara and Cucumber*, on page 177. Cucumber can be integrated with TDD—you'll sometimes see this called outside-in testing. That's a perfectly valid and useful test paradigm, but it's an extension of the classic TDD process.

Testing your application assumes that you know the right answer to specify. And although you sometimes have clear requirements or a definitive source of correct output, other times you don't know what exactly the program needs to do. In this exploratory mode, TDD is less beneficial, because it's hard to write tests if you don't know what assertions to make about the program. Often this lack of direction happens during initial development or during a proof of concept. I also find myself in this position a lot when view-testing—I don't know what to test for until I get some of the view up and visible.

The TDD process has a name for the kind of exploratory code you write while trying to figure out the needed functionality: *spike*, as in, "I don't know if we can do what we need with the Twitter API; let's spend a day working on a spike for it." When working in spike mode, TDD is generally not used, but code written during the spike is not expected to be used in production; it's just a proof of concept to be thrown away and replaced with a version written using TDD.

When view-testing, or in other nonspike situations where I'm not quite sure what output to test for, I often go into a "test-next" mode, where I write the code first but in a TDD-sized small chunk, and then immediately write the test. This works as long as I make the switch between test and code frequently enough to get the benefit of having the code and test inform each other's design.

TDD is not a complete solution for verifying your application. We've already talked about acceptance tests; it's also true that TDD tends to be thin in terms of the quantity of unit tests written. For one thing, in a strict TDD process you would never write a test that you expect to pass before writing more code. In practice, though, you will do this all the time. Sometimes I see and create an abstraction in the code but there are still valid test cases to write. In particular, I'll often write code for potential error conditions even if I think they are already covered in the code. It's a balance because you lose some of the benefit of TDD by creating too many test cases that don't drive code changes. One way to keep the balance is to make a list of the test cases before you start writing the tests—that way you'll remember to cover all the interesting cases.

And some things are just hard. In particular, some parts of your application will be very dependent on an external piece of code in a way that makes it difficult to isolate them for unit testing. Test doubles, which are special kinds of objects that can stand in for objects that are part of your application, are one way to work around this issue; see Chapter 7, *Using Test Doubles as Mocks and Stubs*, on page 117. But there are definitely cases (though they're not common) in which the cost of testing a complex feature is higher than the value of the tests.

Recent discussions in the Rails community have debated whether TDD's design benefits are even valuable. You may have heard the phrase "test-driven design damage." I strongly believe that TDD, and the relatively smaller and more numerous classes that a TDD process often brings, do result in more clear and more valuable code. But the TDD process is not a replacement for good design instincts; it's still possible to create bad code when testing, or even to create bad code in the name of testing.

Words to Live By

* Any change to the program logic should be driven by a failed test.

- If it's not tested, it's broken.

- Testing is supposed to help for the long term. The long term starts tomorrow, or maybe after lunch.

- It's not done until it works.

- Tests are code; refactor them, too.

- Start a bug fix by writing a test.

- Tests monitor the quality of your codebase. If it becomes difficult to write tests, it often means your codebase is too interdependent.

A Word About Tools, Best Practices, and Teaching TDD

There are two test libraries in general use in the Rails community—Minitest and RSpec—meaning I had a choice of which tool to use as the primary library in this book. The book is about how to test Rails in general, and therefore the details of the testing library in use are secondary to most of it, but still, the examples have to be presented using one tool or the other.

Minitest is part of the Ruby Standard Library and is therefore available everywhere you might use Ruby (1.9 and up). It has a straightforward syntax that is the Ruby translation of the original SUnit and JUnit libraries (for Smalltalk and Java, respectively), and it is the default alternative for a new Rails project.

RSpec is a separate testing tool designed to support an emphasis on specifying behavior rather than implementation, sometimes called behavior-driven development (BDD). Rather than using terms like "test" and "assert," RSpec uses "expect" and "describe." BDD emphasizes setting expectations about the code not yet written rather than assertions about code in the past.

RSpec has a quirky, metaprogrammed syntax with a certain "love it or hate it" vibe. It's more flexible, which means more expressive and more complicated, and it has a larger ecosystem of related tools.

The primary testing tool used in this book is RSpec because after going back and forth quite a bit, I've decided that its expressiveness makes it easier to work with over the course of the entire book, even if it has a slightly steeper learning curve. That said, there's a whole chapter on Minitest, and we'll discuss most of the extra tools in a way that references both RSpec and Minitest. Every RSpec example in the downloadable code has a corresponding Minitest version.

That leads to a more general point: sometimes the best practice for learning isn't the best practice for experts. In some cases in this book we'll use relatively verbose or explicit versions of tools or tests to make it clear what the testing is trying to do and how. In particular, for clarity I've tried not to use multiple extra tools at once. For example, we discuss factory_girl as a way to create data for your tests, but we don't use factory_girl in examples that are intended to highlight, say, Capybara. I intend to focus each example on one tool or technique.

Coming Up Next

The next two chapters of this book will walk through a tutorial creating tests for a new Rails application. In Chapter 2, *Test-Driven Development Basics*, on page 13, we'll start testing without using Rails-specific features. Then in Chapter 3, *Test-Driven Rails*, on page 41, we'll start to test Rails functionality. Then we'll talk a bit about what makes testing and tests most valuable.

After that we'll spend a few chapters going through the basic blocks of a Rails program, testing models, then controllers and views. We'll also talk about test doubles, which help prevent slow or dangerous code from being called during test runs.

Then we'll talk about alternative tools, spending a chapter on Minitest and a chapter on the integration-test tools Capybara and Cucumber.

Once we're done talking about tools, we'll cover specific scenarios for testing, including testing for security, testing third-party services, and testing Java-Script. We'll talk about troubleshooting failing tests and how to improve your test environment and run your tests quickly. And we'll end with the very common case where you need to add tests to untested legacy code.

Changes in the Second Edition

A lot has changed in the Rails testing world over the past five years, even if the general principles have stayed more or less the same. The entire community, including me, has had five more years of experience with these tools, building bigger and better applications, learning what tools work, what tools scale, and what tools don't.

This book has been nearly entirely rewritten from its first edition to reflect these changes.

Here's an overview:

- The primary test tool for all examples is now RSpec.

- All tools have been upgraded to their latest versions: Ruby 2.1.2, Rails 4.1.x, Minitest 5.3.x, RSpec 3.1, and so on.

- The opening tutorial was completely rewritten. It's an all-new example that provides, I hope, a more gentle introduction to testing in Rails.

- The code samples are better in general. In the first edition a lot of the samples after the tutorial were not part of the distributed code. Most of the samples in this book tie back to the tutorial and are runnable.

- The JavaScript chapter is almost completely new to reflect changes both in tools and in the scope of JavaScript in most Rails applications.

- I've written all-new chapters on testing external services, testing for security, and debugging and troubleshooting.

- There's a new chapter on running tests more efficiently, looking at both the Spring preloader option and the plain old Ruby object option (which does not involve loading Rails).

- More emphasis on using testing in practice, and somewhat less on duplicating reference information.

- More emphasis on using tests as a guide to design and being more explicit about test design itself.

- Some things that were full chapters in the first edition are now covered sparingly if at all: Shoulda (since it's not really used anymore), Rails core integration tests (in favor of spending more time on Capybara), Rcov, and Rails core performance testing.

## CHAPTER 2

Test-Driven Development Basics

You have a problem.

You are the team leader for a development team that is distributed across multiple locations. You'd like to be able to maintain a common list of tasks for the team. For each task, you'd like to maintain data such as the status of the task, which pair of developers the task is assigned to, and so on. You'd also like to be able to use the past rate of task completion to estimate the project's completion date. For some reason none of the existing tools that do this are suitable (work with me here, folks) and so you've decided to roll your own. We'll call it Gatherer.

As you sit down to start working on Gatherer, your impulse is going to be to start writing code immediately. That's a great impulse, and we're just going to turn it about ten degrees east. Instead of starting off by writing code, we're going to start off by writing tests.

In our introductory chapter we talked about why you might work test-first. In this chapter we'll look at the basic mechanics of a TDD cycle by building a feature in a Rails application. We'll start by creating some business logic with our models, because model logic is the easiest part of a Rails application to test—in fact, most of this chapter won't touch Rails at all. In the next chapter we'll start testing the controller and view parts of the Rails framework.

Infrastructure

First off, we'll need a Rails application. We'll be using Rails 4.1.7 and Ruby 2.1.4; use of Ruby 2.0–specific features will be minimal.

We'll start by generating the Rails application from the command line:

```
% rails new gatherer
```

This will create the initial directory structure and code for a Rails application. It will also run bundle install to load initial gems. I assume that you are already familiar with Rails core concepts, I won't spend a lot of time re-explaining them. If you are not familiar with Rails, *Agile Web Development with Rails [RTH13]* is still the gold standard for getting started.

We need to create our databases. For ease of setup and distribution we'll stick to the Rails default, which is SQLite. (You'll need to have SQLite installed; see http://www.sqlite.org for details if it is not already on your machine.)

```
% cd gatherer
% rake db:create:all
% rake db:migrate
```

We need the db:migrate call even though we haven't actually created a database migration, because it sets up the schema.rb file that Rails uses to rebuild the test database. In Rails 4.1 the test database is automatically maintained when the schema.rb file changes.

The Requirements

The most complex business logic we need to build concerns forecasting a project's progress. We want to be able to predict the end date of a project and determine whether that project is on schedule or not.

In other words, given a project and a set of tasks, some of which are done and some of which are not, use the rate at which tasks are being completed to estimate the project's end date. Also, compare that projected date to a deadline to determine if the project is on time.

This is a good example problem for TDD because, while I have a sense of what the answer is, I don't have a very strong sense of the best way to structure the algorithm. TDD will help, guiding me toward reasonable code design.

Installing RSpec

Before we start testing, we'll need to load RSpec, our testing library.

We'll be talking about RSpec 3, which has some significant syntactical differences from previous versions. We'll largely ignore those differences and focus on only the new syntax.

To add RSpec to a Rails project, add the rspec-rails gem to your Gemfile:

```
group :development, :test do
  gem 'rspec-rails', '~> 3.1'
end
```

The rspec-rails gem depends on the rspec gem proper. The rspec gem is mostly a list of other dependencies where the real work gets done, including rspec-core, rspec-expectations, and rspec-mocks. Sometimes rspec and rspec-rails are updated separately; you might choose to explicitly specify both versions in the Gemfile. Also, rspec goes in the development group as well as the test group so that you can call rspec from the command line, where development mode is the default. (RSpec switches to the test environment as it initializes.)

Install with bundle install. Then we need to generate some installation files using the rspec:install generator:

```
$ bundle install
$ rails generate rspec:install
      create   .rspec
      create   spec
      create   spec/spec_helper.rb
      create   spec/rails_helper.rb
```

This generator creates the following:

- The .rspec file, where RSpec run options go. In RSpec 3.1 the default currently sets two options, --color, which sets terminal output in color, and --require spec_helper, which ensures that the spec_helper file is always required.
- The spec directory, which is where your specs go. RSpec does not automatically create subdirectories like controller and model on installation. The subdirectories can be created manually or will be created by Rails generators as needed.
- The spec_helper.rb and rails_helper.rb files, which contain setup information. The spec_helper.rb file contains general RSpec settings while the rails_helper.rb file, which requires spec_helper, loads the Rails environment and contains settings that depend on Rails. The idea behind having two files is to make it easier to write specs that do not load Rails.

The rspec-rails gem does a couple of other things when loaded in a Rails project:

- Adds a Rake file that changes the default Rake test to run RSpec instead of Minitest and defines a number of subtasks such as spec:models that filter an RSpec run to a subset of the overall RSpec suite.
- Sets itself up as the test framework of choice for the purposes of future Rails generators. Later, when you set up, say, a generated model or resource, RSpec's generators are automatically invoked to create appropriate spec files.

Where to Start?

"Where do I start testing?" is one of the most common questions that people have when they start with TDD. Traditionally, my answer is a somewhat glib "start anywhere." While true, this is less than helpful.

A good option for starting a TDD cycle is to specify the initialization state of the objects or methods under test. Another is the "happy path"—a single representative example of the error-free version of the algorithm. Which starting point you choose depends on how complicated the feature is. In this case it's sufficiently complex that we will start with the initial state and move to the happy path. As a rule of thumb, if it takes more than a couple of steps to define an instance of the application, I'll start with initialization only.

> **Prescription 3** Initializing objects is a good starting place for a TDD process. Another good approach is to use the test to design what you want a successful interaction of the feature to look like.

This application is made up of projects and tasks. A newly created project would have no tasks. What can we say about that brand-new project?

If there are no outstanding tasks, then there's nothing more to do. A project with nothing left to do is done. The initial state, then, is a project with no tasks, and we can specify that the project is done. That's not inevitable; we could specify that a project with no tasks is in some kind of empty state.

We don't have any infrastructure in place yet, so we need to create the test file ourselves—we're deliberately not using Rails generators right now. We're using RSpec, so the spec goes in the spec directory using a file name that is parallel to the application code in the app directory. We think this is a test of a project model, which would be in app/models/project.rb, so we'll put the spec in spec/models/project_spec.rb. We're making very small design decisions here, and so far these decisions are consistent with Rails conventions.

Here's our spec of a project's initial state:

```
basics_rspec/01/gatherer/spec/models/project_spec.rb
Line 1  require 'rails_helper'
     2
     3  RSpec.describe Project do
     4    it "considers a project with no tasks to be done" do
     5      project = Project.new
     6      expect(project.done?).to be_truthy
     7    end
     8  end
```

Let's talk about this spec at two levels: the logistics of the code in RSpec and what this test is doing for us in our TDD process.

This file has four interesting RSpec and Rails features:

- Requiring rails_helper
- Defining a suite with describe
- Writing an RSpec example with it
- Specifying a particular state with expect

On line 1, we require the file rails_helper, which contains Rails-related setup common to all tests. We'll peek into that file in the next chapter, when we talk about more Rails-specific test features. The rails_helper file, in turn, requires a file named spec_helper, which contains non-Rails RSpec setup.

What's a Spec?

What do you call the things you write in an RSpec file? If you are used to TDD and Minitest, the temptation to call them tests can be overwhelming. However, as we've discussed, the BDD planning behind RSpec suggests it's better not to think of your RSpec code as tests, which are things happen after the fact. So, what are they?

The RSpec docs and code refer to the elements of RSpec as "examples." The term I hear most often is simply "spec," as in "I need to write some specs for that feature." I've tried to use "spec" and "example" rather than "test" in this book, but I suspect I'll slip up somewhere. Bear with me.

We use the RSpec.describe method on line 3. In RSpec, the describe method defines a suite of tests that can share a common setup. The describe method takes one argument (typically either a class name or a string) and a block. The argument documents what the test suite is supposed to cover, and the block contains the test suite itself.

As you'll see in a little bit, describe calls can be nested. By convention, the outermost call often has the name of the class under test. In RSpec 3, the outermost describe call should be invoked as RSpec.describe, which is part of a general design change in RSpec 3 to avoid adding methods to Ruby's Kernel and Object namespaces. Nested calls can use just plain describe, since RSpec manages those calls internally.

The actual spec is defined with the it method, which takes an optional string argument that documents the spec, and then a block that is the body of the spec. The string argument is not used internally to identify the spec—you can have multiple specs with the same description string.

RSpec also defines specify as an alias for it. Normally, we'd use it when the method takes a string argument to give the spec a readable natural-language name. (Historically the string argument started with "should," so the name would be something like "it should be valid," but that construct has gotten less popular recently.) For single-line tests in which a string description is unnecessary, we use specify to make the single line read more clearly, such as this:

```
specify { expect(user.name).to eq("fred") }
```

On line 6 we make our first testable specification about the code: expect(project.done?) to be_truthy. The general form of an RSpec expectation is expect(actual_value).to(matcher), with the parentheses around the matcher often omitted in practice.

Let's trace through what RSpec does with our first expectation. First is the expect call itself, expect(project.done?). RSpec defines the expect method, which takes in any object as an argument and returns a special RSpec proxy object called an ExpectationTarget.

The ExpectationTarget holds on to the object that was the argument to expect, and itself responds to two messages: to and not_to. (Okay, technically three messages, since to_not exists as an alias.) Both to and not_to are ordinary Ruby methods that expect as an argument an RSpec matcher. There's nothing special about an RSpec matcher; at base it's just an object that responds to a matches? method. There are several predefined matchers and you can write your own.

In our case, be_truthy is a method defined by RSpec to return the BeTruthy matcher. You could get the same behavior with

```
expect(project.done?).to(RSpec::BuiltIn::BeTruthy.new)
```

but you probably would agree that the idiomatic version reads better.

The ExpectationTarget is now holding on to two objects: the object being matched (in our case, project.done?) and the matcher (be_truthy). When the spec is executed, RSpec calls the matches? method on the matcher, with the object being matched as an argument. If the expectation uses to, then the expectation passes if matches? is true. If the expectation uses not_to, then it checks for a does_not_match? method in the matcher. If there is no such method it falls back to passing if matches? is false. This is shown in the following diagram.

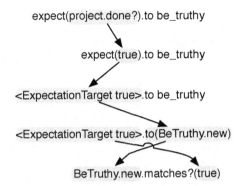

Compared to other testing libraries, RSpec shifts the tone from an assertion, potentially implying already-implemented behavior, to an expectation implying future behavior. The RSpec version, arguably, reads more smoothly (though some strenuously dispute this). Later in this chapter we'll cover some other tricks RSpec uses to make matchers read like natural language.

From an RSpec perspective we're creating an object and asserting an initial condition. What are we doing from a TDD perspective and why is this useful?

Small as it might seem, we've performed a little bit of design. We are starting to define the way parts of our system communicate with each other, and the tests ensure the visibility of important information in our design.

This small test makes three claims about our program:

- There is a class called Project.
- You can query instances of that class as to whether they are done.
- A brand-new instance of Project qualifies as done.

This last assertion isn't inevitable—we could say that you aren't done unless there is at least one completed task, but it's a choice we're making in our application's business logic.

RSpec Predefined Matchers

Before we run the tests, let's take a quick look at RSpec's basic matchers. RSpec predefines a number of matchers. Here's a list of the most useful ones; for a full list visit https://relishapp.com/rspec/rspec-expectations/v/3-0/docs/built-in-matchers.

```
expect(array).to all(matcher)
expect(actual).to be_truthy
expect(actual).to be_falsy
expect(actual).to be_nil
expect(actual).to be_between(min, max)
expect(actual).to be_within(delta).of(actual)
expect { block }.to change(receiver, message, &block)
```

```
expect(actual).to contain_exactly(expected)
expect(actual).to eq(actual)
expect(actual).to have_attributes(key/value pairs)
expect(actual).to include(*expected)
expect(actual).to match(regex)
expect { block }.to raise_error(exception)
expect(actual).to satisfy { block }
```

Most of these mean what they appear to say. The all matcher takes a different matcher as an argument and passes if all elements of the array pass that internal matcher, as in expect([1, 2, 3]).to all(be_truthy). The change matcher passes if the value of receiver.message changes when the block is evaluated. The contain_exactly matcher is true if the expected array and the actual array contain the same elements, regardless of order. The satisfy matcher passes if the block evaluates to true. The matchers that take block arguments are for specifying a side effect of the block's execution—that it raises an error or that it changes a different value—rather than the state of a particular object. Any of these except raise_error can be negated by using not_to instead of to.

RSpec 3 allows you to compose matchers to express compound behavior, and most of these matchers have alternate forms that allow them to read better when composed. Composing matchers allows you to specify, for example, multiple array values in a single statement and get useful error messages.

Here is a contrived example:

```
expect(["cheese", "burger"]).to contain_exactly(
    a_string_matching(/ch/), a_string_matching(/urg/))
```

In this case a_string_matching is an alias for match, and the arguments to contain_exactly are themselves matchers that must match individual elements of the array to allow the entire compound matcher to pass.

Running Our Test

Having written our first test, we'd like to execute it. Although RSpec provides Rake tasks for executing RSpec, I recommend using the rspec command directly to avoid the overhead of starting up Rake. If you use rspec with no arguments, then RSpec will run over the entire spec directory. You can also give RSpec an individual file, directory, or line to run. For full details on those options, see Chapter 15, *Running Tests Faster and Running Faster Tests*, on page 287.

What Happens When We Run the Test?

It fails. We haven't written any code yet.

That's Funny. What Really Happens—Internally?

When you run rspec with no arguments, RSpec loads every file in the spec directory. The following things happen (this process is slightly simplified for clarity):

1. Each file in the spec directory is loaded. Usually these files will contain just these specs, but sometimes you'll define extra helper methods or dummy classes that exist just to support the tests.

2. Each RSpec file typically requires the rails_helper.rb file. The rails_helper.rb file loads the Rails environment itself, as well as the spec_helper.rb, which contains non-Rails RSpec setup. In the default Rails configuration the .rspec file automatically loads spec_helper.rb.

3. By default the rails_helper.rb file sets up transactional fixtures. *Fixtures* are a Rails mechanism that defines global ActiveRecord data that is available to all tests. By default fixtures are added once inside a database transaction that wraps all the tests. At the end of the test the transaction is rolled back, allowing the next test to continue with a pristine state. More on fixtures in *Fixtures*, on page 95.

1. Each top-level call to RSpec.describe creates an internal RSpec object called an *example group*. The creation of the example group causes the block argument to describe to be executed. This may include further calls to describe to create nested example groups.

1. The block argument to describe may also contain calls to it. Each call to it results in the creation of an individual test, which is internally called an "example." The block arguments to it are stored for later execution.

2. Each top-level example group runs. By default the order in which the groups run is random.

Running an example group involves running each example that it contains, and that involves a few steps:

1. Run all before(:example) setup blocks. We'll talk about those more in a moment, when they become useful.

2. Run the example, which is the block argument to it. The method execution ends when a runtime error or a failed assertion is encountered. If neither of those happens, the test method passes. Yay!

3. Run all after(:example) teardown blocks. Teardown blocks are declared similarly to setup blocks, but their use is much less common.

4. Roll back or delete the fixtures as described earlier. The result of each example is passed back to the test runner for display in the console or IDE window running the test.

The following diagram shows the flow.

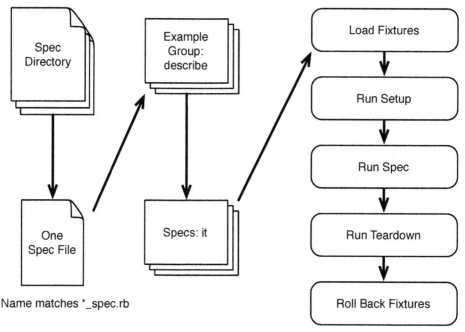

In our specific case, we have one file, one example group, and one spec, and if we run things we fail pretty quickly. Here's the slightly edited output:

```
$ rspec
gatherer/spec/models/project_spec.rb:3:in `<top (required)>':
    uninitialized constant Project
```

We're not even getting to the test run; the use of describe Project at the beginning of our test is failing because we haven't defined Project yet.

Making Our Test Pass

Now it's time to make our first test pass.

But how?

It seems like a straightforward question, but it has a few different answers.

- The purist way: *Do the simplest thing that could possibly work.* In this case "work" means "minimally pass the test without regard to the larger context." Or it might even mean "write the minimum amount of code to clear the current error without regard to the larger context."

- The "practical" way, scare quotes intended: Write the code you know you need to eventually write, effectively skipping steps that seem too small to be valuable.
- The teaching way, which is somewhere in between the other two and lets me best explain how and why test-driven development works without getting bogged down in details or skipping too many steps.

Ultimately, there isn't a one-size-fits-all answer to the question. The goal is to make the test pass in a way that allows us to best discover the solution to the problem and design our code. In practice, the more complicated the problem is and the less I feel I understand the solution, the more purist I get, taking slow steps.

Let's make this test pass. The first error we need to clear is the uninitialized constant: Project error, so put this in app/models/project.rb:

```
class Project
end
```

This is a minimal way to clear the error. (Well, that's technically not true; I could just declare a constant Project = true or something like that, but there's purist and then there's crazy.) But the test still doesn't pass. If we run the tests now, we get this:

```
rspec
F

Failures:

  1) Project considers a project with no tasks to be done
     Failure/Error: expect(project.done?).to be_truthy
     NoMethodError:
       undefined method `done?' for #<Project:0x00000107ce67d0>
     # ./spec/models/project_spec.rb:6:in `block (2 levels) in <top (required)>'

Finished in 0.00104 seconds (files took 1.29 seconds to load)
1 example, 1 failure

Failed examples:

rspec ./spec/models/project_spec.rb:4 #
    Project considers a project with no tasks to be done
```

See that last line starting with rspec? That's where RSpec usefully gives us the exact command-line invocation we need to run just the failing spec.

Our error is that we are calling project.done? and the done? method doesn't exist yet.

That's simple to clear, still in app/models/project.rb:

```
class Project
  def done?
  end
end
```

And when we do this and run rspec again, we finally get a more interesting error:

```
Failure/Error: expect(project.done?).to be_truthy
      expected: truthy value
           got: nil
```

We've now passed out of the realm of syntax and runtime errors and into the realm of assertion failures—our test runs, but the code does not behave as expected. We've expected that the value of project.done? will be truthy, which is to say any Ruby value that evaluates to true. But since our method doesn't return any value, we get nil.

Luckily, that has a simple fix:

```
basics_rspec/01/gatherer/app/models/project.rb
class Project

  def done?
    true
  end

end
```

Which results in this:

```
$ rspec
.

Finished in 0.00105 seconds (files took 1.2 seconds to load)
1 example, 0 failures
```

And the test passes! We're done! Ship it!

Okay, we're not exactly done. We have made the test pass, which actually only gets us two-thirds of the way through the TDD cycle. We've done the failing test step (sometimes this step is called "red") and the passing test step (sometimes called "green") and now we are at the refactoring step. However, we've written almost no code, so we can safely say there are no refactorings indicated at this point.

I suspect that if you are inclined to be skeptical of test-driven development, I haven't convinced you yet. We've gone on for a few pages and written one line of code, and that line of code clearly isn't even final. I reiterate that in practice this doesn't take much time. If we weren't stopping to discuss each step this would take only a couple of minutes, and some of that time—like setting up the Project class—would need to be spent anyway.

In fact, we haven't exactly done nothing—we've defined and documented a subtle part of how our Project class behaves, and we will find out immediately if the class ever breaks that behavior. As I've said, though, documentation and regression are only part of what makes test-driven development powerful. We need to get to the design part. And for that we need to write more tests.

The Second Test

One nice feature of test-driven development is that making one test pass often points the way to the next test. The goal of the next test cycle is to write a test that fails given the current code. At this point the code says that done? is always true, so we should create a case where done? is false.

```
basics_rspec/02/gatherer/spec/models/project_spec.rb
  it "knows that a project with an incomplete task is not done" do
    project = Project.new
    task = Task.new
    project.tasks << task
    expect(project.done?).to be_falsy
  end
end
```

This test is similar to the first one, but now we have a second class, Task, and a related attribute of the Project class, tasks. This time we're assuming that a new task is undone, and therefore a project with an undone task is not done. We could also write the last line expect(project.done?).not_to be_truthy, but that seems harder to read.

Our first failure is that the Task constant is missing. We can clear that up easily.

```
basics_rspec/02/gatherer/app/models/task.rb
class Task

end
```

This leads us to write simple, but still incomplete, done? logic to make the test pass—a project is done if it has no tasks:

basics_rspec/02/gatherer/app/models/project.rb

```ruby
class Project
  attr_accessor :tasks

  def initialize
    @tasks = []
  end

  def done?
    tasks.empty?
  end
end
```

The second test now passes. And we have a clear candidate for our next test—the distinction between complete and incomplete tasks. I'm also thinking about how we get from there to sizing tasks and estimating project due dates.

With the test passing, we enter the refactoring phase. And even with the small amount of code written so far, I'm thinking of two refactoring jobs.

If you've done Rails programming before, you may have noticed that I have not yet made Project and Task subclasses of ActiveRecord::Base, meaning I haven't connected them to the database via ActiveRecord.

My reason for that is a purist one—I haven't added any tests that would need ActiveRecord functionality to pass. (To a slightly lesser extent, I also don't want to further break the flow here to describe the data migrations and the like.) That may seem pedantic—there's a pretty good chance that both these classes will become ActiveRecord classes, but it's not inevitable, and if you are using tests to drive design it makes sense not to let the design leap ahead of the tests, but rather to use the tests to suggest the code's structure.

For example, it's not a completely crazy design to say that Projects might never have data of their own and therefore might never need to be ActiveRecord objects. Somewhat more plausibly, the date-projection code that we're writing now might eventually wind up in some kind of dedicated calculator object separate from the ActiveRecord layer. In either case, there's no need for our design to get ahead of our tests.

Let and Expectations

In addition to examining code for potential refactoring, it's a good idea to look at the tests for duplication. In this case we have a single line of common set-up—namely, project = Project.new, which is shared between the two tests that we have already written. We can fix this and turn our tests into slightly more idiomatic RSpec:

basics_rspec/03/gatherer/spec/models/project_spec.rb

```ruby
require 'rails_helper'

RSpec.describe Project do

  describe "initialization" do
    let(:project) { Project.new }
    let(:task) { Task.new }

    it "considers a project with no test to be done" do
      expect(project).to be_done
    end

    it "knows that a project with an incomplete test is not done" do
      project.tasks << task
      expect(project).not_to be_done
    end
  end
end
```

This version of the test allows me to show two of my favorite parts of RSpec: the let statement and dynamic matchers.

RSpec's let statement cleans up the creation of test data.

Using let, you can make a variable available within the current describe without having to place it inside the before block and without having to make it an instance variable. I use let all the time. I like that it separates the definition of each variable, that it encourages concise initializations, and that the word let allows me to pretend I'm writing in Scheme for a brief moment.

Each let method call takes a symbol argument and a block. The symbol can then be called as if it were a local variable: the first call to the symbol lazily invokes the block and caches the result, and subsequent calls return the same result without reinvoking the block.

In this example we use let twice, first to describe a project and then to describe a task. We can then use project and task in the body of the specs. Even though task isn't used in the first spec, that's perfectly fine—RSpec invokes the let block only when the variable is used.

In essence, a let call is syntactic sugar for defining a method and memoizing the result, like this:

```ruby
def me
  @me ||= User.new(name: "Noel")
end
```

The main gotcha here is that the let block isn't executed unless it's invoked. That's often a good thing since your test won't spend time creating unused objects. You can get in trouble sometimes if you expect that the object already exists. For a contrived problem case, note that this example will fail since the two let blocks are never invoked:

```
describe "user behavior"
  let(:me) { User.new(:name => "Noel") }
  let(:you) { User.new(:name => "Erin") }
  specify { User.count.should == 2 }
end
```

Luckily, RSpec does provides a mechanism in cases where an item must be present even though it is never invoked by name. It's called let!, with a "bang" for "Block Always Needs Gathering," which I just made up and only makes a tiny amount of sense, but you probably won't forget it.

One of my other favorite bits of RSpec is an implicit matcher that RSpec creates by name-mangling if you give it a matcher it doesn't recognize. Any matcher of the form be_whatever or be_a_whatever assumes an associated whatever? method—with a question mark—on the actual object and calls it. The predicate method's return value drives the matcher's behavior. If the matcher is called via to, it passes if the predicate method returns a true value. If the matcher is called via not_to, it passes if the predicate method returns a false value.

In our previous examples we invoked expectations like expect(project.done?).to be_truthy. Since done? is a predicate method, we rewrote those examples to be more direct. This gives us expect(project).to be_done, which almost reads as simple, clear, natural language. Often it's easier to add a predicate method to your object than it is to create a custom matcher in RSpec.

A lot of complexity goes into making the language clear. In addition to allowing be_a and be_an, if the predicate method is in the present tense, such as matches?, you can write the expectation as be_a_match. In this case RSpec will look for match? and then form matches? if it can't find match?.

Similarly, if the predicate method starts with has, RSpec allows your matcher to start with have for readability (so your tests don't look like they've been written by LOLCats); RSpec allows expect(actual).to have_key(:id) rather than expect(actual).to has_key(:id).

RSpec 3 also allows you to chain multiple matchers using and and or, as in expect(actual).to include("a").and match(/.*3.*/), or expect(actual).to eq(3).or eq(5).

You can also pass matchers as arguments to other matchers, or compose matchers to handle an entire data structure using match. The following two snippets are equivalent:

```
expect(actual[0]).to eq(5)
expect(actual[1]).to eq(7)

expect(actual).to match([an_object_eq_to(5), an_object_eq_to(7)])
```

In the bottom snippet, the elements of the array actual are individually matched against an_object_eq_to(5) and an_object_eq_to(7), which are aliases to eq(5) and eq(7). Most of the built-in matchers have aliases to make them more natural-language-like when used as arguments; see http://rubydoc.info/github/rspec/rspec-expectations/RSpec/Matchers for a full list. The all matcher, which looks like expect(actual).to all(be_truthy), takes the matcher argument (in this case be_truthy) and applies it to each element in the object being matched (in this case, actual, which should be enumerable).

I love this language inflection because I feel like it allows me to write tests that are succinct and clear. The composable matchers seem interesting, but I haven't found a use case yet—they are very new to the library. Others find the internal complexity of this feature to be too high a price to pay for the natural-language tests. (Some people also really don't like the natural-language syntax.)

Back on Task

What remains of our definition of done? is the distinction between complete and incomplete tasks. Let's start with that, with a test for Task:

basics_rspec/03/gatherer/spec/models/task_spec.rb
```ruby
require 'rails_helper'

RSpec.describe Task do
  it "can distinguish a completed task" do
    task = Task.new
    expect(task).not_to be_complete
    task.mark_completed
    expect(task).to be_complete
  end
end
```

This test makes two assertions, which I normally try to avoid, but the two assertions in this test are pretty intimately related—it would be awkward to separate them. We create a new Task (expecting that it is not complete at this point), then we complete the task and expect that it is, in fact, complete.

By including both assertions in the same test, we've written a shortcut-proof test—we have to put the real logic in the code to get both halves of this test to pass. More importantly, this test is completely at the API level and makes no claim about the underlying mechanism for representing completed tasks. This is great because it means we can change the implementation without breaking tests as long as the API still works. Overreliance on implementation details is a major cause of test fragility, so when you can describe the behavior rather than the implementation, you should do so.

> **Prescription 4** When possible, write your tests to describe your code's behavior, not its implementation.

We make the test pass with some simple methods in Task:

```
basics_rspec/03/gatherer/app/models/task.rb
class Task
  def initialize
    @completed = false
  end

  def mark_completed
    @completed = true
  end

  def complete?
    @completed
  end
end
```

This implementation probably won't survive long—tasks will probably grow more states—but for now it works.

> **Prescription 5** Keeping your code as simple as possible allows you to focus complexity on the areas that really need complexity.

We can use a very similar test to ensure the project's ability to determine completeness:

```
basics_rspec/04/gatherer/spec/models/project_spec.rb
it "marks a project done if its tasks are done" do
  project.tasks << task
  task.mark_completed
  expect(project).to be_done
end
```

We make the test pass by adding logic to our project's done? method:

basics_rspec/04/gatherer/app/models/project.rb
```
def done?
  tasks.reject(&:complete?).empty?
end
```

I can't think of an easy way to break the done? method as it currently stands, so it is...well, done.

Adding Some Math

Moving on. We need to be able to calculate how much of a project is remaining and the rate of completion, and then put them together to determine a projected end date.

Now that we have the basic infrastructure in place, we can go a little bit faster, which manifests itself in a test that has a little more setup. Our next test is for the project to be able to calculate how much work is remaining.

I like to take a moment before I write a test to think about what the test needs. The typical test structure has three parts:

- Given: What data does the test need? *This test needs a project, at least one complete task, and at least one incomplete task.*
- When: What action is taking place? *We're calculating the remaining work.*
- Then: What behavior do we need to specify? *The work calculation result.*

With that thought exercise over, we write our spec. (Actually there are two assertions and I've split them up.)

basics_rspec/05/gatherer/spec/models/project_spec.rb
```
describe "estimates" do
  let(:project) { Project.new }
  let(:done) { Task.new(size: 2, completed: true) }
  let(:small_not_done) { Task.new(size: 1) }
  let(:large_not_done) { Task.new(size: 4) }

  before(:example) do
    project.tasks = [done, small_not_done, large_not_done]
  end

  it "can calculate total size" do
    expect(project.total_size).to eq(7)
  end

  it "can calculate remaining size" do
    expect(project.remaining_size).to eq(5)
  end
end
```

We'll put the spec in a new describe block in our project_spec.rb file since it has a different setup from the specs we've already written. The let statements combined with the before block set up a project with three tasks, which is a setup common to both of the single-line it blocks. In RSpec, anything in a before(:each) or before(:example) block is executed as part of the setup before each spec.

This is a common RSpec pattern: the "given" data goes in a series of let methods, the "when" action goes in a before block, and then a series of small it statements represent individual assertions. (You can make this more compact by leaving off the string description of each it and turning it into a one-liner.)

A couple of minor style choices make the test easier to manage. All the task objects have meaningful names so that at a glance I can tell each object's reason for being in the test. If the tasks had descriptions or names I'd also give them meaningful data so that if the object gets printed to the terminal it's easy to tell which object it is. The specific score numbers that I'm using for each are deliberate. Each task has a different score, and neither of the two adds up to the third, which is a very small thing that makes it harder to get a false positive test.

> **Prescription 6** Choose your test data and test-variable names to make it easy to diagnose failures when they happen. Meaningful names and data that doesn't overlap are helpful.

This test fails first on the creation of Task.new(size: 2, completed: true). Task isn't an ActiveRecord yet, so we don't have the hash argument by default. If this weren't a book example I would bring in ActiveRecord here, but I don't want to stop to define the migrations since they are irrelevant to the current point. We'll cover ActiveRecord when we bring in more Rails features.

basics_rspec/05/gatherer/app/models/task.rb
```ruby
attr_accessor :size, :completed

def initialize(options = {})
  @completed = options[:completed]
  @size = options[:size]
end
```

We than can make this pass with a couple more single-line methods in Project:

basics_rspec/05/gatherer/app/models/project.rb
```ruby
class Project

  attr_accessor :tasks
```

```
  def initialize
    @tasks = []
  end

  def done?
    tasks.reject(&:complete?).empty?
  end

  def total_size
    tasks.sum(&:size)
  end

  def remaining_size
    tasks.reject(&:complete?).sum(&:size)
  end
end
```

And the test passes.

This time, in the refactoring step we actually have stuff to do. In Project we have two methods, both taking a list of incomplete tasks. We can extract that to common code:

basics_rspec/06/gatherer/app/models/project.rb
```
class Project

  attr_accessor :tasks

  def initialize
    @tasks = []
  end

  def incomplete_tasks
    tasks.reject(&:complete?)
  end

  def done?
    incomplete_tasks.empty?
  end

  def total_size
    tasks.sum(&:size)
  end

  def remaining_size
    incomplete_tasks.sum(&:size)
  end
end
```

This doesn't make our code shorter, but it does wrap a slightly opaque functional call containing a negative condition in a method with a semantically meaningful name. And if the definition of completeness changes, we only have to change one location.

We still have potential duplication in the Project class—two methods that call sum(&:size) on a list of tasks. I don't have an obvious place to put that method, though, short of creating a TaskList class. I don't see creating a TaskList as a simplification at this time, so we'll hold off. (A reviewer suggested this might also lead us to question if our Project class is actually the correct abstraction and if TaskList might be better.)

Our First Date

We've got part of our Project API down; now we need to use that to calculate a projected completion date. The requirement is to calculate the project's end date based on the number of tasks finished in the last three weeks. We'll appropriate the agile term "velocity" to describe the rate of task completion. To make this work, we need to distinguish between tasks that concluded in the last three weeks and tasks that did not.

That means we have to deal with dates.

I'm sorry.

Programming with dates and times is the worst. Time is especially problematic in testing because tests work best when each test run is identical. However, owing to the nature of the universe, the current time inexorably changes from test run to test run. This can lead to all kinds of fun, including tests that fail on or after a particular day or tests that pass only at certain times of day. We'll try to avoid all of that.

We're testing bottom-up, so it's a good idea to start at the smallest unit of code we can think of. In this case, that's having Task instances be aware of whether they have been completed in the three-week window.

In the interest of keeping all of us sane and not walking through another set of trivial tests, I'll present the entire set of Task tests. A task completed in the last three weeks counts toward velocity, which implies two negative cases: an incomplete task and a task that was completed longer ago. To be clear, I wrote and passed them one at a time, but I don't think we need to walk through all those steps a second time.

basics_rspec/07/gatherer/spec/models/task_spec.rb

```
Line 1  describe "velocity" do
    -     let(:task) { Task.new(size: 3) }

    -     it "does not count an incomplete task toward velocity" do
    5       expect(task).not_to be_part_of_velocity
    -         expect(task.points_toward_velocity).to eq(0)
    -     end

    -     it "does not count a long-ago task toward velocity" do
   10       task.mark_completed(6.months.ago)
    -         expect(task).not_to be_part_of_velocity
    -         expect(task.points_toward_velocity).to eq(0)
    -     end

   15     it "counts a recently completed task toward velocity" do
    -         task.mark_completed(1.day.ago)
    -         expect(task).to be_part_of_velocity
    -         expect(task.points_toward_velocity).to eq(3)
    -     end
   20  end
```

A couple of changes to the Task class are implied in these specs.

First off, we've changed the existing mechanism for completing a task. On lines 10 and 16, we've changed the mark_completed call to take an optional date argument indicating the date completed. We'd like to do this without touching the existing tests that use mark_completed with no argument.

We've added two related methods to the Task class: part_of_velocity? (implied by the be_part_of_velocity matcher) and points_toward_velocity. According to our requirements, the part_of_velocity? method returns true if the task has been completed in the last three weeks. As a matter of code style, we're naming the method and testing the behavior rather than testing against the specifics of the implementation. By testing against the behavior, we hope we will be better able to deal with the inevitable requirements changes.

The points_toward_velocity method is trickier. If the task counts toward velocity, then the size of the task is returned; otherwise the method returns zero. This is an example of designing the class interface via tests. The idea is to keep all the logic for tasks inside the Task class. Specifically, I want a project to be able to determine how much time is remaining without having to query the task twice—once to determine the status of the task and again to determine its size.

As a matter of testing style, notice the way dates are specified on lines 10 and 16 of the test file. I'm using the Rails helpers to concisely specify the dates relative to the current time: 6.months.ago for the out-of-velocity task and 1.day.ago for the in-velocity task. If I had specified an explicit date for yesterday, then eventually the passage of time would push that date beyond the three-week threshold and the test would fail. Using relative dates reduces that problem.

There's a different interesting question about the test design and the dates. Neither six months nor one day is particularly close to the boundary between in-velocity and out-of-velocity tasks. Shouldn't I test more days or test something closer to the boundary? This question reflects the difference between testing as a design aid and testing for verification. In strict TDD you would avoid writing a test that you expect to pass, because a passing test doesn't normally drive you to change the code.

I would write a boundary-condition test only if I had reason to think that my implementation might fail in a boundary condition. That is quite possible for dates and times, and often if I'm dealing with SQL date ranges versus Ruby date ranges or if time zones are involved, I add tests near the boundary to attempt to break the implementation and catch an off-by-one error. I wouldn't write a series of tests for every length of time completed one day through six months ago, since I would expect all those tests to pass.

The resulting Task class looks like this:

basics_rspec/07/gatherer/app/models/task.rb
```ruby
class Task
  attr_accessor :size, :completed_at

  def initialize(options = {})
    mark_completed(options[:completed_at]) if options[:completed_at]
    @size = options[:size]
  end

  def mark_completed(date = nil)
    @completed_at = (date || Time.current)
  end

  def complete?
    completed_at.present?
  end

  def part_of_velocity?
    return false unless complete?
    completed_at > 3.weeks.ago
  end

  def points_toward_velocity
    if part_of_velocity? then size else 0 end
  end
end
```

Using the Time Data

With the task tests passing, it's time to switch our attention back to the Project test. We need to make a slight tweak to our project_with_data_test setup so that we have tasks that are in and out of the three-week velocity window:

basics_rspec/07/gatherer/spec/models/project_spec.rb
```
let(:project) { Project.new }
let(:newly_done) { Task.new(size: 3, completed_at: 1.day.ago) }
let(:old_done) { Task.new(size: 2, completed_at: 6.months.ago) }
let(:small_not_done) { Task.new(size: 1) }
let(:large_not_done) { Task.new(size: 4) }

before(:example) do
  project.tasks = [newly_done, old_done, small_not_done, large_not_done]
end
```

We've added one more completed task, and we're using the ability to pass a completed date to differentiate the two. Note that the total size is now 10 instead of 7 and the total-size test needs to be changed accordingly.

Now the calculations we need for determining the projected project status are straightforward math based on this data.

basics_rspec/07/gatherer/spec/models/project_spec.rb
```
Line 1  it "knows its velocity" do
     -    expect(project.completed_velocity).to eq(3)
     -  end
     -
     5  it "knows its rate" do
     -    expect(project.current_rate).to eq(1.0 / 7)
     -  end
     -
     -  it "knows its projected time remaining" do
    10    expect(project.projected_days_remaining).to eq(35)
     -  end
     -
     -  it "knows if it is on schedule" do
     -    project.due_date = 1.week.from_now
    15    expect(project).not_to be_on_schedule
     -    project.due_date = 6.months.from_now
     -    expect(project).to be_on_schedule
     -  end
```

You can quibble with some style choices in these tests. Even though the tests are against the Project class, they have a stealth dependency on the Task class also working. That's not ideal, as it makes it harder to determine the cause if the test fails. In Chapter 7, *Using Test Doubles as Mocks and Stubs*, on page 117, we'll go over some strategies for breaking this kind of dependency in tests.

I also use a couple of different strategies for dealing with math. The assertion on line 6 has a mathematical answer expressed as a math expression in the test (1.0 / 7), while the assertion on line 10 does all the math and spits out the final answer (35). The algebraic version is more clear because it describes the way the answer is derived (and, in this case, makes it easier to express a floating-point answer), whereas the numerical version can seem magical—why 35? However, the downside of having code expressions in test assertions is that it encourages using the test to directly describe the final code, by copying and pasting the code from the test. It's usually better to have the implementation code be as independent as possible from the test itself.

The resulting passing code is a bit anticlimactic—we've pushed almost all the conditional logic to the Task, making our Project code straightforward. This is a good sign and implies that we're factoring the code reasonably.

```
basics_rspec/07/gatherer/app/models/project.rb
def completed_velocity
  tasks.sum(&:points_toward_velocity)
end

def current_rate
  completed_velocity * 1.0 / 21
end

def projected_days_remaining
  remaining_size / current_rate
end

def on_schedule?
  (Date.today + projected_days_remaining) <= due_date
end
```

In addition, we need to add attr_accessor :due_date to the Project class.

This passes the tests and moves us into the refactoring phase. I don't see anything in the code that screams for a refactoring (although one reviewer did suggest turning the rate into a Ruby Rational instance). I'm considering extracting the (Date.today + projected_days_remaining) logic to a method called projected_end_date, but we don't need to do that at the moment.

We also want to look for potentially dangerous special cases to make sure they work—for example, the case where no tasks have been completed. We can put this test, along with the other initialization tests, in our original project_spec.rb file, inside the describe block for initialization.

```
basics_rspec/08/gatherer/spec/models/project_spec.rb
```
```ruby
it "properly estimates a blank project" do
  expect(project.completed_velocity).to eq(0)
  expect(project.current_rate).to eq(0)
  expect(project.projected_days_remaining.nan?).to be_truthy
  expect(project).not_to be_on_schedule
end
```

The first three assertions in this test pass as is; the last one needs some code. The nan? assertion may seem a bit strange. Ruby's divide-by-zero construct is Float::NAN, but the eq matcher fails if you compare Float::NAN to itself, so we're using the provided predicate. Mostly we want to make sure projected_days_remaining doesn't raise an exception if there are no tasks.

We can use the same predicate in the code to make the on_schedule? assertion pass:

```
basics_rspec/08/gatherer/app/models/project.rb
```
```ruby
  def on_schedule?
    return false if projected_days_remaining.nan?
    (Date.today + projected_days_remaining) <= due_date
  end
end
```

And the tests pass, which brings us to the refactoring phase. The first thing to notice is that we have a duplicated piece of data: the 21-day window for determining whether a task counts toward velocity. This data point is referenced in both Project#current_rate and Task#part_of_velocity?. They are pretty clearly the same bit of data—if I changed the time period to two weeks, I'd have to change it in both places.

That said, it's not clear what to do with this information. To me the velocity length feels most like a static constant value owned by the Project class, since velocity applied to a single task makes no sense. In code that looks like the following, with the velocity_length implemented as a class method with a constant return value:

```
basics_rspec/08/gatherer/app/models/project.rb
```
```ruby
def self.velocity_length_in_days
  21
end
```

I'm using a method rather than a constant because this seems very likely to become dynamic at some point in the future. Using a method preserves the API at no additional complexity cost.

The one usage in the Project class changes to this:

basics_rspec/08/gatherer/app/models/project.rb
```
def current_rate
  completed_velocity * 1.0 / Project.velocity_length_in_days
end
```

And the one usage in Task is now as follows:

basics_rspec/08/gatherer/app/models/task.rb
```
def part_of_velocity?
  return false unless complete?
  completed_at > Project.velocity_length_in_days.days.ago
end
```

And the tests pass. This structure eliminates the duplicate value, though the way that particular value is needed by both the Project and Task classes makes me wonder if we really just need a VelocityCalculator class.

What We've Done

Using the TDD process of "write a simple test, write simple code to make it pass, and refactor," we started our Rails application by creating some business logic.

What has the TDD process given us? We started with a requirement and it was not immediately clear how to turn it into an algorithm. By using TDD we were able to attack the problem incrementally, choosing to start in a small, well-understood corner and move outward as our understanding of the problem improved. It allowed us to easily change our code structure as we learned more about the solution.

Most importantly, we wrote better code. The solution we ended up with has short, well-named methods, it has logic in its proper place, and it will be easy to adjust as the requirements change.

Now it's time to integrate this model into an actual web application. Let's do some Rails testing.

## CHAPTER 3

Test-Driven Rails

In the previous chapter we created some basic functionality for a project-management application using test-driven development. The title of this book, though, is *Rails 4 Test Prescriptions*, not *Generic Test Prescriptions*. (As with most generics, if that book did exist, it'd probably be cheaper but with less-interesting packaging.)

In this chapter we will augment our model testing by testing logic in the controller and view layers, and we'll implement tests that cover our entire Rails application from request to response, called *end-to-end* tests. We'll be using a tool called Capybara to help manage our end-to-end testing.

A good test suite consists of a few end-to-end tests, a lot of tests that target a single unit, and relatively few tests that cover an intermediate amount of code. Controller and view tests often wind up in that mushy testing middle. However, by moving logic outside the controller and the views themselves, we can turn those slower and more fragile middle-ground tests into faster and more robust unit tests.

And Now Let's Write Some Rails

To start a test-driven development process, it's important to have some requirements in mind. Without some sense of what your code should be doing, it's hard to write tests to describe behavior.

Requirements-gathering could be an entire book by itself (specifically, this one: *Software Requirements, 2nd Edition [Wie03]*). In our case, we're our own client and we're working on a small project, so we don't exactly need military-grade precision. Here's my informal list of the first few things we'll tackle:

- A user can create a project and seed it with initial tasks using the somewhat contrived syntax of task name:size.

- A user can enter a task, associate it with a project, and see it on the project page.

- A user can change a task's state to mark it as done.

- A project can display its progress and status using the date projection we created in the last chapter.

We'll walk through these one by one, following the basic guideline that any new logic should be driven by a failing test. Let's start with the ability to enter a project.

End-to-End Testing

We'll follow a testing practice called *outside-in testing*, which involves writing an end-to-end test that defines the feature (the "outside"), and then augmenting it with a series of unit tests that drive the actual code and design ("the inside").

A tool called *Capybara* will make our end-to-end tests easier to read and write. Capybara allows for easy interaction with the web page and the document object model (DOM). We'll cover features of Capybara as they come up; for full documentation of Capybara, check out its home page at https://github.com/jnicklas/capybara. We'll also cover Capybara and end-to-end testing in more detail in Chapter 10, *Integration Testing with Capybara and Cucumber*, on page 177.

To get started we need to add the capybara gem:

```
group :test do
  gem "capybara"
end
```

and reinstall the bundle:

```
% bundle install
```

Our first test covers the case where a user adds a project to the system. This task will be very close to Rails boilerplate, so our end-to-end test actually won't need much augmentation from unit tests. Later in this tutorial we'll add features that need more business logic.

Let's plan out what this test needs in terms of given/when/then.

- Given: We're starting with empty data, so no setup
- When: Filling out a form with project data and submitting
- Then: Verifying that the new project shows up on our list of projects with the entered tasks attached

The test looks like this:

```
test_first_rspec/01/gatherer/spec/features/add_project_spec.rb
Line 1  require "rails_helper"

        describe "adding projects" do
          it "allows a user to create a project with tasks" do
5           visit new_project_path
            fill_in "Name", with: "Project Runway"
            fill_in "Tasks", with: "Task 1:3\nTask 2:5"
            click_on("Create Project")
            visit projects_path
10          expect(page).to have_content("Project Runway")
            expect(page).to have_content("8")
          end
        end
```

We call this an "outside" test because it works from outside the Rails stack to define our functionality. We're simulating browser requests and evaluating browser responses. This test is not dependent on our code's structure.

We have no setup in this test. Starting on line 5 and ending on line 8, we use Capybara methods to interact with the application to simulate user interaction.

We start by using the Capybara method visit to simulate a request to our application at the URL that matches the route new_project_path. Once it gets to that page, it uses the Capybara method fill_in to put text in a couple of form fields, then it clicks a button labeled Create Project using the click_on method. We'll talk in more detail about the Capybara API in Chapter 10, *Integration Testing with Capybara and Cucumber*, on page 177. Right now it's enough to get the gist of what the test is doing.

Finally, on line 9, we enter the evaluation phase of the test by visiting a route, projects_path, that represents our project index page and asserting that the title of the new task appears on the page, as does the total size of the project. A task of size 3 points and a task of size 5 points means we're looking for a total of 8 points.

We're not making any assumptions about the layout or presentation of the page—only that the new task name is there. Typically, when doing an end-to-end test the goal is to have the success criteria be based on something that is visible in a response rather than checking the database to see if the object is created.

This is a reasonable end-to-end test. It simulates a simple workflow by filling out a form, submitting it, and validating at least part of the resulting data.

There are several reasons why it's valuable to have a test, like this one, that works from outside the application:

- It makes no assumptions about the structure of the underlying code.

- It forces us to think of our feature in terms of behavior that is visible to a user or client of the application. Not all features have user-facing components, but where they do, being able to specify correct behavior without regard to the implementation is valuable.

- Eventually our unit tests will focus on as small a part of the code as we can manage. Having one test that makes sure all those little pieces correctly pass control between them prevents bugs from living in the gaps between the pieces.

Right now this test will fail—spectacularly. Absolutely none of the component bits are in place. So we'll take this tiny step by tiny step, in each case minimally clearing the current error.

Pending Tests

If it bothers you to see the integration test continue to fail while we write the unit tests that will make it pass, RSpec allows you to specify a test as pending or to skip it altogether. In RSpec, any it method defined without a block is considered to be "pending."

```
it "bends steel in its bare hands"
```

You can temporarily mark an it or describe block as pending by adding :pending as a second argument after the string:

```
it "bends steel in its bare hands", :pending do
  #anything
end
```

Alternatively, you can use the method pending in the spec:

```
it "bends steel in its bare hands" do
  pending "not implemented yet"
end
```

In RSpec 3 all pending specs are actually run if there is code in the block part of the spec. The code is executed, with any failure in the pending spec treated as a pending result, rather than a failure result. However, if the code in the pending spec passes, you'll get an error that effectively means, "You said this was pending, but lo and behold, it works. Maybe it's not actually pending anymore; please remove the pending status."

If you want the spec to not run, and not test for whether it works, employ the preceding syntax but use skip instead of pending. Alternative, you can prefix the method name with x, as in xit or xdescribe. A skipped test will not run, meaning you won't get any notification if the test suddenly starts to pass.

Making Our Test Pass

We can see the first error by running the test using rspec.

```
NameError: undefined local variable or method `new_project_path'
```

Since Project isn't yet a standard ActiveRecord resource with routes, the test (unsurprisingly) can't find new_project_path.

If you were reading the previous chapter and wondering when we would push to creating ActiveRecord models, your time has come. We'll use the Rails resource generator, which creates a controller, migration, route, and the like but doesn't put any code in the generated controller. When we execute the rails generate command, Rails will interactively ask us if we want to override the model project.rb and the model test project_spec.rb. Don't override! We want to keep our existing code and update the model file by hand.

In the interest of sanity, we'll also update Task now. (Otherwise, keeping the tests for both Task and Project passing while one is an ActiveRecord and the other isn't is a pain.)

Here are the exact commands we'll use. Note that the commands need to be on one command line:

```
% rails generate resource project name:string due_date:date
% rails generate resource task project:references \
  title:string size:integer completed_at:datetime
```

We're adding two attributes to the project class: name (which we need for this test) and due_date (which we added in the previous chapter). The Task model tests a title attribute for this test, and size and completed_at attributes from last chapter. Again, don't override the existing files. Rails fans, note that we're using generate resource rather than generate scaffold, meaning we'll get blank controllers and no view files. That's fine since we want to build those via our tests.

Then we change the project.rb file as follows—note that we are removing some code, such as the initialize method, that is no longer needed because ActiveRecord is taking over the functionality. Other methods, such as incomplete_tasks and done?, are still needed.

```
test_first_rspec/01/gatherer/app/models/project.rb
class Project < ActiveRecord::Base

  has_many :tasks

  def self.velocity_length_in_days
    21
  end

  def incomplete_tasks
    tasks.reject(&:complete?)
  end

  def done?
    incomplete_tasks.empty?
  end

  def total_size
    tasks.to_a.sum(&:size)
  end

  def remaining_size
    incomplete_tasks.sum(&:size)
  end

  def completed_velocity
    tasks.to_a.sum(&:points_toward_velocity)
  end

  def current_rate
    completed_velocity * 1.0 / Project.velocity_length_in_days
  end

  def projected_days_remaining
    remaining_size / current_rate
  end

  def on_schedule?
    return false if projected_days_remaining.nan?
    (Date.today + projected_days_remaining) <= due_date
  end
end
```

We've added the superclass ActiveRecord::Base and removed the due_date attr_accessor since ActiveRecord now manages attributes. The relationship to Task is now an ActiveRecord has_many, which means the code that calculates sums over the set of tasks needs to use to_a to convert the relationship to a plain array, or else Rails will give you an ugly deprecation warning.

Similarly, we remove the initializer and attr_accessor to clean up the Task class as follows:

```
test_first_rspec/01/gatherer/app/models/task.rb
class Task < ActiveRecord::Base

  belongs_to :project

  def mark_completed(date = nil)
    self.completed_at = (date || Time.current)
  end

  def complete?
    completed_at.present?
  end

  def part_of_velocity?
    return false unless complete?
    completed_at > Project.velocity_length_in_days.days.ago
  end


  def points_toward_velocity
    if part_of_velocity? then size else 0 end
  end

end
```

We need to run our new migration:

```
% rake db:migrate
```

Versions of Rails before 4.1 will also need to run rake db:test:prepare, which keeps the test database in sync with the main schema. Rails 4.1 does this automatically after a migration is executed.

If you run the tests now, they should still all pass (except for the new integration test), but you'll probably see a couple of pending warnings from boilerplate tests that RSpec puts in the helpers tests. I typically delete these pending warnings on the grounds that the reminder is low value and high annoyance.

The Days Are Action-Packed

Running the tests now gives us a different error since we've defined new_project_path:

```
1) adding projects allows a user to create a project with tasks
   Failure/Error: visit new_project_path
   AbstractController::ActionNotFound:
     The action 'new' could not be found for ProjectsController
   # ./spec/features/add_project_spec.rb:6:in `block (2 levels) in <top (required)>'
```

We need a new action in our Projects controller. Since it is not going to have
logic beyond Rails boilerplate, we don't need to test anything more than the
existing Capybara test does.

`test_first_rspec/01/gatherer/app/controllers/projects_controller.rb`
```ruby
class ProjectsController < ApplicationController

  def new
    @project = Project.new
  end
end
```

Running the specs now triggers an error because Rails expects to find a
template file at /Users/app/views/projects/new.html.erb. After we create a blank file in
that spot, we see an actual Capybara error:

```
1) adding projects allows a user to create a project with tasks
     Failure/Error: fill_in "Name", with: "Project Runway"
     Capybara::ElementNotFound:
       Unable to find field "Name"
   # ./spec/features/add_project_spec.rb:7:in
       `block (2 levels) in <top (required)>'
```

Capybara searches for form items by DOM ID, form name, or the text of the
associated label. We're using the label but, of course, since the view file is
blank it isn't there. We have three form elements to take care of—a text field
for the name, a multiline text area for the tasks, and a submit button.

With the understanding that in a real project we would care about things like
"design" and "making it not look ugly," we'll just put in a basic form that
matches our needs:

`test_first_rspec/01/gatherer/app/views/projects/new.html.erb`
```erb
<h1>New Project</h1>

<%= form_for @project do |f| %>
  <%= f.label :name %>
  <%= f.text_field :name %>
  <br>
  <%= f.label :tasks %>
  <%= text_area_tag :"project[tasks]" %>
  <br>
  <%= f.submit %>
<% end %>
```

This is boilerplate, with one exception—we're creating the text area for tasks by using a text_area_tag rather than the ActiveRecord data-aware text_area method. This is because we're going to do some processing on the list of tasks, and tasks isn't a basic attribute of Project. If you do use f.text_area :tasks, Rails tries to make the value of the text area the value of the tasks relation and places in that text area an ugly Ruby string representation of the empty relation, which is not what we want.

At this point the test will submit the form and fail. Now the test is looking for the create method in the controller that is invoked by submitting the form.

We need to make some decisions. We have some logic that goes beyond Rails boilerplate—namely, we need to parse that list of tasks and create Task instances out of them when the form is submitted. That code needs to go somewhere, and the unit tests we are about to write against that code need to know where that place is. This is where the design thinking comes in our TDD process.

No matter where we put the actual coding logic, Rails will still insist on the existence of a controller, so we have the separate decision of how to test whatever logic winds up in the controller itself.

Let's start with the business logic; we'll come back to the controller.

Three locations are commonly used for business logic that responds to user input beyond the common "pass the params hash to ActiveRecord#create" Rails behavior. Here are our options:

• Put the extra logic in the controller. This is the Rails core team's preferred method, and if there isn't much logic it works perfectly fine. In my experience this location doesn't work as well for complex logic. It's challenging to test, awkward to refactor, and difficult to share if that becomes an issue. It also becomes confusing if there is more than one complicated action in the controller.

• Put the extra logic in a class method of the associated model. This was my go-to move for years. It's somewhat easier to test, but still kind of awkward to refactor—Ruby class method semantics are a pain. It also makes the model more complicated.

• Create a class to encapsulate the logic and workflow. This tends to be my first choice these days. It's the easiest to test and the best able to manage complexity changes as they come. The main downside is you wind up with a lot of little classes, but I don't mind having a lot of little pieces anyway.

So, we're creating a new class. I'll stress here that this design is not the only way to go, and if you feel the complexity of this particular action doesn't warrant its own class, that's fine.

I'd like to show how moving logic outside of Rails objects works in a testing project. There is no consistent generic name for a logic class like this. We're going to call it an action class. Other names you might see in use include service, workflow, context, use case, concern, and factory.

Our action class needs to create a project from a name and a list of tasks. Let's start with the name:

```
test_first_rspec/01/gatherer/spec/actions/creates_project_spec.rb
require "rails_helper"

describe CreatesProject do
  it "creates a project given a name" do
    creator = CreatesProject.new(name: "Project Runway")
    creator.build
    expect(creator.project.name).to eq("Project Runway")
  end
end
```

It's a straightforward test, which is the point. Because the logic isn't in the controller, we don't need to do anything fancy to test it. We're calling the class CreatesProject because I like having action classes that aren't nouns. Alternate naming conventions might include CreateProject, ProjectCreator, or ProjectFactory.

And the passing code looks like this:

```
test_first_rspec/01/gatherer/app/actions/creates_project.rb
class CreatesProject
  attr_accessor :name, :task_string, :project

  def initialize(name: "", task_string: "")
    @name = name
    @task_string = task_string
  end

  def build
    self.project = Project.new(name: name)
  end
end
```

When I create an action object I separate initialization, execution, and saving the result. I do this not just because it allows for easier testing, but also because I find that when I have an object like this there'll come a time when I want to create an object and not save the result. It's also much easier to test features of the action object if I can do so without hitting the database.

We're using Ruby 2.0 keyword arguments in the initializer, as a cheap type check to make sure the arguments passed to the CreatesProject initializer are limited to the ones we want.

Next we test the string-parsing features. If you're following along, you should write these one at a time, making each test pass before writing the next.

```
test_first_rspec/02/gatherer/spec/actions/creates_project_spec.rb
describe "task string parsing" do
  it "handles an empty string" do
    creator = CreatesProject.new(name: "Test", task_string: "")
    tasks = creator.convert_string_to_tasks
    expect(tasks.size).to eq(0)
  end

  it "handles a single string" do
    creator = CreatesProject.new(name: "Test", task_string: "Start things")
    tasks = creator.convert_string_to_tasks
    expect(tasks.size).to eq(1)
    expect(tasks.map(&:title)).to eq(["Start things"])
    expect(tasks.map(&:size)).to eq([1])
  end

  it "handles a single string with size" do
    creator = CreatesProject.new(name: "Test", task_string: "Start things:3")
    tasks = creator.convert_string_to_tasks
    expect(tasks.size).to eq(1)
    expect(tasks.map(&:title)).to eq(["Start things"])
    expect(tasks.map(&:size)).to eq([3])
  end

  it "handles multiple tasks" do
    creator = CreatesProject.new(name: "Test",
        task_string: "Start things:3\nEnd things:2")
    tasks = creator.convert_string_to_tasks
    expect(tasks.size).to eq(2)
    expect(tasks.map(&:title)).to eq(["Start things", "End things"])
    expect(tasks.map(&:size)).to eq([3, 2])
  end

  it "attaches tasks to the project" do
    creator = CreatesProject.new(name: "Test",
                task_string: "Start things:3\nEnd things:2")
    creator.create
    expect(creator.project.tasks.size).to eq(2)
    expect(creator.project).not_to be_a_new_record
  end
end
```

You can see the progression—an empty string parses to an empty list of tasks, a single element has a default size, then the size is set, and multiple tasks are separated by a \n line separator. All those tests call a convert_string_to_tasks method that allows us to test string parsing separate from any other feature of the class. After all that, we do a mini integration test where we explicitly call create to ensure that the task creation is picked up as part of the regular API process.

It is important to test save behavior because sometimes Rails associations behave better when all the objects have been saved, since Rails uses ID numbers to track associated objects, and IDs are assigned only when objects are saved. In tests I often call the Rails save! method, which throws an exception (and therefore fails the test) immediately if the object is invalid. Failing the test as quickly as possible after an error happens is a good idea—if an object fails to save and causes a problem several lines later, that problem is harder to track down.

And back to the code:

```
test_first_rspec/02/gatherer/app/actions/creates_project.rb
class CreatesProject
  attr_accessor :name, :task_string, :project

  def initialize(name: "", task_string: "")
    @name= name
    @task_string = task_string
  end

  def build
    self.project = Project.new(name: name)
    project.tasks = convert_string_to_tasks
    project
  end

  def convert_string_to_tasks
    task_string.split("\n").map do |task_string|
      title, size = task_string.split(":")
      size = 1 if (size.blank? || size.to_i.zero?)
      Task.new(title: title, size: size)
    end
  end

  def create
    build
    project.save
  end
end
```

The only thing I might refactor in the code here would be to break the inside of the loop out into its own method that parses a single string.

Refactoring to Single-Assertion Specs

There's nothing to refactor in the code right now, but we have a series of tests that have a common setup and a common set of assertions. There are a few different ways to manage this duplication in RSpec—including letting it stay if you find the tests most readable this way.

I like to take advantage of the lazy nature of RSpec's let to specify the common action and allow each test to specify an input to the action. This version also splits the assertions into separate specs, using specify as an alias for it for test blocks that don't have (or need) a descriptive comment:

`test_first_rspec/03/gatherer/spec/actions/creates_project_spec.rb`
```ruby
describe "task string parsing" do
  let(:creator) { CreatesProject.new(name: "Test", task_string: task_string) }
  let(:tasks) { creator.convert_string_to_tasks }

  describe "with an empty string" do
    let(:task_string) { "" }
    specify { expect(tasks.size).to eq(0) }
  end

  describe "with a single string" do
    let(:task_string) { "Start things" }
    specify { expect(tasks.size).to eq(1) }
    specify { expect(tasks.map(&:title)).to eq(["Start things"]) }
    specify { expect(tasks.map(&:size)).to eq([1]) }
  end


  describe "with a single string and a size" do
    let(:task_string) { "Start things:3" }
    specify { expect(tasks.size).to eq(1) }
    specify { expect(tasks.map(&:title)).to eq(["Start things"]) }
    specify { expect(tasks.map(&:size)).to eq([3]) }
  end

  describe "with multiple tasks" do
    let(:task_string) { "Start things:3\nEnd things:2" }
    specify { expect(tasks.size).to eq(2) }
    specify { expect(tasks.map(&:title)).to eq(["Start things", "End things"]) }
    specify { expect(tasks.map(&:size)).to eq([3, 2]) }
  end
```

```
describe "attaching tasks to the project" do
  let(:task_string) { "Start things:3\nEnd things:2" }
  it "saves the project and tasks" do
    creator.create
    expect(creator.project.tasks.size).to eq(2)
    expect(creator.project).not_to be_a_new_record
  end
end
end
```

The specs work a little differently in this version. At the top of the describe, we use RSpec's let to define creator in terms of a CreatesProject object and an as-yet-undefined task_string. We then use another let to define tasks in terms of creator.

Each individual test case is now its own describe. Each one uses a let to define the task_string that the creator object is looking for.

The individual assertions are now wrapped in specify calls since the assertion is (arguably) expressive enough not to need another text description. When each assertion references tasks, RSpec calls the let block for tasks, which references creator, lazily triggering that let block—which in turn references task_string, which triggers the let block in that particular test case.

This setup allows each test case to very clearly identify what makes it different from the other cases—the different task_string. In the previous version that information was buried in the noise of the common creation steps. The downside is that the nesting and indirection make it harder to trace execution, especially if you're unfamiliar with this testing style.

This version still has a roughly common set of assertions for each test case, which worries me less (in part because the RSpec remedy doesn't strike me as necessarily easier to read). Later in the book we will discuss custom matchers, which will allow us to combine duplicate assertions.

Myron Marston, the lead maintainer of RSpec, suggested that RSpec compound matchers can let us have the speed of a single spec and the precision of splitting the spec. In particular, he suggested rewriting the multiple-tasks spec as follows:

```
test_first_rspec/02a/gatherer/spec/actions/creates_project_spec.rb
it "handles multiple tasks" do
  creator = CreatesProject.new(name: "Test",
      task_string: "Start things:3\nEnd things:2")
  tasks = creator.convert_string_to_tasks
  expect(tasks).to match([
    an_object_having_attributes(title: "Start things", size: 3),
    an_object_having_attributes(title: "End things", size: 2)])
end
```

In this version, we're using a composite spec to match all the features of the tasks array—each object's size and attributes—in one expectation. Any individual failure will create a reasonably clear error message, and it all runs in a single spec.

Who Controls the Controller?

All our new tests pass, so let's take stock. We still have one test pending—our end-to-end test still doesn't like that the create action can't be found in the ProjectsController. Now we have all the pieces we need to write that action.

Since we've put our business logic in the action object, the controller doesn't have much logic, but it does have some. Specifically, the controller sends data to both the action object and onward to the view layer. Although we haven't stressed the point, the controller also needs to do something in case the action object errors or does something else unexpected. Notice that we've separated responsibilities here—almost nothing that the controller does is dependent on the logic of creating and saving projects.

We'll write a simple controller test. Once we show the tests and make them pass, we'll discuss how the tests might be improved. When we discuss test doubles in Chapter 7, *Using Test Doubles as Mocks and Stubs*, on page 117, we'll revisit controller testing.

RSpec-Rails provides custom example groups that mix in functionality for various Rails testing purposes, including controllers. By default you automatically gain that functionality for all specs in the spec/controllers directory, but you can also manually make any describe block a controller group with RSpec metadata. Here's our first controller spec:

```
test_first_rspec/03/gatherer/spec/controllers/projects_controller_spec.rb
Line 1  require 'rails_helper'

   -    RSpec.describe ProjectsController, type: :controller do

   5      describe "POST create" do
   -        it "creates a project" do
   -          post :create, project: {name: "Runway", tasks: "Start something:2"}
   -          expect(response).to redirect_to(projects_path)
   -          expect(assigns(:action).project.name).to eq("Runway")
  10        end
   -      end

   -    end
```

This test simulates a call to a controller method, and then allows us to make assertions about what the controller does. Unlike the end-to-end test that we wrote at the start of this chapter, the controller test does not go through the entire Rails stack. Instead it skips Rails routing and calls the controller method directly. RSpec controller tests run the controller action but do not, by default, invoke the view. The describe block referencing the controller action is a common convention, without any specific RSpec meaning.

Each line of this test has a feature unique to RSpec controller specs. On line 7 we use a method named post. This method name has a striking resemblance to the HTTP request type POST, and in fact is used to trigger a controller action directly. In this test the post method takes two arguments: a symbol naming the action to be invoked, and a hash representing the request parameters.

In addition to post, we have controller test methods representing the other HTTP request types, such as get, put, and delete. However, the controller test does not verify that the routing engine matches the request type with the action—Rails will happily invoke the action even if the request type would not route to that action from the browser.

The Rails testing engine will run the controller action, setting the params hash to the parameters that you specify in the test. RSpec will stop before the view is executed.

On line 8 we make an assertion about what happens after the controller method completes—specifically that it will redirect to projects_path or /projects. We could also use the matcher render_template to specify that a particular template is invoked as a result of the controller action, which is useful in cases where you are doing something other than the Rails default.

Finally, line 9 specifies the controller's contract with the view, which is to assign an instance variable @action to the actual action object. We're specifying that the action object creates a project by testing the name of that project—we don't need to test any more because further functionality is covered by the tests we already wrote against the action object. The method variable on this takes an argument that matches an instance variable created by the controller. So the controller creates @action and the test can reference that value with assigns(:action).

And that's our controller test. The passing code in the controller looks like the following:

test_first_rspec/03/gatherer/app/controllers/projects_controller.rb

```
def create
  @action = CreatesProject.new(
      name: params[:project][:name],
      task_string: params[:project][:tasks])
  @action.create
  redirect_to projects_path
end
```

There is nothing complicated in the controller action itself; we create an action object, invoke it, and redirect. Since we are explicitly extracting specific values from the params hash, Rails strong parameters are not an issue here.

Testing for Failure

Failure, of course, is always an option, so we need to test for it. I prefer to do failure path testing in unit tests rather than end-to-end tests. Success requires the entire system to work in concert. A failure response can usually be isolated to one component.

We haven't yet talked about tools that will allow us to fake failure—that requires a mock object package. But in this case it's not hard for us to create a real failure by adding a validation that we can then not fulfill.

In the app/models/project.rb file, just add validates :name, presence: true. We'll want all our projects to have names, so this validation seems perfectly reasonable.

Now we trigger a failure by trying to create a project without a name:

test_first_rspec/04/gatherer/spec/controllers/projects_controller_spec.rb

```
Line 1  it "goes back to the form on failure" do
     2    post :create, project: {name: "", tasks: ""}
     3    expect(response).to render_template(:new)
     4    expect(assigns(:project)).to be_present
     5  end
```

We've seen most of this test before. On line 2 we use the same post method to invoke the controller action, but this time with a pair of empty strings in our form. On the next line we use the render_template matcher alluded to earlier to specify nondefault behavior, specifically that we're redisplaying the form by rendering the new action template. Finally, since the new action needs an @project value for it to display, we use be_present to assert that the instance variable is actually assigned.

Making this code work requires us to use the fact that the CreatesProject action returns a Boolean from the save action: true if the action succeeds. (More complex actions would probably maintain their own status as an instance variable.)

```
test_first_rspec/04/gatherer/app/controllers/projects_controller.rb
def create
  @action = CreatesProject.new(
      name: params[:project][:name],
      task_string: params[:project][:tasks])
  success = @action.create
  if success
    redirect_to projects_path
  else
    @project = @action.project
    render :new
  end
end
```

We've added the logic to switch the controller's behavior based on the result of the action. (Some flavors of action objects would place the success and failure responses in the action class rather than the controller.)

I don't think there's any more controller logic to add at this point and I don't have a refactor for the controller code itself, so I think this round is over.

We've been able to cover the controller logic in just these two short tests because we placed the business logic in the action object. If we hadn't, all those tests we wrote for CreatesProject would be part of the controller test suite. As controller tests, they would run slower. More importantly, the tests would potentially be separated from the code where the expected failure would occur, making them less likely to drive design and less likely to be useful in troubleshooting.

That said, there are ways we can make these tests better. In the style of outside-in testing that we're demonstrating here, controller tests like these are being squeezed in two directions. If the controller test does a lot of verification of output, it runs the risk of merely duplicating the original end-to-end test. On the other hand, if the controller winds up interacting with the model layer, it can easily find itself duplicating the model test. Overlapping tests leads to a slower test suite and, again, makes it harder to pinpoint problems when tests fail. Also, it was lucky for us that we were able to trigger a failure in our controller with a relatively simple validation. Sometimes we won't have that luxury.

We want to make the controller test completely isolated from the action object that it interacts with. The key insight is that the controller test needs to test only the behavior of the controller itself—the fact that the controller calls the action object with the correct parameters and uses the values as expected. Whether the action object works correctly or even if it exists is a problem for the action object test. When testing the controller, the controller's behavior is what's important, not the action object.

There are a couple of reasons to isolate the controller test from the rest of the system. One reason is pure speed—calling the action object from the controller test could require creating and saving ActiveRecords. This is relatively slow. And while the difference between a 0.2-second test and a 0.02-second test may not seem like much, after you write a couple hundred of them the difference becomes salient. The second reason is isolation as an end in itself. The more tests that fail based on a single bug or point of regression, the harder it is to isolate and diagnose the real problem.

Prescription 7	Test isolation makes it easier to understand test failures by limiting the scope of potential locations where the failure might have occurred.

If we're sold on the idea that we want to test the controller's behavior separate from whatever it might call, the next question is how. We want to allow the controller to send all the messages it needs to, but to somehow have those messages not actually do anything. To put it another way, instead of having the controller interact with a real action object, we need it to interact with a fake one.

These fake objects are most commonly called *mock objects* or *test doubles*, and they are valuable in a variety of situations where an object you want to interact with is expensive or risky to deal with. We'll talk quite a bit about when to use mock objects in Chapter 7, *Using Test Doubles as Mocks and Stubs*, on page 117. For now, I just want you to be vaguely dissatisfied with this test.

A Test with a View

Meanwhile, we still have this end-to-end test to wrap up. Let's look at that test again:

`test_first_rspec/04/gatherer/spec/features/add_project_spec.rb`
```
require "rails_helper"

describe "adding projects" do

  it "allows a user to create a project with tasks" do
    visit new_project_path
    fill_in "Name", with: "Project Runway"
    fill_in "Tasks", with: "Task 1:3\nTask 2:5"
    click_on("Create Project")
```

```
    visit projects_path
    expect(page).to have_content("Project Runway")
    expect(page).to have_content("8")
  end

end
```

So far we've gotten this test to pass up to the visit projects_path line. This line triggers a visit to the path /projects, which is routed to the index method of the ProjectController. Since we don't have an index method, our current error is The action 'index' could not be found for ProjectsController.

So we'll need the index method:

test_first_rspec/04/gatherer/app/controllers/projects_controller.rb
```
def index
  @projects = Project.all
end
```

And now we have an action without a view, resulting in the error message that starts with ActionView::MissingTemplate: Missing template projects/index,.... To get past this error, we create a blank view file at app/views/projects/index.html.erb.

Now our error is on the following line of the test:

```
adding projects allows a user to create a project with tasks
    Failure/Error: expect(page).to have_content("Project Runway")
      expected to find text "Project Runway" in ""
 # ./spec/features/add_project_spec.rb:11:in `block (2 levels) in <top (required)>'
```

At this point the Capybara test is evaluating the HTML response from our application. We're asking the test to have_content, which is defined by Capybara and which passes if the response either literally contains a string argument or matches a regular-expression argument. Specifically, we're asserting that the output contains the string Project Runway (which is the name of the newly created project) and the string 8 (which is its size).

This is a very weak test. There are all kinds of ways, for example, that the number 8 could appear in our response HTML. To pick one unlikely scenario, our user could be journalist and author Jennifer 8. Lee.[1]) The struggle when view-testing is to find a balance between a test that validates something meaningful about the output and one that isn't so tied to the actual markup that it will break when a designer looks at the page cross-eyed.

Let's make the test pass first, then explore how we can strengthen the test. Passing the test requires a straightforward Rails view:

---

1.   http://en.wikipedia.org/wiki/Jennifer_8._Lee

```
test_first_rspec/04/gatherer/app/views/projects/index.html.erb
<h1>All Projects</h1>
<table>
  <thead>
    <tr>
      <td>Project Name</td>
      <td>Total Project Size</td>
    </tr>
  </thead>
  <tbody>
    <% @projects.each do |project| %>
      <tr>
        <td><%= project.name %></td>
        <td><%= project.total_size %></td>
      </tr>
    <% end %>
  </tbody>
</table>
```

We're not concerned with making this pretty; in a production application, presumably the markup would be more complex.

When this executes, our newly entered project gets its own table row—complete with its name and size.

And our end-to-end test finally passes.

That puts us in a refactoring phase. We didn't write much code in this step, but I'd like to take the opportunity to refactor the last couple of lines of the end-to-end test, using the capybara-rails has_selector matcher. This is a really common work pattern for me. Sometimes I have trouble seeing the shape of a view before I write it, so I write a very loose test and then tighten the test once I see what pieces of the view will exist for me to hook onto.

The has_selector method takes as its argument a jQuery-style selector, with the usual # representing a DOM ID, and a dot (.) representing a DOM class. The assertion passes if the page contains a DOM element that matches the selector. You can also specify a text: option that means the matching DOM element must also contain particular text (or match a particular regular expression).

With has_selector, we can rewrite the test as follows:

```
test_first_rspec/05/gatherer/spec/features/add_project_spec.rb
require "rails_helper"

describe "adding projects" do
  it "allows a user to create a project with tasks" do
    visit new_project_path
```

```
        fill_in "Name", with: "Project Runway"
        fill_in "Tasks", with: "Task 1:3\nTask 2:5"
        click_on("Create Project")
        visit projects_path
        @project = Project.find_by_name("Project Runway")
        expect(page).to have_selector(
            "#project_#{@project.id} .name", text: "Project Runway")
        expect(page).to have_selector(
            "#project_#{@project.id} .total-size", text: "8")
    end
end
```

In our final two lines we're testing for the same text, but now we're forcing it to appear in a specific part of the page. We want each bit of text to be associated with a DOM ID representing the project item—using the Rails-blessed pattern <class>_<id> and then a DOM class representing type. This gives us a stronger test: no longer would a random 8 somewhere on the page cause a pass—now the 8 specifically has to be associated with the size of this project.

However, the test isn't completely brittle—nothing specifies, for example, that the elements are table rows and cells. So if we go off and redesign this page using more modern markup, as long as the size element is subordinate to the project element, the test will still pass.

The view needs only minor changes to make this test pass:

```
test_first_rspec/05/gatherer/app/views/projects/index.html.erb
<h1>All Projects</h1>
<table>
  <thead>
    <tr>
      <td>Project Name</td>
      <td>Total Project Size</td>
    </tr>
  </thead>
  <tbody>
    <% @projects.each do |project| %>
      <tr class="project-row" id="<%= dom_id(project) %>">
        <td class="name"><%= project.name %></td>
        <td class="total-size"><%= project.total_size %></td>
      </tr>
    <% end %>
  </tbody>
</table>
```

We've only added a few DOM IDs and DOM classes.

And with that the test passes again, and I think we've got this feature in the books.

What Have We Done? And What's Next?

We've written an entire (albeit small) piece of Rails functionality, starting with an end-to-end integration test and moving down to unit tests to make each part of the feature work. And it took us only one chapter. It goes a lot faster when you don't stop to explain every line of code.

In the next few chapters we'll look at model testing, controller testing, and view testing, covering the libraries discussed in this chapter in more detail. We'll also discuss related topics, such as placing data in tests, testing for security, and testing JavaScript. After that we'll tackle some wider topics: how to test legacy code, how to keep your tests from becoming legacy code, how to test external services, and the like.

First, though, let's step back for a second and talk about what makes automated testing effective.

## CHAPTER 4

What Makes Great Tests

As the Rails community has matured, Rails developers have become much more likely to work with codebases and test suites that contain many years' worth of work. As a result, there has been a lot of discussion about design strategies to manage complexity over time.

There hasn't been nearly as much discussion about what practices make tests and test suites continue to be valuable over time. As applications grow, as suite runs get longer, as complexity increases, how can you write tests that will be useful in the future and not act as an impediment to future development?

The Big One

The best, most general piece of advice I can give about the style and structure of automated tests is this:

> **Prescription 8** Your tests are also code. Specifically, your tests are code that does not have tests.

Your code is verified by your tests, but your tests are verified by nothing.

Having your tests be as clear and manageable as possible is the only way to keep them honest.

The Big Two

If a programming practice or tool is successful, following or using it will make it easier to:

- add the code I need in the short term.
- continue to add code to the project over time.

All kinds of gems in the Ruby and Rails ecosystem help with the first goal (including Rails itself). Testing is normally thought of as working toward the second goal. That's true, but often people assume the only contribution testing makes toward long-term application health is verification of application logic and prevention of regressions. In fact, over the long term test-driven development tends to pay off as good tests lead toward modular designs.

This means a valuable test saves time and effort over the long term, while a poor test costs time and effort. I've focused on five qualities that tend to make a test save time and effort. The absence of these qualities, on the other hand, is often a sign that the test could be a problem in the future.

The More Detailed Five: SWIFT Tests

I like to use five criteria to evaluate test quality. I've even managed to turn them into an acronym that is only slightly contrived: SWIFT.

- Straightforward
- Well defined
- Independent
- Fast
- Truthful

Let's explore those in more detail.

[S]traightforward

A test is *straightforward* if its purpose is immediately understandable.

Straightforwardness in testing goes beyond just having clear code. A straightforward test is also clear about how it fits into the larger test suite. Every test should have a point: it should test something different from the other tests, and that purpose should be easy to discern from reading the test.

Here is a test that is not straightforward:

```
## Don't do this
it "should add to 37" do
  expect(User.all_total_points).to eq(37)
end
```

Where does the 37 come from? It's part of the global setup. If you were to peek into this fake example's user fixture file, you'd see that somehow the totals of the points of all the users in that file add up to 37. The test passes. Yay?

There are two relevant problems with this test:

- The 37 is a magic literal that apparently comes from nowhere.
- The test's name is utterly opaque about whether this is a test for the main-line case, a test for a common error condition, or a test that exists only because the coder was bored and thought it would be fun.

Combine these problems, and it quickly becomes next to impossible to fix the test a few months later when a change to the User class or the fixture file breaks it.

Naming tests is critical to being straightforward. Creating data locally and explicitly also helps. With most factory tools (see *Factories*, on page 101), default values are preset, so the description of an object created in the test can be limited to defining only the attributes that are actually important to the behavior being tested. Showing those attributes in the test is an important clue to the programmer's intent. Rewriting the preceding test with a little more information might result in this:

```
it "rounds total points to the nearest integer" do
  User.create(:points => 32.1)
  User.create(:points => 5.3)
  expect(User.all_total_points).to eq(37)
end
```

It's not poetry, but at the very least an interested reader now knows where that pesky 37 comes from and where the test fits in the grand scheme of things. The reader might then have a better chance of fixing the test if something breaks. The test is also more independent since it no longer relies on global fixtures—making it less likely to break.

Long tests or long setups tend to muddy the water and make it hard to identify the critical parts of the test. The same principles that guide refactoring and cleaning up code apply to tests. This is especially true of the rule that states "A method should only do one thing," which here means splitting up test setups into semantically meaningful parts, as well as keeping each test focused on one particular goal.

On the other hand, if you can't write short tests, consider the possibility that it is the code's fault and you need to do some redesign. If it's hard to set up a short test, that often indicates the code has too many internal dependencies.

There's an old programming adage that goes like this: "Debugging is twice as hard as writing the code in the first place. Therefore, if you write the code as cleverly as possible, you are, by definition, not smart enough to debug it." (I got the quote from http://quotes.cat-v.org/programming/, but the original source is Brian W. Kernighan and P.J. Plauger's *The Elements of Programming Style*.)

Because tests don't have their own tests, this quote suggests that you should keep your tests simple to give yourself cognitive room to understand them.

In particular, this guideline argues against using clever tricks to reduce duplication among multiple tests that share a similar structure. If you find yourself starting to metaprogram to generate multiple tests in your suite, you'll probably find that complexity working against you at some point. You never want to have to decide whether a bug is in your test or in the code. And when—not if—you do find a bug in your test suite, it's easier to fix if the test code is simple.

We'll talk more about clarity issues throughout the book. In particular, the issue will come up when we discuss factories versus fixtures as ways of adding test data in Chapter 6, *Adding Data to Tests*, on page 93.

[W]ell Defined

A test is *well defined* if running the same test repeatedly gives the same result. If your tests are not well defined, the symptom will be intermittent, seemingly random test failures (sometimes called Heisenbugs, Heisenspecs, or Rando Calrissians).

Three classic causes of repeatability problems are time and date testing, random numbers, and third-party or Ajax calls. In all cases the issue is that your test data changes from test to test. Dates and times have a nasty habit of monotonically increasing, while random data stubbornly insists on being random. Similarly, tests that depend on a third-party service or even test code that makes Ajax calls back to your own application can vary from test run to test run, causing intermittent failures.

Dates and times tend to lead to intermittent failures when certain magic time boundaries are crossed. You can also get tests that fail at particular times of day or when run in certain time zones. Random numbers, in contrast, make it somewhat difficult to test both the randomness of the number and that the randomly generated number is used properly in whatever calculation requires it.

The test plan is similar for dates, randomness, and external services—really, it applies to any constantly changing dataset. We test changing data with a combination of encapsulation and mocking. We encapsulate the data by creating a service object that wraps around the changing functionality. By mediating access to the changing functionality, we make it easier to stub or mock the output values. Stubbing the values provides the consistency we need for testing.

We might, for example, create a RandomStream class that wraps Ruby's rand() method:

```
class RandomStream
  def next
    rand()
  end
end
```

This example is a little oversimplified—normally we'd be encapsulating RandomStream. With your own wrapper class, you can provide more specific methods tuned to your use case, something like def random_phone_number. First you unit-test the stream class to verify that the class works as expected. Then any class that uses RandomStream can be provided mock random values to allow for easier and more stable testing.

The exact mix of encapsulation and mocking varies. Timecop is a Ruby gem that stubs the time and date classes with no encapsulation—in Rails 4.1, ActiveSupport has a similar feature. This allows us to specify an exact value for the current time for testing purposes. That said, nearly every time I talk about Timecop in a public forum, someone points out that creating a time service is a superior solution.

We'll discuss this pattern for wrapping a potentially variable external service in more detail in Chapter 12, *Testing External Services*, on page 229. We'll cover mock objects in Chapter 7, *Using Test Doubles as Mocks and Stubs*, on page 117, and we'll talk more about debugging intermittent test failures in Chapter 14, *Troubleshooting and Debugging*, on page 273.

[I]ndependent

A test is *independent* if it does not depend on any other tests or external data to run. An independent test suite gives the same results no matter the order in which the tests are run, and tends to limit the scope of test failures to only tests that cover a buggy method.

In contrast, a very dependent test suite could trigger failures throughout your tests from a single change in one part of an application. A clear sign that your tests are not independent is if you have test failures that happen only when the test suite is run in a particular order—in fully independent tests, the order in which they are run should not matter. Another sign is a single line of code breaking multiple tests.

The biggest impediment to independence in the test suite itself is the use of global data. Rails fixtures are not the only possible cause of global data in a

Rails test suite, but they are a common cause. Somewhat less common in a Rails context is using a tool or third-party library in a setup and not tearing it down.

Outside the test suite, if the application code is not well encapsulated it may be difficult or impossible to make the tests fully independent of one another.

[F]ast

It's easy to overlook the importance of pure speed in the long-term mainte-nance of a test suite or a TDD practice. In the beginning it doesn't make much difference. When you have only a few methods under test, the difference between a second per test and a tenth of a second per test is almost imper-ceptible. The difference between a one-minute suite and a six-second suite is easier to discern.

From there, the sky's the limit. I worked in one Rails shop where nobody really knew how long the tests ran in development because they farmed the test suite out to a server farm that was more powerful than most production web servers I've seen. This is bad.

Slow test suites hurt you in a variety of ways.

There are startup costs. In the sample TDD session we went through in Chapter 2, *Test-Driven Development Basics*, on page 13, and Chapter 3, *Test-Driven Rails*, on page 41, we went back and forth to run the tests a lot. In practice I went back and forth even more frequently. Over the course of writing that tutorial, I ran the tests dozens of times. Imagine what happens if it takes even 10 seconds to start a test run. Or a minute, which is not out of the question for a larger Rails app. I've worked on JRuby-based applications that took well over a minute to start.

TDD is about flow in the moment, and the ability to go back and forth between running tests and writing code without breaking focus is crucial to being able to use TDD as a design tool. If you can check Twitter while your tests are running, you just aren't going to get the full value of the TDD process.

Tests get slow for a number of reasons, but the most important in a Rails context are as follows:

- Startup time
- Dependencies within the code that require a lot of objects to be created to invoke the method under test
- Extensive use of the database or other external services during a test

Not only do large object trees slow down the test at runtime, but setting up large amounts of data makes writing the tests more labor-intensive. And if writing the tests becomes burdensome, you aren't going to do it.

Speeding tests up often means isolating application logic from the Rails stack so that logic can be tested without loading the entire Rails stack or without retrieving test data from the database. As with a lot of good testing practices, this isolation results in more robust code that is easier to change moving forward.

Since test speed is so important for successful TDD, throughout the book we'll discuss ways to write fast tests. In particular, the discussion of creating data in Chapter 6, *Adding Data to Tests*, on page 93, and the discussion of testing environments in Chapter 15, *Running Tests Faster and Running Faster Tests*, on page 287, will be concerned with creating fast tests.

[T]ruthful

A *truthful* test accurately reflects the underlying code—it passes when the underlying code works, and fails when it does not. This is easier said than done.

A frequent cause of brittle tests is targeting assertions at surface features that might change even if the underlying logic stays the same. The classic example along these lines is view testing, in which we base the assertion on the creative text on the page (which will frequently change even though the basic logic stays the same):

```
it "shows the project section" do
  get :dashboard
  expect(response).to have_selector("h2", :text => "My Projects")
end
```

It seems like a perfectly valid test right up until somebody determines that "My Projects" is a lame header and decides to go with "My Happy Fun-Time Projects," breaking our test. You are often better served by testing something that's slightly insulated from surface changes, such as a DOM ID.

```
it "shows the project section" do
  get :dashboard
  expect(response).to have_selector("h2#projects")
end
```

The basic issue here is not limited to view testing. There are areas of model testing in which testing to a surface feature might be brittle in the face of trivial changes to the model (as opposed to tests that are brittle in the face of changes to the test data itself, which we've already discussed).

The other side of robustness is not just a test that fails when the logic is good, but a test that stubbornly continues to pass even if the underlying code is bad—a tautology, in other words.

Speaking of tautologies, mock objects have their own special robustness issues. It's easy to create a tautology by using a mock object. It's also easy to create a brittle test because a mock object often creates a hard expectation of what methods will be called on it. If you add an unexpected method call to the code being tested, you can get mock-object failures simply because an unexpected method has been called. I've had changes to a login filter cause hundreds of test failures because mock users going through the login filter bounced off the new call.

Using SWIFT Tests

Writing effective test suites is hard. The complexity and runtime of a typical test suite increases slowly, and often you don't realize you have a serious problem until it's too late. Paying attention to detail in keeping individual tests simple and fast will pay off over time.

The goal of your test suite is to allow you to use tests to improve the design and for the existing tests to empower you to make changes with less fear of introducing new bugs. If your test suite is slow, complicated, or fragile, then you lose the ability of your tests to help you with either of these things. In the worst case, you can find yourself still needing to maintain a test suite but having that test suite slow down development because of how hard it is to keep the tests synchronized with the code.

Being strict about writing tests first, writing tests against behavior and not implementation, and taking time to make the tests simple and fast will all help keep your test suite useful and healthy over the course of a long project.

## CHAPTER 5

Testing Models

A standard Rails application uses a design pattern called *MVC*, which stands for model-view-controller. Each of the three sections in the MVC pattern is a separate layer of code, which has its own responsibilities and communicates with the other layers as infrequently as possible. In Rails, the model layer contains both business logic and persistence logic, with the persistence logic being handled by ActiveRecord. Typically, all of your ActiveRecord objects will be part of the model layer, but not everything in the model layer is an ActiveRecord object. The model layer can include various services, value objects, or other classes that encapsulate logic and use ActiveRecord objects for storage.

We'll start our tour of testing the Rails stack with the model layer because model tests have the fewest dependencies on Rails-specific features and are often the easiest place to start testing your application. Standard Rails model tests are very nearly vanilla RSpec. Features specific to Rails include a few new matchers and the ability to set up initial data.

We'll talk about testing ActiveRecord features such as associations and models. And we'll talk about separating logic from persistence and why that can be a valuable practice for both testing and application development.

What Can We Do in a Model Test?

An RSpec file in the spec/models directory is automatically of type: :model, which gives you...not a whole lot of new behavior, actually. There is an add-on gem called rspec-activemodel-mocks, which is maintained by the RSpec core team and includes some mock-object tools specific to use with ActiveModel.

What Should I Test in a Model Test?

Models. Next question?

Okay, Funny Man, What Makes a Good Set of Model Tests?

There are a lot of different, sometimes conflicting, goals for tests. It's hard to know where to start your TDD process, how many tests to write, and when you are done. The classic description of the process—write a simple test, make it pass, then refactor—doesn't provide a lot of affirmative guidance or direction for the larger process of adding a feature.

A TDD Metaprocess

Here's a metaprocess that reflects how I write a new business logic feature. (I handle view logic a little differently.) This process is more of a guideline than a hard-and-fast checklist. As the logic we are working on gets more complex, and the less we know about the implementation when we start, the closer we should stick to this process and the smaller the steps we should take.

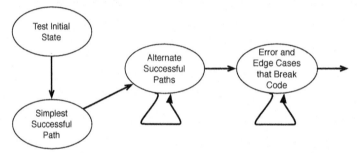

Often the best place to start is with a test that describes an initial state of the system, without invoking logic. This is especially useful if you are test-driving a new class, so the first test just sets up the class and verifies the initial state of instance variables. If you are working in an existing class, this step may not be necessary.

Next, determine the main cases that drive the new logic. Sometimes there will be only one primary case, like "calculate the total value of a user's purchase." Sometimes there will be many; "calculate tax on a purchase" might have lots of cases based on the user's location or the items being purchased.

Take that list and write tests for the main cases one at a time. I do not recommend writing multiple failing tests simultaneously—that turns out to be confusing. It can be helpful to use comments or pending tests to at least note what the future tests will be. Ideally these tests are small—if they need a lot of setup, you probably should be testing a smaller unit of code.

Sometimes you'll pass the first test by putting in a solution that is deliberately specific to the test, like doing nothing but returning the integer makes the test pass. Gary Bernhardt of Destroy All Software calls this technique "sliming."[1] This can be helpful in keeping your code close to the tests—again, especially when the algorithm is complex.

Prescription 9	If you find yourself writing tests that already pass given the current state of the code, that often means you're writing too much code in each pass.

The goal in these tests is to first make the test pass quickly without worrying much about niceties of implementation. Once each test passes, look for opportunities to refactor—we'll talk more about that in the next section.

When the main cases are done, you try to think of ways to break the existing code. Sometimes you'll notice something as you're writing code to pass a previous test, like, "Hey, I wonder what would happen if this argument were nil?" Write a test that describes what the output should be and make it pass. Refactoring gets increasingly important here because special cases and error conditions tend to make code complex, and managing that complexity becomes really important to future versions of the code. The advantage of waiting to do special cases at the end is that you already have tests to cover the normal cases, so you can use those to check your new code each step of the way.

When you can no longer think of a way to break your code, you're likely done with this feature and ready to move on to the next. If you haven't been doing so, run the entire test suite to make sure you didn't inadvertently break something. Then take one further look at the code for larger-scale refactoring.

Refactoring Models

In a TDD process, much of the design takes place during the refactoring step. A lot of this design happens under the guise of cleanup—looking at parts of the code that seem overly complicated or poorly structured and figuring out how best to rearrange them.

Just because the refactoring step includes cleanup doesn't mean you can skip this step when you're in a hurry. Don't do that. Refactoring is not a luxury that you can throw aside. Refactoring is where you think about your code and how best to structure it. Skipping refactoring will slowly start to hurt, and by the time you notice the problem, it'll be much harder to clean up than if you had addressed it early.

---

1.   http://www.destroyallsoftware.com

> **Prescription 10** Refactoring is where a lot of design happens in TDD, and it's easiest to do in small steps. Skip it at your peril.

At the most abstract level, you're looking for three things: complexity to break up, duplication to combine, and abstractions waiting to be born.

Break Up Complexity

Complexity will often initially manifest itself as long methods or long lines of code. If you are doing a "quick to green" first pass of the code to make the tests pass, there will often be a line of code with lots of method chaining or the like. It's almost always a good idea to break up long methods or long lines by extracting part of the code into its own method. In addition to simplifying the original method, you have the opportunity to give the method you're creating a name that is meaningful in the domain and that can make your code self-documenting.

Booleans, local variables, and inline comments are almost always candidates for extraction:

- Any compound Boolean logic expression goes in its own method. It's much harder than you might think for people to understand what a compound expression does. Give people reading your code a fighting chance by hiding the expression behind a name that expresses the code's intent, such as valid_name? or has_purchased_before?.

- Local variables are relatively easy to break out into methods with the same name as the variable—in Ruby, code that uses the variable doesn't need to change if the variable becomes a method with no arguments. Having a lot of local variables is a huge drag on complex refactorings—you'll be surprised at how much more flexible your code feels if you minimize the number of local variables in methods. (I first encountered this idea, along with a lot of other great refactoring ideas, in *Refactoring: Improving the Design of Existing Code [FBBO99]*.)

- In long methods, sometimes a single-line comment breaks up the method by describing what the next part does. This nearly always is better extracted to a separate method with a name based on the comment's contents. Instead of one twenty-five-line method, you wind up with a five-line method that calls five other five-line methods, each of which does one thing, and each of which has a name that is meaningful in the context of the application domain.

> **Prescription 11** Try to extract methods when you see compound Booleans, local variables, or inline comments.

Combine Duplication

You need to look out for three kinds of duplication: duplication of fact, duplication of logic, and duplication of structure.

Duplication of fact is usually easy to see and fix. A common case would be a "magic number" used by multiple parts of the code, such as a conversion factor or a maximum value. Often a status variable has only a few valid values, and the list of those values is duplicated:

```
validates :size, numericality: {less_than_or_equal_to: 5}

def possible_sizes
  (1 .. 5)
end
```

The remedy for duplication of fact is also usually simple—make the value a constant or a method with a constant return value, like this:

```
MAX_POINT_COUNT = 5

validates :size, numericality: {less_than_or_equal_to: MAX_POINT_COUNT}

def possible_sizes
  (1 .. MAX_POINT_COUNT)
 end
```

Or, alternatively, like this:

```
VALID_POINT_RANGE = 1 .. 5
validates :size, inclusion: {in: VALID_POINT_RANGE}
```

That said, at some point the extra character count for a constant is ridiculous and Java-like in the worst way. For string and symbol constants, if the constant value is effectively identical to the symbol (as in ACTIVE_STATUS = :active), I'll often leave the duplication. I'm not saying I recommend that; I'm just saying I do it.

I also often make the constant value an instance method with a static return value rather than a Ruby constant, like this:

```
def max_point_count
  5
end
```

I do this because then max_point_count has the same lookup semantics as any other instance value, and it often reads better to make a value owned by the instance rather than the class. It's also easier to change if the constant turns out to be less than constant in the future.

Duplication of logic is similar to duplication of fact, but instead of looking for simple values we're looking for longer structures. This will often include compound Boolean statements used as guards in multiple methods (in our task-manager example, this might be something about whether a task has been completed) or simple calculations that are used in multiple places (such as converting task size to time based on the project's rate of completion).

In this example, the same Boolean test is applied twice and it's easy to imagine it being used many more times:

```
class User
  def maximum_posts
    if status == :trusted then 10 else 5 end
  end

  def urls_in_replies
    if status == :trusted then 3 else 0 end
  end
end
```

One task here is move the duplicated logic into its own method and call the method from each location (in this case def trusted?). I recommend being aggressive about this—you'll sometimes see advice that you should just notice duplication on the second instance and refactor on the third instance. In my experience, that just means you wind up with twice as much duplication as you should have. (See the next section for other ideas about reused Booleans.)

Keep in mind that not every piece of logic that is spelled the same in Ruby is actually duplication. It's possible for early forms of two pieces of logic to look similar but eventually evolve in separate directions. A great example of this is Rails controller scaffolding. Every RESTful controller starts with the same boilerplate code for the seven RESTful actions. And there have been innumerable attempts to remove that duplication by creating a common abstraction. Most of those attempts eventually wind up in a tangle of special case logic because each controller eventually needs to have different features.

Find Missing Abstractions

Duplication of structure often means there's a missing abstraction, which in Ruby generally means you can move some code into a new class.

One symptom is a set of instance attributes that are always used together—especially if the same group of attributes is being passed to multiple methods. Use of a common set of variables often indicates that you want a new class with those friendly attributes as the instance attributes.

Another common symptom is a group of methods that all share a prefix or a suffix, such as logger_init, logger_print, and logger_read. Often this means you need a class corresponding to the common word.

In ActiveRecord, one side effect of discovering friendly attributes is the creation of value objects, which are immutable instances that represent parts of your data. For example, a start_date and end_date are often used together and could easily be combined into a DateRange class.

Also, how often do you write something like this?

```ruby
class User < ActiveRecord::Base
  def full_name
    "#{first_name} #{last_name}"
  end

  def sort_name
    "#{last_name}, #{first_name}"
  end
end
```

You could try this:

```ruby
class Name
  attr_reader :first_name, :last_name

  def initialize(first_name, last_name)
    @first_name, @last_name = first_name, last_name
  end

  def full_name
    "#{first_name} #{last_name}"
  end

  def sort_name
    "#{last_name}, #{first_name}"
  end
end

class User < ActiveRecord::Base
  delegate :full_name, :sort_name, to: :name
  def name
    Name.new(first_name, last_name)
  end
end
```

If you have existing tests on User in that situation, those tests should continue to pass.

Normally I don't change tests when I refactor—the goal is to test functionality, not implementation. I will sometimes make an exception to this rule if I move the code to a new class, especially if I expect the new class to be shared often.

When you break out related attributes into their own class, as in this Name example, you'll often find it's much easier to add complexity when you have a dedicated place for that logic. When you need middle names or titles, it's easier to manage that in a separate class than it would be if you had a half implementation of names in multiple classes.

You'll also find that these small classes are easy to test because Name no longer has a dependency on the database or any other code. Without dependencies, it's easy to set up and write fast tests for name logic.

```
it "generates sortable names" do
  name = Name.new("Noel", "Rappin")
  expect(name.sort_name).to eq("Rappin, Noel")
end
```

The tests for the new Name class are quick to write and to run. The easier it is to write tests, the more tests you'll write.

Also look out for repeated if statements or other conditionals that switch on the same values. A common example is continually checking for a nil value. Another is frequent checking against a status variable. Our task tracker, for example, might have a lot of methods that do this:

```
if status == :completed
  calculate_completed_time
else
  calculate_incompleted_time
end
```

Every program needs the occasional if statement. But if you're continually checking an object's state to determine what to do next, consider the possibility that you have a new set of classes. For example, the preceding snippet implies the existence of something like CompleteTask and IncompleteTask. (Or maybe completeness and incompleteness affect only part of the class functionality, so you get something like CompleteTaskCalculator and IncompleteTaskCalculator.)

Once you've separated functionality into separate classes, an object-oriented program is supposed to switch based on class, using message passing and polymorphism:

```ruby
def calculator
  if complete?
    CompleteTaskCalculator.new(self)
  else
    IncompleteTaskCalculator.new(self)
  end
end

def calculate
  calculator.calculate_time
end
```

In the second example we still have an if statement about the logic between complete and incomplete tasks, but only one. Any further difference between complete and incomplete tasks is handled in the difference between the two calculator classes. If you're testing for completion in many places, this form can be more clear.

Again, these classes typically don't depend on the database making them easy to write fast tests for, and you'll often find these classes attracting behavior—once they exist, it's easier to see what behavior belongs there.

A Note on Assertions per Test

You'll often find that a common setup results in multiple assertions in a test. This is particularly true of integration tests. For example, when we created a new project we asserted that the project existed and had a specific relationship with newly created tasks.

There are two contrasting styles for writing tests with multiple assertions. In one style the setup and all the assertions are part of the same test. If we were trying to test changes when we mark a task complete, then having all the assertions in the same test might look like this:

```ruby
it "marks a task complete" do
  task = tasks(:incomplete)
  task.mark_complete
  expect(task).to be_complete
  expect(task).to be_blocked
  expect(task.end_date).to eq(Date.today.to_s(:db))
  expect(task.most_recent_log.end_state).to eq("completed")
end
```

In contrast, we could put each assertion in a separate test and put the common setup in a setup block. Using the same set of assertions in separate tests looks like the following:

```
describe "task completion" do
  let(:task) {tasks(:incomplete)}
  before(:example) { task.mark_complete }
  specify { expect(task).to be_complete }
  specify { expect(task).to be_blocked }
  specify { expect(task.end_date).to eq(Date.today.to_s(:db)) }
  specify { expect(task.most_recent_log.end_state).to eq("completed") }
end
```

We've already seen this pattern a bit, where the variable is defined in a let method, with some additional configuration happening in a before method.

The tradeoff is pretty plain: the one-assertion-per-test style has the advantage that each assertion can fail independently—when all the assertions are in a single test, the test bails on the first failure. In the all-in-one test, if expect(task).to be_complete fails, you won't even get to the check for expect(task).to be_blocked. If all the assertions are in separate tests, everything runs independently but it's harder to determine how tests are related. There are two significant downsides to the one-assertion style: first, there can be a significant speed difference since the single-assertion-per-test version will run the common setup multiple times, and second, the one-assertion style can become difficult to read, especially if the setup and test wind up with some distance between them.

Often I compromise by making my first pass at TDD in the one-assertion-per-test style, which forces me to work in baby steps and gives me a more accurate picture of what tests are failing. When I'm confident in the correctness of the code, I consolidate related assertions, giving me the speed benefit moving forward. Another compromise is the use of compound RSpec matchers or the has_attributes matcher to create a single assertion out of what might otherwise be multiple assertions.

That said, expectations that genuinely cover different branches of the application logic should be handled in separate specs. Avoid changing local variables inside a spec just to test different logic in the same test. That means you would want to keep these specs separate:

```
it "knows full names" do
  user = User.create(:first_name => "Fred", :last_name => "Flintstone")
  expect(user.full_name).to eq("Fred Flintstone")
end

it "knows full names with a middle initial" do
  user = User.create(:first_name => "Fred", :last_name => "Flintstone"
      :middle_initial => "D")
  expect(user.full_name).to eq("Fred D. Flintstone")
end
```

```
it "knows full name where there's no first name" do
  user = User.create(:last_name => "Flintstone")
  expect(user.full_name).to eq("Flintstone")
end
```

Continually changing the value of user to put all those assertions in the same branch makes for a test that is very hard to read and understand.

Testing What Rails Gives You

Rails provides built-in functionality for associations and validations, which leads to questions about how to effectively and usefully test those features in your application.

The answer in both cases is similar, and goes back to the basic principle that we're testing functionality and not implementation. Although I do not normally write tests just to show the existence of a particular association or validation, I do sometimes write tests that show those features in action. For associations, this means showing the association in use. For validations, it means testing the overall logic of what makes an instance valid.

The testing gem shoulda-matchers, defines matchers that specifically test for the existence of validations and associations, like so:[2]

```
describe Task do
  it { should belong_to(:project) }
  it { should belong_to(:user) }
  it { should ensure_length_of(:name) }
end
```

Tests like that are not particularly valuable for a TDD process because they are not about the design of new features. If you're doing the TDD process, you shouldn't start from the idea that your Task belongs to a Project. Rather, as you describe features the relationship is implied from the feature tests that you're writing. More operationally, this means that in a good TDD process, any condition in the code that would cause a direct test like those Shoulda matchers to fail would also cause another test to fail. In which case, what's the point of the Shoulda matcher?

To briefly and halfheartedly argue the other side, you often don't need to go through a whole TDD process to know that a relationship or a validation should exist, and these tests don't cost very much to write. And to rebut myself, part of doing the TDD process is to force you to examine the things

---

2. https://github.com/thoughtbot/shoulda-matchers

you think you know and prove that they are really necessary. In particular, if I see a lot of those should belong_to lines of code in a test suite, rightly or wrongly I'm going to be worried about the test suite's effectiveness.

Validations are a little different since the validity of a piece of data is often a legitimate and complex piece of business logic and the Rails helpers cover only a set of common cases. I think you can make validations in your code work efficiently with the TDD process if you focus on the functional part—"this object is valid" versus "this object is not," rather than the "I'm using a Rails numerical validator" part. Also, consider using a Rails database-blocking validation only as a last resort when you sincerely believe it's worth potentially raising an exception rather than having this data in your database.

This means I would typically test for the functional effect of an invalid object rather than the implementation fact of the existence of a Rails validation. The functional effect is often along the lines of an object or objects not saving to the database. If we wanted to augment our project tracker's project creation to require that all the tasks for the new project have a size, we might try something like this:

```
it "doesn't allow  creation of a task without a size" do
  creator = CreatesProject.new(name: "Test", task_string: "size:no_size")
  creator.create
  expect(creator.project.tasks.map(&:title)).to eq(["size"])
end
```

In this test, we're validating that the second task, with the clever name no size, does not get added to the project. This test works whether the size limitation is implemented as a Rails validation or as some kind of filter that the CreatesProject class manages. Again, we're testing the behavior, not the implementation. This strategy works for all kinds of Rails validations, including uniqueness (create two objects and validate that the second one doesn't save). When I create a custom validator, though, as either a method or a separate class, it goes through the same TDD process as any other method.

Testing ActiveRecord Finders

ActiveRecord provides a rich set of methods that are wrappers around SQL statements sent to your database. These methods are collectively referred to as *finders*. One great feature of ActiveRecord finders is that they can be composed, allowing you to express a compound statement like "bring me the most recently completed five large tasks" as Task.where(status: completed).order("completed_at DESC").where("size > 3").limit(5).

You can even compose the finders if you extract them to their own methods in pieces:

```ruby
class Task < ActiveRecord::Base

  def self.completed
    where(status: :completed)
  end

  def self.large
    where("size > 3")
  end

  def self.most_recent
    order("completed_at DESC")
  end

  def self.recent_done_and_large
    completed.large.most_recent.limit(5)
  end
end
```

Being able to compose this logic is awesome. But finder methods occupy an awkward place between methods you might write and Rails core features, leading to the question of how best to test them.

Here are some guidelines.

Be aggressive about extracting compound finder statements to their own method, in much the same way and for much the same reason as I recommended for compound Boolean logic. The methods are easier to understand and reuse if they are bound together behind a method name that defines the intent of the method. When we talk about mock objects you'll also see that having finders called behind other methods makes it much easier to avoid touching the database when you don't need to.

If a finder is extracted during refactoring and an existing test already covers its functionality, you may not need a new test to cover it. Like any other method extracted in refactoring, you aren't adding logic. Again, though, if the finder method winds up in a different class than that covered by the existing test, consider transferring the test logic.

If you are test-driving the finder method directly, you have two issues in tension. On one hand, you need to create enough objects to feel confident that the finder method is being tested. On the other, ActiveRecord finder methods need to touch the database, which makes the test slow, so you want to create as few objects as possible. Don't shy away from creating ActiveRecord objects when you are legitimately testing database retrieval behavior, but don't create more objects than you need to.

If you are testing a method that finds objects based on criteria, start with a test that creates two objects. That's one object you expect the method to find and one that you do not, which allows you to cover the logic from both sides:

```
it "finds completed tasks" do
  complete = Task.create(completed_at: 1.day.ago, title: "Completed")
  incomplete = Task.create(completed_at: nil, title: "Not Completed")
  expect(Task.complete.map(&:title)).to eq(["Completed"])
end
```

The test creates two objects and asserts that the Task.complete method finds only one of them. The last line of the test does something that is a little idiosyncratic but that I've found useful. Specifically, it converts the list of ActiveRecord objects (Task.complete) to a list of strings (map.(&:title)).

More generally, I'm converting a complex object to a simple one for the purpose of testing. I do this for increased readability—to some extent in the test, but much more so in the test output. If this test fails as written, the output will look something like this:

```
  1) Failure:
Expected: ["Completed"]
  Actual: []
```

Whereas if I had not converted the last line, the error would be more like this:

```
-[#<Task id: 980190963, project_id: nil, title: "Completed",
size: nil, completed_at: "2013-12-14 21:47:22",
created_at: "2013-12-15 21:47:22",
updated_at: "2013-12-15 21:47:22">]
+[]
```

I submit that the first error message makes it easier to determine what's going on.

Once you've written your initial two-object test, write another test only if you can think of another pair of objects that would fail given the current code, such as if your finder had compound logic. If we were writing a method to find tasks that were both "completed" and "large," we might start with a test that has one object with both of those criteria and one with neither, and then write a second test that has an object with both criteria and an object that only has one of the two criteria.

We're trying to avoid a combinatorial explosion where we create 16 objects to test a finder with four elements. Going two at a time and creating new pairs only if there's still a potential failure keeps each test small and easy to understand.

If you're testing for sort logic, you have to work around the fact that the order in which you add data to the database in setup is the order in which you get the objects back when you don't explicitly specify an order (because the default order is ascending by ID). If you input your data in the same order as the expected output, then the test passes before you do anything. That is bad.

If I need to test sort behavior, I create three objects: expected middle value first, expected high value second, and expected low value third. This pattern is out of order no matter which way we go, so a test for sorting will correctly fail until the logic is in place.

Testing Shared Modules and ActiveSupport Concerns

Often you'll have multiple models in your application that share some kind of common feature set. For example, you may have multiple object types that can be purchased, tagged, or commented on. You can use standard Ruby modules for this shared behavior. If the shared behavior has both class and instance methods, Rails provides ActiveSupport::Concern, which allows you to easily use a common pattern to mix multiple kinds of behavior from one module.

Testing this shared behavior can be a challenge. You don't want to have to rewrite the shared behavior specs for each class that shares the mixed-in module. At the same time, if the shared feature depends on data being available in each class, that dependency is testable logic.

RSpec has a powerful mechanism for sharing specs across multiple objects that have common functionality, simply called the *shared example*. You can use shared examples to run the same set of specs in multiple describe blocks, whether the common feature is encapsulated in a module or not.

Shared examples in RSpec have two parts: the definition and the usage. Shared examples must be defined before they are used. In a Rails context the easiest way to do that is to put the shared examples inside the spec/support directory since the Rails default rails_helper.rb file loads everything in that directory before any specs are run.

Let's create a contrived example, suggesting that we want projects and tasks to respond to a similar set of adjectives about their size. We create a shared group with the method shared_examples taking a string argument and a block.

```
model/01/gatherer/spec/support/size_group.rb
RSpec.shared_examples "sizeable" do
  let(:instance) { described_class.new }

  it "knows a one-point story is small" do
    allow(instance).to receive(:size).and_return(1)
    expect(instance).to be_small
  end

  it "knows a five-point story is epic" do
    allow(instance).to receive(:size).and_return(5)
    expect(instance).to be_epic
  end
end
```

The block inside the shared_examples method is very similar to a describe block. Inside, you can use let to define variables or it to define specs. The only unusual thing about this block is that rather than create an object explicitly, our let statement at the top is creating a generic instance using the described_class, which is the class referenced by the innermost describe whose argument is a class. Most of the time this will be the initial RSpec.describe. We're also "setting" the size via a mock, on the theory that while tasks have a setter for their size, projects don't.

To use the shared example group, all you need to do is declare it. RSpec defines multiple equivalent methods for doing so (and even allows you to define your own), one of which is it_should_behave_like followed by the name of the group. Here's what that looks like in the task_spec file:

```
model/01/gatherer/spec/models/task_spec.rb
RSpec.describe Task do

  it_should_behave_like "sizeable"
```

When task_spec is executed, the shared group is invoked with Task as the described_class, and the test will look for the small? and epic? methods to pass the test. The following code will pass:

```
model/01/gatherer/app/models/task.rb
def epic?
  size >= 5
end

def small?
  size <= 1
end
```

There are a couple of other ways to invoke a shared example group—RSpec defines synonymous methods include_examples and it_behaves_like. You can also use RSpec metadata, which we'll discuss in Chapter 15, *Running Tests Faster and Running Faster Tests*, on page 287.

When invoking the group, you can also have the it_should_behave_like method take a block argument. Inside that block, you can use let statements to define variables, which are then visible to the shared example specs. In other words, an alternative to creating an instance with described_class is to place the burden on the calling spec to create a variable and give it an appropriate name in the it block.

Write Your Own RSpec Matchers

RSpec's built-in matchers are flexible, but sometimes you have behavior patterns you specify multiple times in your code and the existing matchers don't quite cover it. Sometimes this is because the specification requires multiple steps, and sometimes it's because the generic matcher doesn't quite match the code's intent.

RSpec provides tools for creating your own custom matchers to cover just such an eventuality. A basic matcher is really simple. Let's say we wanted a custom matcher to measure project size in points. Rather than say expect(project.size).to eq(5) we'd say expect(project).to be_of_size(5). It's a little contrived, but work with me.

Normally custom matchers are placed in the spec/support folder, which can be imported when RSpec starts. To import your matcher, you need to explicitly require the custom matcher file in your rails_helper file. RSpec 3.1 contains a commented line in the rails_helper that you can uncomment to have the entire spec/support directory loaded automatically. You can also choose to directly import individual matcher files at the beginning of the spec files that use them.

Here's an example of converting our size comparisons to an RSpec custom matcher:

```
model/01/gatherer/spec/support/size_matcher.rb
RSpec::Matchers.define :be_of_size do |expected|
  match do |actual|
    actual.total_size == expected
  end
end
```

The definition starts with a call to RSpec::Matchers.define, pssing it the name of the matcher and a block. The block takes an argument that will eventually be the expected value—the value passed to the matcher when called.

Inside the block, the match method is called with a block. That block takes one argument, actual, which is the value passed to expect when the matcher is invoked. The block is expected to do something with the expected and actual values and return true if they match according to the definition of the matcher being written. In this case, we're calling total_size on the actual value, presumably a Project, and comparing it to the expected value for an equality match. If the matcher takes multiple expected arguments, then the outer block definition should name all the arguments: define :have_sizes do |first, second|.

Remember: the expected value is the value defined by the test, and the actual value is the value defined by the code. Here is the form in which the matcher gets called:

```
expect(actual_value).to be_of_size(expected_value)
```

We can then use this in a test, just like any other matcher:

model/01/gatherer/spec/models/project_spec.rb
```
it "can calculate total size" do
  expect(project).to be_of_size(10)
  expect(project).not_to be_of_size(5)
end
```

In the first call 10 is the expected value and project is the actual value. In the second call we're using not_to to negate the matcher, and 5 is the expected value.

There are, of course, additional options. You can call other methods inside the define block to further specify behavior. For instance, you can override the messages RSpec will use when the matcher is displayed:

model/02/gatherer/spec/support/size_matcher.rb
```
RSpec::Matchers.define :be_of_size do |expected|
  match do |actual|
    actual.total_size == expected
  end

  description do
    "have tasks totaling #{expected} points"
  end

  failure_message do |actual|
    "expected project #{actual.name} to have size #{expected}"
  end
```

```
    failure_message_when_negated do |actual|
      "expected project #{actual.name} not to have size #{expected}"
    end
end
```

We're using three different customizations here: description takes no arguments and returns a string used by RSpec formatters that display the matcher's description. The other two are displayed by RSpec when the matcher fails, with failure_message being printed when a to match fails, and failure_message_on_negation being printed when a not_to match fails. You can also adjust the failure message by calling the method diffable in the matcher block—no arguments, no block. Effectively, you are declaring the matcher to be diffable, which means that on failure the expected and actual arguments are displayed in a diff format. RSpec uses this in the built-in string and array matchers.

If you want to be able to chain additional methods after the initial matcher to specify further arguments, then you use the chain method inside the matcher block:

```
model/03/gatherer/spec/support/size_matcher.rb
RSpec::Matchers.define :be_of_size do |expected|
  match do |actual|
    size_to_check = @incomplete ? actual.remaining_size : actual.total_size
    size_to_check == expected
  end

  description do
    "have tasks totaling #{expected} points"
  end

  failure_message do |actual|
    "expected project #{actual.name} to have size #{expected}"
  end

  failure_message_when_negated do |actual|
    "expected project #{actual.name} not to have size #{expected}"
  end

  chain :for_incomplete_tasks_only do
    @incomplete = true
  end
end
```

The chain method takes an argument and a block, with the argument being the name of the method you want to chain. Any arguments to that method become arguments to the block—in our case the method has no arguments. Typically, inside a chained method you set instance variables, which are then referenced inside the match method to affect the match. Our for_incomplete_tasks_only method sets a flag used to determine how to query the project for the size being tested.

The new method can then be chained onto the matcher:

`model/03/gatherer/spec/models/project_spec.rb`
```ruby
it "can calculate total size" do
  expect(project).to be_of_size(10)
  expect(project).to be_of_size(5).for_incomplete_tasks_only
end
```

Modeling Data

These guidelines should give you some direction as you test-drive new business logic in your Rails application. Every test you write, however, depends on some data to run. Getting useful data into the test cleanly and quickly turns out to be kind of complicated. In the next chapter we will discuss several ways of managing test data.

## CHAPTER 6

Adding Data to Tests

Creating test data sounds like it should be the easiest thing ever. We already have ActiveRecord#create, right? Not quite. To be useful, the data that you generate for your tests needs to support the goals of testing. You should be able to create the data quickly and easily, both in the amount of typing it takes to create data and the speed at which the test runs. The data should be the same every time you generate it, should be specific to a set of tests, and should be an accurate representation of the objects that will be used when the code runs outside of tests.

Nothing against ActiveRecord#create, but if it is the only way you get data into your tests, you're going to have some problems. These problems include tests with a lot of extraneous details, slow tests, and tests that are brittle against future changes to your model's definition.

In this chapter we'll discuss two techniques that are in wide use in the Rails community for creating data. Defined by the Rails framework, *fixtures* are used to rapidly create global data. As you'll see, fixtures solve some of the problems of creating test data, but cause different ones. Specifically, fixtures are fast and easy to use but are global to all tests.

The Rails community has created a set of *factory* tools, which use some variant on the factory design pattern to create data. Factories' strengths overlap with but are slightly different from fixtures' strengths; factories are also easy to create but can be slow to run.

In the next chapter we'll explore a completely different way to think about your test's inputs when we talk about *mock objects*.

As with many testing decisions, no one answer works for all situations; there's a variety of tools with different strengths that can be used well or poorly.

What's the Problem?

What's the big deal if I want to use normal, ordinary ActiveRecord#create in my tests? I use it in my code. What could go wrong?

Since you asked...

We'll start with a simple test involving two users:

```
it "can tell which user is older" do
  eldest = User.create(date_of_birth: '1971-01-22')
  youngest = User.create(date_of_birth: '1973-08-31')
  expect(User.find_eldest).to eq(eldest)
  expect(User.find_youngest).to eq(youngest)
end
```

That test is deliberately simple, so as not to distract from the data-creation issue. The only weird thing here is that we are testing a hypothetical finder method, find_eldest, that actually goes into the database, so it's necessary for the test that the objects actually make it all the way into the database.

You make the test pass and forget about it. The test silently continues to pass every time you run your test suite.

And then...

You add authentication. And even though this test has nothing to do with authentication, it fails. Instead of returning eldest, the find_eldest call in the first assertion returns nil.

The problem is that adding authentication adds two new validations: a requirement that a user must have an email address and a password. Our test data no longer matches those requirements, so the objects aren't saved to the database, and therefore the finder methods can't find them; hence the nil.

With a heavy sigh, we add the required fields to the test:

```
it "can tell which user is older" do
  eldest = User.create!(date_of_birth: '1971-01-22',
      email: "eldest@example.com", password: "password")
  youngest = User.create!(date_of_birth: '1973-08-31'
      email: "youngest@example.com", password: "password")
  expect(User.find_eldest).to eq(eldest)
  expect(User.find_youngest).to eq(youngest)
end
```

Okay...that's not horrible. It's not great, but life marches on. We've switched to create! so now at least any further validation will fail at the point of creation, which makes diagnosing the failure much easier.

Some time later, marketing insists on full demographic data for all your users, including height in centimeters, zip code, and handedness. (Handedness? Sure, let's say your company makes golf clubs.) And the database guy insists that means that all demographic categories must be required in the database. Now the test looks like this:

```
it "can tell which user is older" do
  eldest = User.create!(date_of_birth: '1971-01-22',
      email: "eldest@example.com", password: "password",
      height: 185, zip_code: "60642", handedness: "left")
  youngest = User.create!(date_of_birth: '1973-08-31'
      email: "youngest@example.com", password: "password",
      height: 178, zip_code: "60642", handedness: "ambidextrous")
  expect(User.find_eldest).to eq(eldest)
  expect(User.find_youngest).to eq(youngest)
end
```

This is starting to get out of hand. Now not only do you need to type three lines of text in a test just to create a single user, but it's also nearly impossible to pick out of this data the one attribute—date of birth—that is actually relevant for the test.

Not only that, but this problem happens every time we create a user in a test and every time we add a new validation to users. In other words, all the time.

We'd like a way to specify a known valid object so that there is at most one place to update when new validations get created. Fixtures and factories are two different mechanisms for solving this problem.

Fixtures

Rails has always made it very easy to manage a database just for test data, which is automatically cleared between tests. (While there's no denying this is tremendously useful, it has also lulled all of us into feeling that a test that touches the database—a huge third-party dependency—is somehow a *unit* test.) One of the most valuable ways in which Ruby on Rails has supported automated testing is through the use of easily created data that is accessible to all the tests in your system, no matter when or where you write those tests, using *fixtures* specified in a YAML file. (YAML stands for *YAML Ain't Markup Language*.)[1] It's sometimes hard for an experienced Rails programmer to

---

1. http://www.yaml.org

remember just how exciting the YAML fixtures used to seem. You can just set up data once? In an easy format? And it's always there? Amazing.

Over time, the infatuation with fixtures has dimmed a bit, but they are still a quick and easy way to get data into your tests.

What's a Fixture?

Generically, a fixture is any baseline state known to exist at the beginning of a test. The existence of a fixed state makes it possible to write tests that make assumptions based on that particular set of data. In Rails, the term "fixture" refers to a specific mechanism to easily define a set of objects that will exist globally for all tests. These fixtures are defined in a set of YAML files that are automatically written to the database and converted to ActiveRecord objects at the beginning of each test run.

Under normal circumstances, each ActiveRecord model in your application will have an associated fixture file. The fixture file is in YAML format, a data-description format often used as an easier-to-type alternative to XML. The details of YAML syntax are both way outside the scope of this book and largely irrelevant to fixtures. YAML contains a number of advanced features that don't concern us here.

Each model in your system has a fixture file named after the plural version of the model. So, if we wanted fixtures for our Projects and Task models, they would go in spec/fixtures/projects.yml and spec/fixtures/tasks.yml, respectively. (If you are using Minitest, that's test/fixtures/ for the directory.) If you use Rails generators to create your model, then a fixture file is created for you with some boilerplate values for each attribute.

Each entry in a fixture file starts with an identifier, with the attributes for that entry subordinate to the identifier. Here's a sample for Project:

```
runway:
  name: Project Runway
  due_date: 2013-12-18

book:
  name: Write the book
  due_date: 2014-04-14
```

YAML syntax is somewhat reminiscent of Python, both in the colon used to separate key/value pairs and in the use of indentation to mark the bounds of each entry. The fact that the line book: is outdented two spaces indicates to the YAML parser that a new entry has begun. Strings do not need to be enclosed in quotation marks (except for strings the YAML parser would find ambiguous, such as if the string value also contains a colon and a space). It doesn't hurt to add the quotation marks if you find it more readable, though.

You can specify a multiline string by putting a pipe character (|) on the line with the attribute name. The multiline string can then be written over the next set of lines; each line must be indented relative to the line with the attribute name. Once again, outdenting indicates the end of the string.

```
runway:
  name: Project Runway
  due_date: 2013-12-18
  description: |
    The awesomest project ever.
    It's really, really great.
```

The Rails fixture-creation process uses information in your database to coerce the values to the proper type. I write dates in SQL format (yyyy-mm-dd), though any format readable by Ruby's Date.parse() will work.

The identifier that introduces each record is then used to access the individual fixture entry within your tests. Assuming that this is the Project class, you'd be able to retrieve these entries throughout your test suite as projects(:runway) and projects(:book), respectively. Unless you like trying to figure out what's special about projects(:project_10), I recommend meaningful entry names, especially for entries that expose special cases, like this: projects(:project_with_no_due_date).

The YAML data is converted to a database record directly, without using ActiveRecord#new or ActiveRecord#create. (To be clear, when you use the data in your tests, the objects you get are ActiveRecord models—ActiveRecord is bypassed only when the fixture is first converted to a database record.) This means you can't use arbitrary methods of the model as attributes in the fixture the way you can in a create call.

Fixture attributes have to be either actual database columns or ActiveRecord associations explicitly defined in the model. Removing a database column from your model and forgetting to take it out of the fixtures results in your test suite erroring out when loaded. The fixture-loading mechanism also bypasses any validations you have created on your ActiveRecord, meaning there is no way to guarantee the validity of fixture data on load short of explicitly testing each fixture yourself.

You do not need to specify the id for a fixture (although you can if you want). If you do not specify an id explicitly, the id is generated for you based on the entry's YAML identifier name. If you allow Rails to generate these ids, you get a side benefit: an easy way of specifying relationships between fixture objects. If your two model classes have an explicitly defined ActiveRecord relationship, you can use the fixture identifier of one object to define the relationship in the other object. In this snippet from a potential tasks.yml, I'm defining the task as having a relationship with the project defined as projects(:book):

```
chapter:
  title: Write a chapter
  project: book
```

If the relationship is has_many, the multiple values in the relationship can be specified as a comma-delimited list. This is true even if the two objects are in a has_and_belongs_to_many relationship via a join table, although a has_many :through relationship does need to have the join model entry explicitly specified.

Fixture files are also interpreted as ERB (Embedded Ruby) files, which means you can have dynamic attributes like this:

```
runway:
  name: Project Runway
  due_date: <%= 1.month.from_now %>
```

Or you can specify multiple entries dynamically, like this:

```
<% 10.times do |i| %>
task_<%=i%>:
  name: "Task <%= i %>"
<% end %>
```

In the second case, notice that the identifier still needs to be at the leftmost column; you can't indent the inside of the block the way normal Ruby style would suggest. Don't loop inside fixture files; it gets confusing really quickly. If you find yourself needing dynamic data functionality like this, you are probably better off with a factory tool.

Loading Fixture Data

By default, all your defined fixtures are loaded into the database once at the beginning of your test run. Rails starts a database transaction at the beginning of each test. At the end of each test the transaction is rolled back, restoring the initial state very quickly.

The transactional behavior of fixtures is a problem if you are actually trying to test transactional behavior in your application. In that case the fixture transaction will overwhelm the transaction you're trying to test. If you need less-aggressive transaction behavior, you can go into the spec/spec_helper.rb file and add the line config.use_transactional_fixtures = false. There's no way to change this behavior to be fine-grained enough to use the nontransactional behavior for only a single spec. Again, if you need to test transactional behavior, fixtures may not be your best bet.

Why Fixtures Are Great

Fixtures have a bad reputation in some circles, but they do have their good points. Used judiciously, fixtures are a fast way to create background static data.

Fixtures Are Fast

One reason to use fixtures in a modern Rails application is how fast they are. They add overhead only when the Rails framework is loaded; there's no real cost to having fixtures persist between tests, so there's no particular downside to having a lot of objects defined in fixture files.

Well, there's *one* downside, which is sometimes you might write a test that assumes the database table is blank, so you'd test something that's supposed to create an object and then test that there's exactly one object in the database. The existence of fixture data will break that test because you'll start with objects in the database. One workaround is to explicitly test the change between the initial state and the ending state rather than assuming the before value is zero.

Fixture speed makes fixtures ideal for setting up reasonably complicated object-relationship trees that you might use in your tests. That said, if you are truly unit-testing, you likely don't need complicated object-relationship trees. (If you are acceptance-testing, on the other hand...hold that thought.)

Fixtures Are Always There

You can count on fixtures always being available anywhere in your test suite. In many unit-testing situations that's not a big deal because you don't create a lot of data for each test.

However, some applications rely on the existence of some kind of mostly static data that's stored in the database. Often this is metadata, product types, or user types. It's stored in the database to make it easy to modify, but most of the time it's static data. If your application assumes that kind of data will always be there, setting that data up via fixtures will be faster and easier than re-creating the data for each test.

> **Prescription 12** Fixtures are particularly useful for global semi-static data stored in the database.

Why Fixtures Are a Pain

As great as fixtures are when you're starting out, using them long term on complex projects exposes problems. Here are some things to keep an eye on.

Fixtures Are Global

There is only one set of fixtures in a default Rails application, so the temptation to add new data points to the fixture set every time you need a corner case is overwhelming. The problem is that every time you add a user to test what happens when a left-handed user sends a message to a user who has a friend relationship and lives in Fiji (or whatever oddball scenario you need), every other test has to deal with that data point being part of the test data.

Fixtures Are Spread Out

Fixtures live in their own directory, and each model has its own fixture file. That's fine until you start needing to manage connections and a simple setup of a user commenting on a post related to a given article quickly spans across four fixture files, with no easy way to trace the relationships. I'm a big fan of "small and plentiful" over "large and few" when it comes to code structure, but even I find fixtures too spread out sometimes.

Fixtures Are Distant

If you are doing a complex test based on the specific fixture lineup, you'll often wind up with the end data being based on the fixture setup in such a way that, when reading the test, it's not clear exactly how the final value is derived. You need to go back to the fixture files to understand the calculation.

Fixtures Are Brittle

Of course, once you add that left-handed user to your fixture set, you're guaranteed to break any test that depends on the exact makeup of the entire user population. Tests for searching and reporting are notorious culprits here. There aren't many more effective ways to kill your team's enthusiasm for testing than having to fix 25 tests on the other side of the project every time you add new sample data.

Sounds grim, right? It's not. Not only are fixtures perfectly suitable for simple projects, but the Rails community has responded to the weaknesses of fixtures by creating factory tools that can replace them in creating test data.

Factories

Generically, the factory pattern refers to a class or module in your application whose sole purpose is to safely and correctly create other objects in your application. Outside of tests, factories are frequently used to encapsulate complex object-creation logic. Inside of Rails tests, factories are used to provide templates for creating valid objects.

Rather than specifying all the test data exactly, the factory tool provides a blueprint for creating a sample instance of your model. When you need data for a specific test, you call a factory method, which gives you an object based on your blueprint. You can override the blueprint to identify any specific attribute values required to make your test work out. Calling the factory method is simple enough to make it feasible to set up a useful amount of data in each test.

The most common factory tools used for Rails testing are factory_girl and its Rails library, factory_girl_rails.[2] [3] The current version is 4.3.0.

Let's talk first about how to set up and use factory_girl, and once we have the basics down we'll talk about how to use it effectively.

Installing factory_girl

To install factory_girl in a Rails project, include the following in the Gemfile:

```
gem 'factory_girl_rails'
```

In a Rails project, factory files are automatically loaded if they are in spec/factories.rb or spec/factories/*.rb. (In Minitest land, that would be test/factories.rb or test/factories/*.rb.) Factories defined any other place need to be explicitly required into the program.

There's one optional configuration, which is to place the following line inside the configuration definition in spec/rails_helper.rb:

```
config.include FactoryGirl::Syntax::Methods
```

If enabled, you can use the factory_girl creation methods without the FactoryGirl prefix—this will make more sense in a little bit. I avoid using this line; I'm accustomed to the more verbose syntax.

---

2.   https://github.com/thoughtbot/factory_girl
3.   https://github.com/thoughtbot/factory_girl_rails

Basic Factory Definition

All the definitions of your factories go inside a call to the method FactoryGirl.define, which takes a block argument. Inside that block, you can declare factories to define default data. Each factory declaration takes its own block argument in which you can define default values on an attribute-by-attribute basis.

A very simple example for our task builder might look like this:

```
FactoryGirl.define do
  factory :project do
    name "Project Runway"
    due_date Date.parse("2014-01-12")
  end
end
```

Note the absence of equals signs—these are not assignments. Technically they are method calls, so if it makes it more readable to write the lines like name("Project Runway"), go for it.

Factory_girl assumes there is an ActiveRecord class with the same name as the one you give the factory. When the factory is invoked, the resulting object is of that class.

If you want to have the factory refer to an arbitrary class, you can specify the class when the factory is defined:

```
FactoryGirl.define do
  factory :big_project, class: Project do
    name: "Big Project"
  end
end
```

In the previous factory, all the values are static and are determined when the factory file is loaded. If you want a dynamic value to be determined when an individual factory object is created, just pass a block instead of a value; the block will be evaluated when each new factory is called.

```
FactoryGirl.define do
  factory :project do
    name "Project Runway"
    due_date { Date.today - rand(50) }
  end
end
```

You can also refer to a previously assigned value later in the factory.

```
FactoryGirl.define do
  factory :project do
    name "Project Runway"
```

```
    due_date { Date.today - rand(50) }
    slug { "#{name.downcase.gsub(" ", "_")}" }
  end
end
```

What's nice about this is that the factory will always use the value in the name attribute to calculate the slug, even if you pass the name in yourself rather than use the default value. So this factory could be used as follows:

```
it "uses factory girl slug block" do
  project = FactoryGirl.create(:project, name: "Book To Write")
  expect(project.slug).to eq("book_to_write")
end
```

If you used the include FactoryGirl::Syntax::Methods call alluded to previously, then you could write the first line as project = create(:project, name: "Book To Write"). I prefer the explicit reminder that factory_girl is being used.

Inside the factory, you can call any attribute in the model that has a setter method; in other words, unlike fixtures, any virtual attribute in the model (such as the unencrypted password attribute of a secure user model) is fair game.

Basic Factory Creation

Factory_girl provides four ways of turning a factory into a Ruby object. For the project factory we were just looking at, the four ways are as follows:

- build(:project), which returns a model instance that has not been saved to the database.
- create(:project), which returns a model instance and saves it to the database.
- attributes_for(:project), which returns a hash of all the attributes in the factory that are suitable for passing to ActiveRecord#new or ActiveRecord#create. This method is most often useful for creating a hash that will be sent as params to a controller test.
- build_stubbed(:project), which is almost magical. Like build, it returns an unsaved model object. Unlike build, it assigns a fake ActiveRecord ID to the model and stubs out database-interaction methods (like save) such that the test raises an exception if they are called.

All four of these build strategies allow you to pass key/value pairs to override the factory value for a given attribute:

```
project = FactoryGirl.build_stubbed(:project, name: "New Project")
expect(project.name).to eq("New Project")
```

When building the object from the factory, I consider it useful to explicitly list any attribute whose value is essential to the test. I do this even if the attribute has the same value as the factory default because I like having the explicit value in the test, where it can easily be seen.

All the build strategies will also yield the new object to a block in case you want to do more custom processing:

```
project = FactoryGirl.build_stubbed(:project) do |p|
  p.tasks << FactoryGirl.build_stubbed(:task)
end
```

I don't use this form very much, though I think it would be helpful if you had additional creation logic on a new test object.

This is the strategy by which I determine which of these methods to use:

- Use attribute_for only in the specialized case of needing a valid set of hash attributes. Again, in my experience that's most likely in a controller test.
- Use create only if the object absolutely must be in the database. Typically, this is because the test code must be able to access it via an ActiveRecord finder. However, create is much slower than any of the other methods, so it's also worth thinking about whether there's a way to structure the code so that persistent data is not needed for the test.
- In all other cases, use build_stubbed, which does everything build does, plus more. Because a build_stubbed object has a Rails ID, you can build up real Rails associations and still not have to take the speed hit of saving to the database.

> **Prescription 13**
> Your go-to build strategy for factory_girl should be build_stubbed unless there is a need for the object to be in the database during the test.

If you need to create a set of objects together, all the build strategies have two special forms: *_pair and *_list. The pair methods, like create_pair(:project) or build_stubbed_pair(:project), create exactly two objects of the given factory. You can still pass key/value pairs to the method, in which case the attribute overrides are applied to both objects. The list methods create an arbitrary number of items, denoted by an integer argument after the name of the factory, as in create_list(:project, 5), which creates five projects. As with the pair methods, key/values can be passed in and are applied to the entire list.

Associations and Factories

Factory_girl has a powerful set of features for adding associations to factories. We'll talk about them because they are so powerful and you might see code that uses them. Then we'll talk about why you should be careful about using them.

The simplest case is also a common one: the class being created has a belongs_to association with the same name as a factory. In that case, you just include that name in the factory:

```
FactoryGirl.define do
  factory :task do
    title: "To Something"
    size: 3
    project
  end
end
```

In this case, calling task = FactoryGirl.create(:task) would also implicitly call task.project = FactoryGirl.create(:project).

If you want to explicitly specify the project when calling the task factory, you can do so the same way you would for any other attribute—namely, via task = FactoryGirl.create(:task, project: Project.new). If the association is specified in the factory definition but you don't want any value in the test, then you need to set the association to nil, as in: task = FactoryGirl.create(:task, project: nil).

If the association name doesn't match the factory name or if you want to specify default attributes of the associated object, you can use the longer form of the association statement in the factory definition:

```
FactoryGirl.define do
  factory :task do
    title: "To Something"
    size: 3
    project
    association :doer, factory: :user, name: "Task Doer"
  end
end
```

The syntax is association, followed by the name of the association in the ActiveRecord model and then a bunch of key/value pairs, with the factory key being used by factory_girl to determine which factory to use to create the associated object.

This gets tricky in the build strategy used for the subordinate object. As you might expect, calling the parent factory (in this case Task) with create causes the associated factory (in this case Project) to also be instantiated using create.

By default, however, even if you call the parent factory with build, the subordinate factory is still called with create. This is a side effect of how Rails manages associations. The associated object needs an ID so that the parent object can link to it, and in Rails you get an ActiveRecord ID only when an ActiveRecord instance is saved to the database.

As a result, even if you use the build strategy specifically to avoid slow and unnecessary database interaction, if the factory has associations you will still save objects to the database. Since those associated factories may themselves have associations, if you aren't careful you can end up saving a lot of objects to the database, resulting in prohibitively slow tests.

It's exactly this characteristic of factory_girl that has made it unwelcome in some circles, particularly if the people in those circles have to maintain large, unwieldy test suites. Factory-association misuse can be a big cause of a slow test suite, as tests create many more objects than they need to because of factory_girl associations.

There are a few ways to avoid unnecessary database creation of associated objects.

If you use the longer form of specifying the association, you can explicitly specify the build strategy:

```
FactoryGirl.define do
  factory :task do
    title: "To Something"
    size: 3
    project
    association :doer, factory: :user, strategy: :build
  end
end
```

If you go this route, you may have problems because the associated object won't have an ID. In this specific case, for example, the Task object will have its user attribute set but not its user_id. If your code is expecting the user_id to be set—for example, because user_id is faster to access than user—this may cause problems in your tests.

Since the build_stubbed strategy assigns an ID to the objects being created, using build_stubbed sidesteps the whole issue. If a factory with associations is instantiated using build_stubbed, then by default all the associations are also invoked using build_stubbed. That solves the problem as long as you always use build_stubbed.

My preferred strategy is to not specify attributes in factories at all, and if I need associated objects in a specific test, I explicitly add them to the test at the point they're needed.

Why?

- The surest way to keep factory_girl from creating large object trees is to not define large object trees.
- Tests that require multiple degrees of associated objects often indicate improperly factored code. Making it a little harder to write associations in tests nudges me in the direction of code that can be tested without associations.

 Avoid defining associations automatically in factory_girl definitions. Set them test by test, as needed. You'll wind up with more manageable test data.

The only downside is that there's a little more typing involved in some tests.

DRY Factories

Once you have more than a couple of factories in your application, you want to make sure you can manage complexity and duplication. Factory_girl has a number of features to allow you to do just that.

Sequences

A common problem is the creation of multiple objects that require unique values. This most often happens with unique user attributes such as a login or email address. To allow the easy creation of unique attributes, factory_girl allows you to define an attribute as part of a sequence of values.

The short version of the syntax looks like this:

```
FactoryGirl.define do
  factory :task do
    sequence(:title) { |n| "Task #{n}" }
  end
end
```

Calling sequence inside a factory takes one argument (which is the attribute whose values are being sequenced) and a block. When the factory is invoked, the block is called with a new value and the block's return value is set to be the value of the attribute. The start value is 1 by default, but a second argument to sequence can be used to specify an arbitrary value, which is usually a number but can be any object that responds to next.

When a sequence is defined inside a factory, it can be used in only that one place; however, sequences can also be defined outside of factories and reused:

```
FactoryGirl.define do
  sequence :email do |n|
    "user_#{n}@test.com"
  end

  factory :user do
    name "Fred Flintstone"
    email
  end
end
```

The use of email inside the factory is a shortcut that assumes the sequence and the attribute have the same name. If so, the sequence is triggered and the next value becomes the value of the attributes. If the sequence and the attribute have different names, then you need to invoke the sequence explicitly by calling generate inside an attribute's block:

```
factory :task do
  title "Finish Chapter"
  user_email { generate(:email) }
end
```

Inherited Factories

Often you'll need to create multiple factories from the same class—a classic example is the ability to create different kinds of users, such as regular users versus administrators.

The most direct way to create slightly different factories in the same class is via factory_girl's inheritance feature. If you define a factory as having another factory as a parent, it takes all the attributes set in that parent but then allows you to override those attributes in the child factory. Effectively, factory_girl inheritance allows you to group common attributes so they can be reused:

```
FactoryGirl.define do
  factory :task do
    sequence(:title) { |n| "Task #{n}" }
  end

  factory :big_task, parent: :task do
    size 5
  end
```

```
    factory :small_task, parent: :task do
      size 1
    end
  end
end
```

In the preceding set of factories, big_task and small_task share the sequence being used to generate unique titles, but they each define their own size value.

In addition to explicitly setting the parent, you can achieve the same effect by nesting the child factories inside the parent definition, like so:

```
FactoryGirl.define do
  factory :task do
    sequence(:title) { |n| "Task #{n}" }

    factory :big_task do
      size 5
    end

    factory :small_task do
      size 1
    end
  end
end
```

In case creating a parent factory and child factories seems a little backwards to you, factory_girl also allows you to group a set of common attributes into a single chunk, called a *trait*, which can be used inside other factories. This makes sense if you have groups of attributes with values that are orthogonal to each other.

Traits can be used as though they were single attributes. Creating a noncontrived example is tricky without making our sample classes much more complex than they currently are—just realize that each trait could hold multiple attributes here:

```
FactoryGirl.define do
  factory :task do
    sequence(:title) { |n| "Task #{n}" }

    trait :small do
      size 1
    end

    trait :large do
      size 5
    end
```

```ruby
    trait :soon do
      due_date { 1.day.from_now }
    end

    trait :later do
      due_date { 1.month.from_now }
    end

    factory :trivial do
      small
      later
    end

    factory :panic do
      large
      soon
    end
  end
end
```

The last couple of factories can be written slightly differently:

```ruby
factory :trivial, traits: [:small, :later]
factory :panic, traits: [:large, :soon]
```

Having just one attribute per trait doesn't show the feature in its best light, but you have the basic tradeoff of verbose versus succinct. Traits take some extra definition but give meaningful names to groups of attributes that you might reuse. The good side is the meaningful name; the downside is the extra typing and added complexity of the factory.

As factories get even more complex, factory_girl offers a few other techniques to manage them, including the ability to have postcreation callbacks, create custom build strategies, and have dummy attributes that are used only to control the factory creation. I suspect that these are useful only in somewhat specialized cases, so we won't go into them in more detail. The factory_girl documentation can help you if you're curious.[4]

Preventing Factory Abuse

The initial temptation when using factories is to continue to build large trees of objects—this is particularly true if you're converting a project that was using fixtures. The best way to use factories is to create only the smallest amount of data needed to expose the issue in each test. This practice speeds

---

4.   https://github.com/thoughtbot/factory_girl/blob/master/GETTING_STARTED.md

up the tests, makes the issue easy to see rather than burying it among dozens of fixtures, and makes the correctness of the tests themselves easier to verify.

Dates and Times

Date and time logic has a well-deserved reputation as some of the most complex and irritating logic in any application. Testing calendar logic—including time-based reports, automatic logouts, and "1 day ago" text displays—can be a particular headache, but you can do a couple of things to simplify the time-logic beast.

Part of the Problem

We have a YAML file with some projects:

```
runway:
  name: Project Runway
  start_date: 2015-01-20

greenlight:
  name: Project Greenlight
  start_date: 2015-02-04

gutenberg:
  name: Project Gutenberg
  start_date: 2015-01-31
```

We'd like to test some time-based code that might be used in a search or report result; this goes in test/unit/project_test.rb:

```
it "finds recently started projects" do
  actual = Project.find_recently_started(6.months)
  expect(actual.size).to eq(3)
end
```

Here's code that makes the test pass, from app/models/project.rb:

```
def self.find_recently_started(time_span)
  old_time = Date.today - time_span
  all(conditions: ["start_date > ?", old_time.to_s(:db)])
end
```

On January 20, 2015, the test passes. And on the 21st it will pass, and it will pass the day after that....

Six months later, about June 20th (when we've probably long forgotten about this test, this sample data, and maybe even this entire project), the test will fail. And we'll spend way too much time trying to figure out what happened, until we remember the date issue and realize that the January 20 sample has moved out of the six-month time span specified in the test. Of course, changing all the dates just pushes the problem forward and gives us time to forget all about it again.

This issue may sound silly, but like many of the more ridiculous examples in the book, this happened to me and can end up costing a lot of time. I've seen tests that fail at a particular time of day (because time zones used inconsistently push part of the code into the next day). I've seen tests that pass in Chicago but fail in California. I've seen tests that fail on the first day of a new month and a new year—and, of course, tests that fail on the boundary in and out of daylight savings time. Most of this can be prevented.

When I was young and foolish and got paid to write Java, I solved this problem by adding an optional argument to every method that had a default value of Date.today, allowing an optional time to explicitly be passed to the method for testing. This is a lot of work (although, interestingly, I think the Ruby community is coming back to allowing this kind of optional argument injection as a regular practice). Here are a few other options for dealing with date and time data.

Using Relative Dates

Using relative dates in your test data is often a way to work around date and time weirdness. You can do this with fixtures, factories, or just the objects you create in your tests.

Since Rails fixture files are evaluated as ERB files before loading, you can specify dynamic dates:

```
runway:
  name: Project Runway
  start_date: <%= 1.month.ago %>

greenlight:
  name: Project Greenlight
  start_date: <%= 1.week.ago %>

gutenberg:
  name: Project Gutenberg
  start_date: <%= 1.day.ago %>
```

With fixtures written like this, the previous test will always work since the start_date of the projects will never fall out of the six-month range.

You can do something similar in factory_girl:

```
factory :project do
  name "Project Runway"
  start_date { 1.week.ago }
end
```

Although this technique works quite well for keeping test data a consistent relative distance from the test time, it's less helpful if you're trying to test based on the exact value of one of the dates—for example, if you're testing an output value or format. With the first, static set of fixture data, you could write the following:

```
it "displays project date in this goofy format" do
  expect(projects(:runway).goofy_start_date).to eq("2010 1 January")
end
```

This test is a lot more difficult to write if you don't explicitly know the value of the project's start_date.

Stubbing Time

Another option for managing date logic in tests is to "freeze" time by using a stub to explicitly specify what time Ruby reports when you ask for the current time. Rails 4.1 has also added support for this feature with the methods ActiveSupport::Testing::TimeHelpers#travel and ActiveSupport::Testing::TimeHelpers#travel_to. In the past I've used the Timecop gem,[5] but in the interest of keeping things in-house, as it were, I'll use the newer ActiveSupport syntax.

The travel_to method is effectively a super-specific mock-object package: it stubs out Date.today and Time.now, allowing you to explicitly set the effective date for your tests. Using this, the original test could be rewritten as follows:

```
it "finds recently started projects" do
  travel_to(Date.parse("2015-02-10"))
  actual = Project.find_recently_started(6.months)
  expect(actual.size).to eq(3)
end
```

The travel_to method stubs the current date and time methods to the date passed as the argument: in this case, February 10, 2015. Time does not move for the duration of the test.

A separate method, travel, allows you to specify the duration of the time change rather than the absolute target, as in travel 1.month. This is particularly useful when you need time to pass during the course of a test, as in loan calculations or whatever.

---

5. https://github.com/travisjeffery/timecop

The method travel_back resets time to its original state.

The Timecop gem has a third option that changes the time but allows the system time to move forward from that point onward, which is useful when you need two things to happen with different timestamps. Along those lines, it's sometimes useful to put the following line in a setup method:

```
travel_to(Date.today)
```

And then the other half in the teardown method:

```
travel_back
```

This ensures that the current time doesn't change for the duration of each test. Again, with certain timing-related issues, that consistency eliminates a possible source of intermittent test failures or just plain confusion.

The argument to travel_to is a Date, Time, DateTime, or anything that accepts the message to_time. The argument to travel is an integer number of seconds that is added to the current time.

Both methods also take blocks such that the fake time is good only for the duration of the block:

```
it "reports based on start date" do
  travel_to(Date.parse("2015-02-10")) do
    actual = Project.find_started_in_last(6.months)
    expect(actual.size).to eq(3)
  end
end
```

The time-travel methods can be in your setup or in an individual test. You can use travel to change the time in the middle of a test to speed up an ongoing process:

```
it "knows if the project is over" do
  p = Project.new(:start_date => Date.today,
      :end_date = Date.today + 8.weeks)
  expect(p).not_to be_complete
  travel(10.weeks)
  expect(p).to be_complete
end
```

These methods let you keep explicit dates in your test data without causing problems later. The only downside is that if you have many tests setting time to different days, it can get somewhat confusing in the aggregate. It's easier if you use the same start date consistently. (On a solo project, you might use your birthday, for instance, but that's probably overly cute for a team project.) A more minor problem is that the line at the end of your test runs that says how long the test suite took may be hopelessly messed up because of the continued tweaking of Time.now.

Comparing Time

Ruby, not content with a simple date and time system, has three separate classes that manage date and time data. The Time class is a thin wrapper around the same Unix C library that pretty much every language exposes. (Motto: "Annoying programmers since 1983!") The Ruby-specific classes Date and DateTime are more flexible and have a more coherent API but are slower.

For Rails testing purposes, the relevant points are that ActiveRecord uses Date and DateTime (depending on the specifics of the underlying database column). Comparing a Date to a DateTime instance will always fail, as will trying to add or subtract them. And most of the Rails ActiveSupport methods (such as 5.days.ago) return DateTime. In testing this can lead to a lot of annoying failures, especially when you have a Date column with no time information—which is recommended if the time is not important.

In general, it's a good idea to compare dates and times by converting them using to_s(:db). It avoids the irritating question of object equality and you get more readable tests and error messages. When the exact time of the time object is in question, try to force the issue by using the Rails ActiveSupport methods to_date, to_time, and to_datetime. At worst, this means something like 5.days.ago.to_ date.to_s(:db), which may read a touch awkwardly but is a robust test with a decent error message on failure.

Setting Rails Timestamps

One trick worth mentioning when testing dates is to explicitly set the created_at attribute of your ActiveRecord model. Normally created_at is a timestamp automatically generated by Rails, and it's often used for the kind of time-based reporting alluded to in the rest of this section. Since it's automatically created at the current time, you can get into some weird situations if the other dates in the test are explicitly set in the past. Even without that complication, you may still need to explicitly set created_at to use the attribute to test time-based features.

You can set created_at in the fixture file, just like any other attribute; specify it in ActiveRecord::create, ActiveRecord::new, or a factory blueprint; or just reset with an assignment or update method.

Setting updated_at is trickier. Under normal circumstances, if you try to explicitly set updated_at Rails will automatically reset it on save, which defeats the purpose. To change this behavior, set the class variable for your class with code like Project.record_timestamps = false, using the name of your class as the message receiver sometime before you save the object with a modified update time. After the save, reset things to normal with Project.record_timestamps = true.

Fixtures vs. Factories vs. Test Doubles

To sum up, Rails provides fixtures as an exceptionally simple way to create a set of test data that can be shared across multiple tests. However, fixtures are so simple that they tend to not be adaptable to more complex product needs. Factory tools, which take a little bit more initial setup, allow for more flexibility at some cost in test performance. The two structures are not mutually exclusive. One pattern for combining them is to create a complex scenario in fixtures for use in integration or complex controller tests, and to use factories for unit tests or simpler controller tests.

Fixtures and factory tools allow you to get test data into your database to create a known baseline for testing. However, in some cases you may not want to place data in the database. Using the database in a test may be undesirable for performance reasons, for philosophical reasons (some people don't consider it reasonable to touch the database in a "unit" test), or where logistical reasons make objects hard to create. In the next chapter we'll explore test doubles, which allow tests to proceed by faking not the data but rather the method calls that produce the data.

## CHAPTER 7

Using Test Doubles as Mocks and Stubs

We have a problem. We want to add credit-card processing to our project application so that we can make money. Testing the credit-card functionality presents immediate difficulties. For one thing, we don't want to accidentally make a credit-card purchase during testing—that would be bad. But even if the purchase gateway provides a test sandbox, we still don't want to depend on it for our unit tests to run. That network call is slow and we don't want our passing tests to depend on the status of a remote server.

We have a different problem. We'd like to build our code in a very modular kind of way. In doing so, we'd like our tests to be as isolated as possible from dependencies on other parts of the code. For example, we might have controller logic that calls a model but that we want to test without depending on the model. We want our controller test to work even if the model is broken—even if the model code does not yet exist.

The solution to both of these problems is a *test double*, sometimes called a *mock object*.

A test double is a "fake" object used in place of a "real" object for the purposes of automated testing. A double might be used when the real object is unavailable or difficult to access from a test environment. Or you might use a double to create a specific application state that would be otherwise difficult to trigger in a test environment, such as a database or network failure.

Doubles can also be used strategically to limit a test's execution to the object and method specifically under test. Used in that manner, doubles drive a different style of testing, where the test is verifying the behavior of the system during the test rather than the state of the system at the end of the test.

Test doubles can be a bit of a contentious issue, with different people giving conflicting advice about the best way to use them when testing. I'd like to give you enough information to make informed decisions about who to agree with. (Though I hope you'll agree with me.) We'll start by discussing the mechanics of test doubles, using the RSpec-Mock library. Then we'll discuss different ways to use doubles to solve both of the testing issues described previously. Chapter 9, *Minitest*, on page 161, will cover the basics of the Mocha mocking library, for use with Minitest.

Mock Objects Defined

One complicating factor in dealing with test doubles is that pretty much everybody who creates a tool feels perfectly free to use slightly different naming conventions than everybody else. Here are the names that I use, which are—of course—also the correct ones. (Actually, I believe this naming structure is the creation of Gerard Meszaros in *xUnit Test Patterns [Mes07]*.)

The generic term for any object used as a stand-in for another object is *test double*, by analogy to "stunt double" and with the same connotation of a cheaper or more focused replacement for a more expensive real object. Colloquially, "mock object" is also sometimes used as a generic term but, confusingly, is also the name of a specific type of test double.

A *stub* is a fake object that returns a predetermined value for a method call without calling the actual method on an actual object. In RSpec we can stub a method on an existing object as follows:

```
allow(thing).to receive(:name).and_return("Fred")
```

That line of code says that if you call thing.name, you'll get Fred as a result. Crucially, the actual thing.name method is not touched, so whatever value the "real" method would return is not relevant; the Fred response comes from the stub, not the actual object. If thing.name is not called in the test, nothing happens.

A *mock* is similar to a stub, but in addition to returning the fake value, a mock object sets a testable expectation that the method being replaced will actually be called in the test. If the method is not called, the mock object triggers a test failure. You can write the following snippet to create a mocked method call instead of a stub, using expect instead of allow:

```
expect(thing).to receive(:name).and_return("Fred")
```

If you use the mock then call thing.name in your test, you still get Fred and the actual thing.name method is still untouched. But if you don't call thing.name in the test, the test fails with an unfulfilled expectation error.

In other words, setting a stub on a method is passive and says, "Ignore the real implementation of this method and return this value," while setting a mock on a method is aggressive and says, "This method will return this value, and you better call the method, or else!"

The reason you might set an expectation on whether a method is called is that once you've stubbed the method, it makes no sense to write an assertion like this one:

```
allow(thing).to receive(:name).and_return("Fred")
expect(thing.name).to eq("Fred")
```

In this case, you're just testing that the stub works as advertised—this test can't fail. But if you do this:

```
expect(thing).to receive(:name).and_return("Fred")
```

Then the code is required to behave a certain way—namely, it has to call thing.name in order to pass the test.

There is a third test-double pattern, called a *spy*. A spy is often declared like a stub, but allows you to specify a testable expectation later in the test. Typically, we would place the body of the test in between.

```
allow(thing).to receive(:name).and_return("Fred")
# body of test
expect(thing).to have_received(:name)
```

In this test, the first line defines the stub and the last line sets the expectation. In RSpec the method being spied on must be declared as a stub before you check to see if it has been received.

Using spies mitigates a common criticism of mock-object testing, which is that it can be difficult to look at a mock test and see exactly what behavior is being tested for. The spy explicitly declares the behavior that is expected. Spies are also more consistent with the given/when/then test structure we've used elsewhere, allowing the stub to be declared in the "given" section and the expectation to be set separately in the "then" part of the test.

Creating Stubs

A stub is a replacement for all or part of an object that prevents a normal method call from happening and instead returns a value that is preset when the stub is created. In RSpec, as in many Ruby double libraries, there are two kinds of fake objects. You can create entire objects that exist only to be stubs, which we'll call *full doubles*, or you can stub specific methods of existing objects, which we'll call *partial doubles*.

A partial double is useful when you want to use a "real" ActiveRecord object but you have one or two dangerous or expensive methods you want to bypass. A full double is useful when you're testing that your code works with a specific API rather than a specific object—by passing in a generic object that responds to only certain methods, you make it hard for the code to assume anything about the structure of the objects being coordinated with.

Prescription 15 — Use partial doubles when you want to ensure most of your real object behavior. Use full doubles when the behavior of the stubbed object doesn't matter—only its public interface does.

Full Stubs

In RSpec you create full doubles with the double method, which is available anywhere. The double method takes an optional string argument, which is a name for the double, and then key/value pairs representing messages that can be sent to the double. Since Ruby uses duck typing—which is to say it cares not about the type of objects but only about whether objects respond to the messages sent to them—a stub object created in such a way can be inserted into your application as a replacement for a real object:

```
it "can create doubles" do
  twin = double(first_name: "Paul", weight: 100)
  expect(double.first_name).to eq("Paul")
end
```

The double method takes an optional hash argument, the keys being messages the stub will respond to and the values being the return values of those messages. These are stubbed methods, meaning that failure to use them will not trigger an error. (Alternatively, you can use the same allow and expect methods on the double that you can on any other object.) The assertion in the last line of the snippet is true because the stub has been preset to respond to the name message with "Paul."

This spec is a very bad way to use stubs; I've set up a nice little tautology and I haven't learned anything about any larger system around this test.

By default RSpec doubles are "strict," meaning that if you call the stub with a method that is not in the hash argument, RSpec will return an error. If that's not the behavior you want, RSpec provides the as_null_object method, which instead returns the double itself for methods not in the hash argument. Using as_null_object makes sense in the case where there's a large number of potential methods to be stubbed but where the values make so little difference that specifying them reduces the test's readability.

Null-object test doubles automatically spy on all methods, which is useful enough when using spies that RSpec 3.1 provides spy(name) as an alternate method of writing double(name).as_null_object.

For when you know your double needs to mimic a specific object, RSpec provides the concept of a *verifying* double. A verifying double checks to see whether messages passed to the double are actually real methods in the application. RSpec has a few methods to allow you to declare what to verify the double against:

```
instance_twin = instance_double("User")
instance_twin = instance_double(User)
class_twin = class_double("User")
class_twin = class_double(User)
object_twin = object_double(User.new)
```

Each of these three methods behaves slightly differently. The instance_double method takes a class's string name. The resulting double only responds to methods that could be passed to an instance of that class. If you attempt to send the resulting double a method that is not implemented by that class, the test will error with a message that says something like "User does not implement method." The class_double method is similar but verifies against class methods on the existing class (or module), rather than instance methods. Note instance_double will not recognize methods defined via method_missing. (When matching, instance_double uses method_defined? while class_double uses respond_to? on the class itself.)

In addition to verifying the existence of the method, RSpec double verification ensures that the arguments passed to the method are valid. The doubled method will also have the same public/protected/private visibility as the original method.

If you use the string version of a constant name and the constant doesn't exist, RSpec will ignore the string and treat the double like a normal, unverified double. If you'd like a failure if you use a string constant name that doesn't exist, add the line mocks.verify_doubled_constant_names = true to the appropriate section in the spec_helper.rb file. (By default the section that manages mocks is wrapped in a multiline comment; you'll need to remove the comment lines.)

If you want to verify against a class that has methods dynamically defined with method_missing, you can use object_double, which has an instance of the class as an argument and therefore allows RSpec to call respond_to? on that instance to determine whether the call to the stub is valid.

All three of these methods have spy forms—instance_spy, class_spy, and object_spy—which add as_null_object to the double, giving you verification that a method passed to the spy exists without having to specify a return value.

Partial Stubs

You might use a full double object to stand in for an entire object that is unavailable or prohibitively expensive to create or call in the test environment. In Ruby, though, you would more often take advantage of the way Ruby allows you to open up existing classes and objects to add or override methods. It's easy to take a "real" object and stub out only the methods you need. This is extraordinarily useful when it comes to actual uses of stub objects.

In RSpec this is managed with the allow method:

mocks/01/gatherer/spec/models/project_spec.rb
```
Line 1  it "stubs an object" do
     2    project = Project.new(name: "Project Greenlight")
     3    allow(project).to receive(:name)
     4    expect(project.name).to be_nil
     5  end
```

This test passes: line 3 sets up the stub, and the stub intercepts the project.name call in line 4 to return nil and never even gets to the project name.

In RSpec 3.0 if you set mocks.verify_partial_doubles in the configuration file, then partial doubles will also be verified, meaning the test will fail if the double is asked to stub a method the object does not respond to.

Having a stub that always returns nil is pointless, so RSpec allows you to specify a return value for the stubbed method using the following syntax:

mocks/01/gatherer/spec/models/project_spec.rb
```
Line 1  it "stubs an object again" do
     2    project = Project.new(name: "Project Greenlight")
     3    allow(project).to receive(:name).and_return("Fred")
     4    expect(project.name).to eq("Fred")
     5  end
```

Line 3 is doing the heavy lifting here, tying the return value Fred to the method :name. The allow method returns a proxy to the real object, which responds to a number of methods that let you annotate the stub. The and_return method is an annotation message that associates the return value with the method.

Since classes in Ruby are really just objects themselves, you'd probably expect that you can stub classes just like you can instance objects. You'd be right:

```
mocks/01/gatherer/spec/models/project_spec.rb
```

```ruby
Line 1   it "stubs the class" do
    2      allow(Project).to receive(:find).and_return(
    3          Project.new(name: "Project Greenlight"))
    4      project = Project.find(1)
    5      expect(project.name).to eq("Project Greenlight")
    6   end
```

In this test, the class Project is being stubbed to return a specific project instance whenever find is called. In line 4 the find method is, in fact, called, and returns that object.

Let's pause here and examine what we've done in this test. We're using find to get an ActiveRecord object. And because we're stubbing find we're not touching the actual database. Using the database is, for testing purposes, slow. Very slow. And this is one strategy for avoiding the database. In the meantime, remember that this stub shouldn't be used to verify that the find method works; it should be used by other tests that need the find method along the way to the logic that is under test.

That said, in practice you also should avoid stubbing the find method because it's part of an external library—you might be better off creating a model method that has a more meaningful and specific behavior and stubbing that method.

On a related note, if you wanted to create multiple partial stubs from the same class and have them all behave the same way, you could do so with the method allow_any_instance_of, as you see here:

```
allow_any_instance_of(Project).to receive(:save).and_return(false)
```

You should use allow_any_instance_of very sparingly, as it often implies that you don't really understand what the underlying code is doing or where objects might come from. However, when you're testing legacy code you may genuinely not know where the object comes from, and allow_any_instance_of might be a lesser evil. Also, sometimes framework concerns in Rails make using allow_any_instance_of easier than managing the set of objects that might be returned by some distant method. In either case, though, consider the possibility of refactoring the code or test to avoid allow_any_instance_of. The RSpec docs explicitly recommend not using this feature if possible, since it is "the most complicated feature of rspec-mocks, and has historically received the most bug reports."

> **Prescription 16** The use of the allow_any_instance_of stub modifier often means the underlying code being tested could be refactored with a more useful method to stub.

A very common use of stub objects is to simulate exception conditions. If you want your stubbed method to raise an exception, you can use the and_raise method, which takes an exception class and an optional message:

```
allow(stubby).to receive(:user_count).and_raise(Exception, "oops")
```

Mock Expectations

A mock object retains the basic idea of the stub—returning a specified value without actually calling a live method—and adds the requirement that the specified method must be called during the test. In other words, a mock is like a stub with attitude, expecting—nay, demanding—that its parameters be matched in the test or else we get a test failure.

In RSpec you use the expect method to create mock expectations. This can be applied to full or partial doubles:

```
it "expects stuff" do
  mocky = double("Mock")
  expect(mocky).to receive(:name).and_return("Paul")
  expect(mocky).to receive(:weight).and_return(100)
  expect(mocky.name).to eq("Paul")
end
```

This test fails:

```
Failures:
  1) Project expects stuff
     Failure/Error: expect(mocky).to receive(:weight).and_return(100)
       (Double "Mock").weight(any args)
           expected: 1 time with any arguments
           received: 0 times with any arguments
```

The test sets up two mock expectations, mocky.name and mocky.weight, but only one of those two mocked methods is called in the test. Hence, it's an unsatisfied expectation. To make the test pass, add a call to mocky.weight:

```
it "expects stuff" do
  mocky = double("Mock")
  expect(mocky).to receive(:name).and_return("Paul")
  expect(mocky).to receive(:weight).and_return(100)
  expect(mocky.name).to eq("Paul")
  expect(mocky.weight).to eq(100)
end
```

This also works for existing objects:

mocks/01/gatherer/spec/models/project_spec.rb
```
it "mocks an object" do
  mock_project = Project.new(name: "Project Greenlight")
  expect(mock_project).to receive(:name).and_return("Fred")
  expect(mock_project.name).to eq("Fred")
end
```

All the modifiers we've seen so far, such as and_return and and_raise, as well as ones we haven't seen, such as with, can be added to a mock just like they can to a stub.

By default, the expects method sets a validation that the associated method is called exactly once during the test. In case that does not meet your testing needs, RSpec has methods that let you specify the number of calls to the method. These methods are largely self-explanatory:

```
proj = Project.new
expect(proj).to receive(:name).once
expect(proj).to receive(:name).twice
expect(proj).to receive(:name).at_least(:once)
expect(proj).to receive(:name).at_least(:twice)
expect(proj).to receive(:name).at_least(n).times
expect(proj).to receive(:name).at_most(:once)
expect(proj).to receive(:name).at_most(:twice)
expect(proj).to receive(:name).at_most(n).times
expect(proj).not_to receive(:name)
```

In practice, the default behavior is good for most usages (I'd worry if I started needing these decorators a lot), though not_to is sometimes useful to guarantee that a particular expensive method is not called. Note that a stub is equivalent to a mock expectation defined with at_least(0).times.

Using Mocks to Simulate Rails Save

You can use mock objects to rectify what used to be a nagging annoyance in the standard Rails scaffolds (well, it annoyed me). The Rails-generated tests for a scaffolded controller created with rails generate scaffold controller do not cover the failure conditions for create and update. I've always assumed, with no real justification, this oversight was because the easiest way to test these is with a mock package and the Rails team didn't want to mandate one particular package.

We've already mandated a mock package. And we've already written a failure test for ProjectController#create (see *Testing for Failure*, on page 57). But if you'll recall, we had to think of a case in which the save would fail. (The RSpec-generated scaffold tests cover failure similarly, with the need for you to create a set of invalid parameters for an object.)

We won't always be able to do that so easily, but we can mock objects to ensure a failing create. I'll throw in the failing update test even though we didn't put update in our controller in the earlier tutorial—it's still a test structure you might find useful.

Our controller test for create will take advantage of the fact that we're using an external action object.

Let's think about these tests from a given/when/then perspective.

- Given: The create test needs some way to simulate failure. In the earlier tutorial, we used a set of form values that were invalid. In this case we'll use a stub. The update test needs an existing object and a way to simulate failure on update.
- When: The "when" action in this test is the actual save or update_attributes call. For the create controller action, where the ActiveRecord save happens inside the CreatesProject object, we just need to simulate a save failure.
- Then: The temptation is to test that new objects are not created and existing objects are not updated. Those values represent the ending state of the action. Since we are stubbing save and update_attributes, however, testing the state is pointless—the object is not being saved because the real save method is prevented from being called by the stub. Instead we're testing the controller, and we want to test the controller's response—namely, that a failed create action goes back to the new form and a failed update goes back to edit.

Here are the tests:

mocks/01/gatherer/spec/controllers/projects_controller_spec.rb
```
Line 1  it "fails create gracefully" do
          action_stub = double(create: false, project: Project.new)
          expect(CreatesProject).to receive(:new).and_return(action_stub)
          post :create, :project => {name: 'Project Runway'}
     5    expect(response).to render_template(:new)
        end


        it "fails update gracefully" do
          sample = Project.create!(name: "Test Project")
    10    expect(sample).to receive(:update_attributes).and_return(false)
          allow(Project).to receive(:find).and_return(sample)
          patch :update, id: sample.id, project: {name: "Fred"}
          expect(response).to render_template(:edit)
        end
```

The create test starts on line 2 by defining a full double that will stand in for the CreatesProject action. All we need that double to do is respond to the create method with false and respond to the project method with a dummy Project. On the next line we stub CreatesProject#new to return the action_stub when the controller method tries to create the action. We then call the create normally. When the create method executes, the stub is returned in place of the action; the controller method interprets as failure the false result when create is called on the action, and the new template is invoked.

The update test is similar, except that it doesn't have a separate action object; it just calls the regular ActiveRecord update_attributes. We create a dummy object, in this case a Project. (It's going into the database because doing so is the simplest, if not the fastest, way to give the object an ID.) We then set up the failure condition on line 10 by stubbing update_attributes on the new object to return false. And then we stub Project#find on line 11 so that the controller action will return the stubbed object we've created. Otherwise, the controller action would go to the database and create a new instance of the same object. That new object would not have the update_attribute stub, and presumably would not fail when updated. We then call the update normally. The controller takes the stubbed object, interprets the failure of update_attribute, and invokes the edit template.

For reference, here's the scaffolded update method that passes this test:

mocks/01/gatherer/app/controllers/projects_controller.rb
```ruby
def update
  @project = Project.find(params[:id])
  if @project.update_attributes(params[:project])
    redirect_to @project, notice: "'project was successfully updated.'"
  else
    render action: 'edit'
  end
end
```

You also need a blank template file at app/views/projects/edit.html.erb, since it's referenced by the controller method.

There's a slight difference between the two tests: the update method is stubbing ActiveRecord classes that are not part of our application proper. This should give us pause. Normally we'd start looking for ways to wrap that behavior in an extracted method so we can stub the extracted method. However, in this case the update_attributes is so simple that the extraction would make the overall code more complex, so it's probably not worth it.

> **Prescription 17** If you're stubbing methods that do not belong to your program, think about whether the code would be better if restructured to wrap the external behavior.

We'll expand on this technique in Chapter 12, *Testing External Services*, on page 229, where we'll show when to use test doubles in testing external services.

Using Mocks to Specify Behavior

In addition to merely replacing expensive method calls, mock objects enable a different style of testing where you validate the application's behavior rather than its ending state. In most of the tests we've seen throughout the book, the test validates the result of a computation: it's testing whether something is true at the end of an action. When using mocks, however, we have the opportunity to test the process's behavior during the test rather than the outcome.

Let's look at an example. Back in *Who Controls the Controller?*, on page 55, we wrote the following test of our ProjectsController:

```
mocks/01/gatherer/spec/controllers/projects_controller_spec.rb
it "creates a project" do
  post :create, project: {name: "Runway", tasks: "Start something:2"}
  expect(response).to redirect_to(projects_path)
  expect(assigns(:action).project.name).to eq("Runway")
end
```

At the time I mumbled something about being careful not to duplicate test-model functionality, and said we'd do something different after we'd covered more tools. Guess what—we've covered a new tool, and now it's time for us to apply it to the controller test.

This test makes two assertions—that the successful creation redirects to the projects listing page and that an instance variable named @actions is correctly set with the proper project name. Actually, let's split that last assumption into two parts. The controller is a) setting a particular instance variable and b) giving it a value matching the incoming data.

Setting the instance variable is part of the controller's logic because it's an expectation that the view template will have when it renders; it will expect to have a particular value at @actions. However, the specific value that goes there isn't really the controller's responsibility. The controller is acting as a conduit. Its job is to just get the value from some data source and pass it on. Using the controller test to verify the value is misplaced.

What is the controller's responsibility? The controller is just a conduit. By testing that the controller sets @actions, we're testing the output of the conduit. The input of the conduit, though, is verified not by the state of the variable at the end of the controller call, but by the way in which that value is obtained. In other words, the controller's responsibility is to meet a contract on both ends—it's responsible for setting a particular value to satisfy the view, and it's responsible for calling some other place in the system to acquire data.

Specifically, the controller calls CreatesProject.new and then calls create on the resulting action. Crucially, we leave the fact that CreatesProject accurately creates a project to the tests for that object (tests we wrote when we added the CreatesProject functionality). So all we need to do here is specify that the controller calls the appropriate methods.

Enter mocks. We use mock objects to set an expectation for the controller's behavior during the user action. This will look similar to our failure test from the last section, but I'm going to emphasize a different part of the test:

```
mocks/01/gatherer/spec/controllers/projects_controller_spec.rb
Line 1   it "creates a project (mock version)" do
     2     fake_action = instance_double(CreatesProject, create: true)
     3     expect(CreatesProject).to receive(:new)
     4         .with(name: "Runway", task_string: "start something:2")
     5         .and_return(fake_action)
     6     post :create, project: {name: "Runway", tasks: "start something:2"}
     7     expect(response).to redirect_to(projects_path)
     8     expect(assigns(:action)).not_to be_nil
     9   end
```

Well, we're still making the same controller call to create and we're still testing the redirection. Everything else has changed.

On lines 2 and 3 we create our doubles. We need to do this in two steps because the controller both instantiates a CreatesProject object and calls create on it. At the end of the test, on line 8, we've changed the test for the @action; now all we're testing is that the variable is set to something non-nil. That seems like a weaker test, but it's actually a more accurate representation of the controller's responsibilities.

The power of this test is in the mock expectations. We're validating all of the following:

- The controller calls CreatesProject.new.
- That call passes a name and a task_string as key/value pairs based on the incoming parameters.
- The controller calls create on the return value of CreatesProject.new.

That's a fairly detailed description of the controller's responsibilities.

This test makes only a minimal attempt to validate the objects outside of the controller. The use of instance_double to create the test double guarantees the test will fail if the controller calls a method on the action item that doesn't exist, but makes no other claim about what the action item does. That's great in that a bug in CreatesProject will trigger only one test failure, making it easier to track down. But it's terrifying in that it's possible for this test to pass without the underlying code working.

Because it is possible to have tests pass due only to mismatches between the API and the test double, generally I do this kind of testing based on setting mock expectations only if there is a separate integration test tying together all the small, focused unit tests.

A plus for this test is speed. Since it doesn't actually contact the model layer, it's probably going to be fast.

A downside is readability. It can be genuinely hard to look at a mocked test and determine exactly what is being validated. Using spies can help here because spies force you to be explicit about the expectations you're claiming in the test.

Finally, an elaborate edifice of mocked methods runs the risk of causing the test to depend on very specific details of the method structure of the object being mocked. This can make the test brittle in the face of refactorings that might change the object's methods. Good API design and an awareness of this potential problem go a long way toward mitigating the issue.

I'm hesitant to put a "don't do this" example here, but we could easily have made this test far more brittle if we'd started to worry about tasks being part of projects:

```
it "don't do this" do
  fake_action = double(create: true,
      project: double(name: "Fred", tasks: [double(title: "Start", size: 2)]))
  # and so on…
```

In this snippet, fake_action isn't merely concerned with reporting success; it also wants to stub the project and have the project stub the array of tasks. This is where test doubles become a pain. The preceding snippet is hard to set up, it's hard to read, and it's very brittle against changes to object internals. If you find yourself needing to write nested mocks like this, try to restructure your code to reduce dependencies.

Prescription 18	A stubbed method that returns a stub is usually okay. A stubbed method that returns a stub that itself contains a stub probably means your code is too dependent on the internals of other objects.

More Expectation Annotations

RSpec allows a number of different annotations to the expectation part of declaring a test double. You can specify more complex return values or a variety of arguments to the stubbed method.

Stubbing Return Values

A couple of advanced usages of returns might be valuable now and again. If you have multiple return values specified, the stubbed method returns them one at a time:

`mocks/01/gatherer/spec/models/project_spec.rb`
```
it "stubs with multiple returns" do
  project = Project.new
  allow(project).to receive(:user_count).and_return(1, 2)
  assert_equal(1, project.user_count)
  assert_equal(2, project.user_count)
  assert_equal(2, project.user_count)
end
```

The return values of the stubbed method walk through the values passed to and_return. Note that the values don't cycle; the last value is repeated over and over again.

RSpec can do a couple of other occasionally useful things with return values. If the method being stubbed takes a block and you want to cause the stubbed method to yield a particular set of arguments to the block, you can do so with and_yield:

```
`allow(project).to receive(:method).and_yield("arg")`
```

The expectation is that some method takes a block argument, and we want to pass through method and send arg to the block.

You can also call the original method implementation with and_call_original, as in expect(project).to receive(:name).and_call_original. You would do this (rarely) if you were mostly interested in setting the expectation that the object is being called rather than changing the behavior of the object.

Finally, you can pass a block to receive, in which case the block is executed to be the method's value:

```
first_name = "Noel"
last_name = "Rappin"
allow(project).to receive(:name) { first_name + last_name }
```

In theory this gives you some flexibility to manage the method's output. In practice it may mean it's time to abandon RSpec mocks in favor of a dummy object via OpenStruct, or that it's time to rethink the code design.

Mocks with Arguments

You can tune an RSpec double to return different values based on the parameters passed to the method using the with method to filter incoming calls.

In its simplest form, shown earlier in the chapter, the with method takes one or more arguments. When the stubbed method is called, RSpec searches for a match between the arguments passed and the declared double and returns the value matching those arguments.

Take care: by setting expectations tied to specific input values, you are limiting the RSpec double to only those input values. For instance, our earlier example of stubbing methods calls find(1). If we change the double to expect a different number, the test will fail:

```
it "stubs the class" do
  allow(Project).to receive(:find).with(3).and_return(
      Project.new(:name => "Project Greenlight"))
  project = Project.find(1)
  expect(project.name).to eq("Project Greenlight")
end
```

We've added with(3) to the double declaration, leading to this:

```
1) Project stubs the class
   Failure/Error: project = Project.find(1)
     <Project(id: integer, name: string, due_date: date, created_at: datetime,
       updated_at: datetime) (class)> received :find with unexpected arguments
       expected: (3)
            got: (1)
     Please stub a default value first if message
         might be received with other args as well.
```

This message is saying that RSpec doesn't know what to do if find is called with the argument 1, but it would know what to do with the argument 3. In other words, we did something RSpec didn't expect, and RSpec doesn't like surprises.

You can have multiple stubs of the same method that use with to expect differ-ent arguments and return different values. As implied by the last line of the preceding error message, a stub without a with argument is considered a default and is used if nothing else matches:

```
it "stubs the class" do
  allow(Project).to receive(:find).with(1).and_return(
      Project.new(:name => "Project Greenlight"))
  allow(Project).to receive(:find).with(3).and_return(
      Project.new(:name => "Project Runway"))
  allow(Project).to receive(:find).and_raise(ActiveRecord::RecordNotFound)
  project = Project.find(1)
  expect(project.name).to eq("Project Greenlight")
end
```

Using with does not constrain the eventual return value. You can use both returns or raises after a with call.

You need to be careful here—using with makes RSpec powerful and flexible, but in general testing with mock objects works best if they are weak and rigid. The use of a complicated mock object suggests the existence of an overly complex dependency in your code.

Many of these matchers make more sense when you're talking about mock expectations rather than just stubs. When you're actually validating the behavior of the object being mocked, having a tighter filter on the incoming values you expect makes more sense.

RSpec allows you to use many things besides literal values as the arguments to a with call. Here are a few. You can see a full list at https://relishapp.com/rspec/rspec-mocks/v/3-0/docs/setting-constraints/matching-arguments. Many of these arguments are actually RSpec matchers that are being used to match against potential arguments to a double in the same way they match against expectations.

- If you expect the method to be called with no arguments, use with(no_args).
- If you don't care what an argument is as long as it's there, use anything, as in with("foo", anything).
- Any Ruby object that implements triple-equal (===) can be used and will match anything it's === to. This will most commonly be regular expres-sions, such as with(/\d{3}/), but could also be classes or Proc objects.
- A hash that includes a particular key can be matched with with(hash_including(key: value)).
- Any RSpec matcher can be used.

Mock Tips

My opinion about the best way to use mock objects changes every few months. I'll try some mocks, they'll work well, I'll start using more mocks, they'll start getting in the way, I'll back off, and then I'll think, "Let's try some mocks." This cycle has been going for years and I have no reason to think it's going to change anytime soon.

That said, some guidelines always hold true.

The Ownership Rule

Don't mock what you don't own. In other words, use test doubles only to replace methods that are actually part of your application, and not part of an external framework. (Note that we violated this rule in this chapter when we stubbed ActiveRecord methods like update_attributes.)

> **Prescription 19** Don't mock what you don't own.

One reason to mock only methods you control is, well, that you control them. One danger in mocking methods is that your mock either doesn't receive or doesn't return a reasonable value from the method being replaced. If the method in question belongs to a third-party framework, the chance that it will change without you knowing increases and thus the test becomes more brittle.

More importantly, mocking a method you don't own couples your test to the internal details of the third-party framework. By implication, this means the method being tested is also coupled to those internal details. That is bad, not just if the third-party tool changes, but also if you want to refactor your code; the dependency will make that change more complicated.

The solution, in most cases, is to create a method or class in your application that calls the third-party tool and stubs that method (while also writing tests to ensure that the wrapper does the right thing). We'll see a larger example of this technique in Chapter 12, *Testing External Services*, on page 229. However, in a smaller case you can do this as easily as follows:

```
class Project
  def self.create_from_controller(params)
    create(params)
  end
end
```

And then in a test:

```
it "creates a project" do
  allow(Project).to receive(:create_from_controller).and_return(Project.new)
end
```

I admit that, oversimplified like this, the technique seems like overkill. (All object-oriented techniques seem like overkill until you suddenly realize you needed them six months ago.) If you create a method like this wrapper, however, you'll often find that the functionality is shared in multiple places, giving you one point of contact with the third-party tool rather than several. You'll also find that these methods attract what would otherwise be duplicated behavior. Both of these are good things.

When to Mock, When to Stub

If you're using your fake objects to take the place of real objects that are hard or impossible to create in a test environment, it's probably a good idea to use stubs rather than mocks. If you're actually using the fake value as an input to a different process, then you should test that process directly using the fake value rather than a mock. Adding the mock expectation just gives you another thing that can break, which in this use case is probably not related to what you're testing.

On the other side, if you are testing the relationship between different systems of your code, tend to use mocks to verify the behavior of one part of the code as it calls the other.

Mocks are particularly good at testing across boundaries between subsystems. For example, controller testing to isolate the controller test from the behavior of the model, essentially only testing that the controller makes a specific model call and using the model test to verify model behavior. Among the benefits of using mocks this way is you are encouraged to make the interface between your controllers and models as simple as possible. However, it does mean that the controller test knows more about your model than it otherwise might, which may make the model code harder to change.

You also need to be careful of mocking methods that have side effects or that call other methods that might be interesting. The mock bypasses the original method, which means no side effect and no calling the internal method.

Pro tip: saving to the database and outputting to the response stream are both side effects.

Be very nervous if you're specifying a value as a result of a mock and then asserting the existence of the very same value. One of the biggest potential problems with any test suite is false positives, and testing results with mocked values is a really efficient way to generate false positives.

Mocks Are Design Canaries

Test-driven development in general and mock objects in particular are sensitive indicators of your application code's quality. As the code becomes more complex and tightly coupled, the tests become harder and harder to write.

When you're using a true mock to encapsulate a test and isolate it from methods that are not under test, try to limit the number of methods you're mocking in one test. The more mocks, the more vulnerable the test will be to changes in the actual code. A lot of mocks may indicate that your test is trying to do too much or might indicate a poor object-oriented design where one class is asking for too many details of a different class.

In this section of the book we covered model testing. We talked about the services Rails provides for testing models, and we discussed fixtures and factories as mechanisms for creating consistent test data. With this chapter we've started to transition from testing models to testing the user-facing parts of the application. Mock testing is useful for testing models, but it becomes especially useful when trying to shield the various layers of your application from each other.

In the next section we'll be discussing testing the controller and view layers. Mock objects can be a very important part of controller testing; creating mock models allows the controller tests to proceed independently of the model test.

## CHAPTER 8

Testing Controllers and Views

Rails applications follow a model-view-controller, or MVC, pattern. The view layer has the responsibility of presenting data to the user, which in a server-side web application usually means generating HTML. Ideally, the view layer does this with minimal interaction with the model. The controller takes in information about the user request, contacts the appropriate parts of the model layer for data, and passes that information on to the view layer. The following is a very simplified diagram.

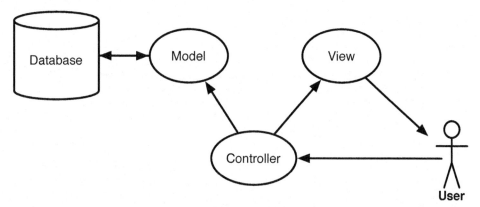

Testing Rails controllers and views is more challenging than testing Rails models. You can see from the diagram that controllers and views both interact with the external users, whereas models are more inherently isolated. In Rails, controller and view instances are typically created by the framework itself and are not easy to create in isolation during a test. (As far as the Rails developer is concerned, the view instance is mostly just a template.) Controller and view calls often are more interesting for their side effects than for the value they return. Also, individual controller actions and view templates are often too large to be meaningfully unit-tested.

While the Rails framework and third-party testing tools allow us to interact with controller actions and view templates in our test environment, the issues of isolation and size still exist. A discussion of how to best test views and controllers, therefore, often turns into a discussion about what code belongs in the controller and view and what should be extracted into a different object. The object extracted to, which is not a part of the Rails framework, is sometimes referred to as a PORO: Plain Old Ruby Object. The issue of how to best deconstruct or refactor controller and view code is somewhat contentious within the Rails community.

We've discussed the idea that the most useful tests test either an entire end-to-end process or a single unit. Controller and view tests are easy to put in the middle ground and are therefore notoriously brittle and hard to manage.

Testing Controllers

We've already written a few controller tests as part of our earlier testing walkthroughs. Let's take a look at one of them:

```
display/01/gatherer/spec/controllers/projects_controller_spec.rb
Line 1  require 'rails_helper'
2
3  RSpec.describe ProjectsController, type: :controller do
4
5    describe "POST create" do
6      it "creates a project" do
7        post :create, project: {name: "Runway", tasks: "Start something:2"}
8        expect(response).to redirect_to(projects_path)
9        expect(assigns(:action).project.name).to eq("Runway")
10     end
```

This test is simple but has most of the features of a basic controller test. Like many tests we have seen, controller tests have three parts. First, the controller test may create data needed to cover a particular logic path. We don't need any data for this test, but we will see examples of generating controller-specific test data in our next examples. Second, on line 7 the code performs an action. Specifically, it simulates a post request to the controller's create action with one argument, the hash {name: "Runway", tasks: "start something:2"}, which represents the parameters being passed to the action as part of the request.

Finally, on lines 8 and 9, our test makes assertions about the controller's behavior. Broadly, we care about two kinds of behavior. We care about what template or other action the controller passes control to. The redirect_to matcher is one of a few assertions added by RSpec in controller test groups to specify that transfer of control. We may also care that the controller specifies particular instance variables for use by a view template. The assigns method is also managed by RSpec controller groups to enable assertions to be made about those values.

What to Test in a Controller Test

Ideally, your controllers are relatively simple. The complicated functionality is in a model or other object and is being tested in your unit tests for those objects. One reason this is a best practice is that models are easier to test than controllers because they are generally easier to extract and use independently in a test framework.

> **Prescription 20** A controller test should test controller behavior. A controller test should not fail because of problems in the model.

A controller test that overlaps with model behavior is part of the awkward middle ground of testing that we're trying to avoid. If the controller test is actually going to the database, then the test is slower than it needs to be, and if a model failure can cascade into the controller tests, then it's harder than it needs to be to isolate the problem.

A controller test should have one or more of the following goals:

- Verifying that a normal, basic user request triggers expected model calls and passes the necessary data to the view.
- Verifying that an ill-formed or otherwise invalid user request is handled properly, for whatever definition of "properly" fits your app.
- Verifying security, such as requiring logins for pages as needed and testing that users who enter a URL for a resource they shouldn't be able to see are blocked or diverted. We will discuss this more in Chapter 11, *Testing for Security*, on page 205.

Simulating Requests in a Controller Test

Most of your controller tests in Rails will surround a simulated request. To make this simulation easier, Rails provides a controller test method for each HTTP verb: delete, get, head, patch, post, and put. Each of these methods works the same way. (Internally, they all dispatch to a common method that does all the work.) A full call to one of these methods has five arguments, though you'll often just use the first three:

```
get :show, {id: @task.id}, {user_id: "3",
    current_project: @project.id.to_s}, {notice: "flash test"}
```

The method name, get, is the HTTP verb being simulated—sort of. While the controller test will set the HTTP verb if for some reason you query the Rails request object, it does not check the Rails routing table to see if that action is reachable using that HTTP verb. As a result, you can't test routing via a controller test. Rails does provide a mechanism for testing routes, which we'll cover in *Testing Routes*, on page 143.

The first argument—in this case :show—is the controller action being called. The second argument, {id: @task.id}, is a hash that becomes the params hash in the controller action. In the controller action called from this test, you would expect params[:id] to equal @task.id. The Rails form name-parsing trick is not used here—if you want to simulate a form upload, you use a multilevel hash directly, as in user: {name: "Noel", email: "noel@noelrappin.com"}, which implies params[:user][:name] == "Noel" in the controller.

Any value passed in this hash argument is converted to a string—specifically, to_param is called on it. So you can do something like id: 3, confident that it will be "3" in the controller. This, by the way, is a welcome change in recent versions of Rails; older versions did not do this conversion, which led to occasional heads pounding against walls.

If one of the arguments is an uploaded file—say, from a multipart form—you can simulate that using the Rails helper fixture_file_upload(filename, mime_type), like this:

```
post :create, logo: fixture_file_upload('/test/data/logo.png', 'image/png')
```

If you're using a third-party tool, such as Paperclip or CarrierWave to manage uploads, those tools typically have more specific testing helpers.

The fourth and fifth arguments to these controller methods are optional and rarely used. The fourth argument sets key/value pairs for the session object, which is useful in testing multistep processes that use the session for continuity. The fifth argument represents the Rails flash object, which is useful...well, never, but if for some reason the incoming flash is important for your logic, there it is.

You may occasionally want to do something fancier to the simulated request. In a controller test you have access to the request object as @request, and access to the controller object as @controller. (As you'll see in *Evaluating Controller Results*, on page 141, you also have the @response object.) You can get at the HTTP headers using the hash @request.headers.

There is one more controller action method, xml_http_request (also aliased to xhr). This simulates a classic Ajax call to the controller and has a slightly different signature:

```
it "makes an ajax call" do
  xhr :post, :create, :task => {:id => "3"}
end
```

The method name is xhr, the first argument is the HTTP verb associated with the xhr call, and the remaining arguments are the arguments to all the other controller-calling methods in the same order: action, params, session, and flash. The xhr call sets the appropriate headers such that the Rails controller will appropriately be able to consider the request an Ajax request (meaning .js format blocks will be triggered), then simulates the call based on its arguments.

Evaluating Controller Results

A controller test has three things you might want to validate after the controller action:

- Did it return the expected HTTP status code? RSpec provides the response.status object and the have_http_status matcher for this purpose.

- Did it pass control to the expected template or redirected controller action? Here we have the render_template and redirect_to matchers.

- Did it set the values that the view will expect? For this we have the special hash objects assigns, cookies, flash, and session.

Often you'll combine more than one of these in the same test:

```
it "is a successful index request with no filters" do
  get :index
  expect(response).to have_http_status(:success)
  expect(response).to render_template(:index)
end
```

Asserting Controller Response Type

Let's talk about these three types of assertions in more detail:

We can use have_http_status to verify the HTTP response code sent back to the browser from Rails. Normally we use this assertion to ensure that our controller correctly distinguishes between success and redirect or error cases.

The value passed to have_http_status is usually one of four special symbols:

Symbol	HTTP Code Equivalent	Symbol	HTTP Code Equivalent
:success	200–299	:redirect	300–399
:missing	404	:error	500–599

If you need to test for a more specific response, you can pass either the exact HTTP code number or one of the associated symbols defined by Rack.[1] Note that RSpec uses the codes defined by SYMBOL_TO_STATUS_CODE. The most common case I've had for specific HTTP codes is the need to distinguish between 301 permanent redirects (:moved-permanently) and other redirects.

Asserting Which View Is Rendered

The render_template matcher is used to determine whether the controller is passing control to the expected view template. The method has a simple form and then some optional complexity. In the simple form, render_template is passed a template name that is specified exactly as it would be in the controller, using render :action—the template name can be a string or a symbol. If the argument is just a single string or symbol, then it is checked against the name of the main template that rendered the action.

Normally I will not employ render_template when the controller action is just using the implicit Rails default and ceding to a view of the same name. I will use render_template when I expect the controller will need to explicitly pass control to a specific template, with the most common case being a create action that is successful and renders a show template.

When you expect the controller to redirect, you can use redirect_to to assert the exact nature of the redirect. The argument to redirect_to is pretty much anything Rails can convert to a URL, although the method's behavior is slightly different based on what the argument actually is. The code for redirect_to explicitly includes have_http_status(:redirect), so you don't need to duplicate that assertion.

If the argument to redirect_to is the name of a URL because it's a string or a method for a Rails named route, or because it's an object that has a Rails RESTful route, then the assertion passes if and only if the redirecting URL exactly matches the asserted URL. For testing purposes, Rails will assume that the application's local hostname is http://www.example.com. If that's too exact a test for your taste, you can pass a hash to redirect_to, which specifies the :controller, :action, and any parameters. If the argument is a hash, then

---

1.   https://github.com/rack/rack/blob/master/lib/rack/utils.rb

assert_redirected_to checks only the exact key/value pairs in the hash; other parts of the URL are not checked.

Rails controller tests do not—repeat, *do not*—follow the redirect. Any data-validation tests you write apply only to the method before the redirect occurs. If you need your test to follow the redirection for some reason, you are cordially invited to try something in an integration test; see Chapter 10, *Integration Testing with Capybara and Cucumber*, on page 177.

Asserting Controller Data

Rails allows you to verify the data generated by the controller action being tested with the four items mentioned earlier: assigns, session, cookies, and flash. Of these, assigns, which gives access to instance variables declared by the controller, is the most commonly used. A typical use might look like this, with a common use of assigns and an admittedly contrived use of session:

```
it "shows a task" do
  task = Task.create!
  get :show, id: task.id
  expect(response).to have_http_status(:success)
  expect(assigns(:task).id).to eq(task.id)
  expect(session[:previous_page]).to eq("task/show")
end
```

The cookies and flash special variables are used similarly, though I don't write tests for the flash very often. The cookie hash has key/value pairs only for cookies. If you want to test other cookie attributes, you need to access them via the request object.

Testing Routes

Although the basics of Rails routing are simple, the desire to customize Rails' response to URLs can lead to confusion about exactly what your application is going to do when converting between a URL and a Rails action. Rails provides a way to specify route behavior in a test.

Routing tests are not typically part of my TDD process—usually my integration test implicitly covers the routing. That said, sometimes routing gets complicated and has some logic of its own (especially if you're trying to replicate an existing URL scheme), so it's nice to have this as part of your test suite.

RSpec-Rails puts route tests in the spec/routing directory. The primary matcher that RSpec-Rails uses for route testing is route_to. Here's a sample test that includes all seven default RESTful routes for the project resource:

```
display/01/gatherer/spec/routing/project_routing_spec.rb
require 'rails_helper'

RSpec.describe "project routing" do
  it "routes projects" do
    expect(get: "/projects").to route_to(
        controller: "projects", action: "index")
    expect(post: "/projects").to route_to(
        controller: "projects", action: "create")
    expect(get: "/projects/new").to route_to(
        controller: "projects", action: "new")
    expect(get: "/projects/1").to route_to(
        controller: "projects", action: "show", id: "1")
    expect(get: "/projects/1/edit").to route_to(
        controller: "projects", action: "edit", id: "1")
    expect(patch: "/projects/1").to route_to(
        controller: "projects", action: "update", id: "1")
    expect(delete: "/projects/1").to route_to(
        controller: "projects", action: "destroy", id: "1")
  end
end
```

All of these are using the same form. The argument to expect is a key/value pair where the key is the HTTP verb and the value is the string form of the route. The argument to route_to is a set of key/value pairs where the keys are the parts of the calculated route (including controller, action, and what have you) and the values are, well, the values.

The route_to matcher tests the routes in both directions. It checks that when you send the path through the routing engine, you get the controller, action, and other variables specified. It also checks that the set of controller, action, and other variables sent through the router results in the path string (which is why you might need to specify query-string elements). It's not clear to me why a route might pass in one direction and not the other.

RSpec also provides a be_routable method, which is designed to be used in the negative to show that a specific path—say, the Rails default—is not recognized:

```
expect(get: "/projects/search/fred").not_to be_routable
```

Testing Helper Methods

Helper modules are the storage attic of Rails applications. They are designed to contain reusable bits of view logic. This might include view-specific representations of data, or conditional logic that governs how content is displayed. Helper modules tend to get filled with all kinds of clutter that doesn't seem to belong anywhere else. Because they are a little tricky to set up for testing, helper methods often aren't tested even when they contain significant amounts of logic.

RSpec helper tests go in spec/helpers. There's not a whole lot of special magic here—just a helper object that you use to call your helper methods.

Let's say we want to change our project view so behind-schedule projects show up differently. We could do that in a helper. My normal practice is to add a CSS class to the output for both the regular and behind-schedule cases, to give the design maximum freedom to display as desired.

Here's a test for that helper:

```
display/01/gatherer/spec/helpers/projects_helper_spec.rb
require 'rails_helper'

RSpec.describe ProjectsHelper, :type => :helper do
  let(:project) { Project.new(name: "Project Runway") }

  it "augments with status info" do
    allow(project).to receive(:on_schedule?).and_return(true)
    actual = helper.name_with_status(project)
    expect(actual).to have_selector("span.on_schedule", text: "Project Runway")
  end

end
```

In this test we're creating a new project using a standard ActiveRecord new method. Rather than define a bunch of tasks that would mean the new project is on schedule, we just stub the on_schedule? method on line 7 to return true. This has the advantage of being faster than creating a bunch of objects and, I think, being more clear as to the exact state of the project being tested.

We're using the have_selector matcher again to compare the expected HTML with the generated HTML. We'll cover have_selector in more detail when we talk about Capybara.

That test will fail because we haven't defined the name_with_status helper. Let's define one:

```
display/01/gatherer/app/helpers/projects_helper.rb
module ProjectsHelper

  def name_with_status(project)
    content_tag(:span, project.name, class: 'on_schedule')
  end
end
```

The test passes; now let's add a second test for the remaining case. This test will look familiar.

display/02/gatherer/spec/helpers/projects_helper_spec.rb
```
it "augments project name with status info when behind schedule" do
  allow(project).to receive(:on_schedule?).and_return(false)
  actual = helper.name_with_status(project)
  expect(actual).to have_selector("span.behind_schedule", text: "Project Runway")
end
```

It passes with the following:

display/02/gatherer/app/helpers/projects_helper.rb
```
module ProjectsHelper
  def name_with_status(project)
    dom_class = project.on_schedule? ? 'on_schedule' : 'behind_schedule'
    content_tag(:span, project.name, class: dom_class)
  end
end
```

One gotcha that you need to worry about when view-testing is using Rails-internal view methods like url_for. Although all core Rails helpers are automatically loaded into the ActionView test environment, one or two have significant dependencies on the real controller object and therefore fail with opaque error messages during helper testing. The most notable of these is url_for. One workaround is to override url_for by defining it in your own test case. (The method signature is def url_for(options = {}).) The return value is up to you; a simple stub response is often good enough.

Sometimes helper methods take a block, which is expected to be ERB text. One common use of this kind of helper is access control, in which the logic in the helper determines whether the code in the block is invoked. Blocks also are very helpful as wrapper code for HTML that might surround many different kinds of text—a rounded-rectangle effect, for example.

Here's a simple example of a helper that takes a block:

```
def if_logged_in
  yield if logged_in?
end
```

Which would be invoked like so:

```
<% if_logged_in do %>
  <%= link_to "logout", logout_path %>
<% end %>
```

To test the if_logged_in helper, we take advantage of the fact that the yield statement is the last statement of the helper and therefore is the return value, and of the fact that Ruby will let us pass any arbitrary string into the block, giving us tests that look like this:

```
it "does not display if not logged_in" do
  expect(logged_in?).to be_falsy
  expect(if_logged_in { "logged in" }).to be_nil
end

it "displays if logged in" do
  login_as users(:quentin)
  expect(logged_in?).to be_truthy
  expect(if_logged_in { "logged in" }).to eq("logged in")
end
```

The first test asserts that the block is not invoked, so the helper returns nil. The second asserts that the block is invoked, just returning the value passed into the block.

You have to be a little careful here because these tests are just testing the helper method's return value, not what is sent to the output stream. The output-stream part is a side effect of the process, but it is stored in a variable called output_buffer, which you can access via testing. So you could write the preceding tests as follows:

```
it "does not display if not logged_in" do
  expect(logged_in?).to be_falsy
  if_logged_in { "logged in" }
  expect(output_buffer).to be_nil
end

it "displays if logged in" do
  login_as users(:quentin)
  expect(logged_in?).to be_truthy
  if_logged_in { "logged in" }
  expect(output_buffer).to eq("logged in")
end
```

If for some reason your helper method requires a specific instance variable to be set, cut that out immediately; it's a bad idea. However, if you must and you want to test it in RSpec, use the assigns method, as in assigns(:project) = Project.new.

Testing Views and View Markup

We've tested a helper for project status, but when we go to the browser the new status DOM elements don't show up. This is because we haven't placed our new helper in the view template itself. Naturally, we would like our dazzling two-line helper to be incorporated into the view.

From a TDD perspective, we have a few options:

- Write no further tests, and just insert the helper into the view template. Technically we're not adding logic, so we can kind of squeak by with this one. I don't mean to be glib here—having no extra test may be the right choice when the test is a) expensive, b) trivial in the larger scheme of things, and c) easy to visually inspect.

- Write an integration test using Capybara, as we saw in Chapter 3, *Test-Driven Rails*, on page 41, and will see again in Chapter 10, *Integration Testing with Capybara and Cucumber*, on page 177. If we've been using outside-in development, we may already have an integration test in place.

- Write a Rails view test. This has the advantage of being somewhat faster than the integration test, and we may be able to piggyback it on existing controller tests.

RSpec allows you to specify view tests independent of controllers (though you can get views to run from controller tests, it's not the default and it's not recommended). The RSpec convention is to place view tests in the spec/views folder, with one spec file to a view file, so the view in app/views/projects/index.html.erb is specified in spec/views/projects/index.html.erb_spec.rb.

I rarely write these tests. I find the file structure hard to maintain, and what logic I do have in views is often tested between objects like presenters and integration tests. In general, I find full TDD on views difficult—I often have to see a scratch implementation of a view before I know exactly what to test. That said, they are surprisingly easy to write because they have no dependency on any other part of the code. So let's try one.

Let's take a second to plan this test. What does it need to do?

- Given: We need just two projects, one that is on schedule and one that's not. That allows us to verify both halves of the helper. The projects we create need to be visible to the controller method, meaning we either need to put the data in the database or do some clever mocking. (Fixtures could be used too, but I don't want to create fixtures because I don't want this project data to be global.) Let's start with the database; it's simpler for the moment.

- When: We just need to hit the index action of the controller.

- Then: Our on-schedule project has the on-schedule DOM class and our behind-schedule class has the behind-schedule one.

In code, that becomes the following:

```
display/02/gatherer/spec/views/projects/index.html.erb_spec.rb
require 'rails_helper'

describe "projects/index" do
  let(:completed_task) { Task.create!(completed_at: 1.day.ago, size: 1) }
  let(:on_schedule) { Project.create!(due_date: 1.year.from_now,
      name: "On Schedule", tasks: [completed_task]) }
  let(:incomplete_task) { Task.create!(size: 1) }
  let(:behind_schedule) { Project.create!(due_date: 1.day.from_now,
      name: "Behind Schedule", tasks: [incomplete_task]) }

  it "renders the index page with correct dom elements" do
    @projects = [on_schedule, behind_schedule]
    render
    expect(rendered).to have_selector(
        "#project_#{on_schedule.id} .on_schedule")
    expect(rendered).to have_selector(
        "#project_#{behind_schedule.id} .behind_schedule")
  end
end
```

I cheated here in one respect—the have_selector matcher is not part of core RSpec; it's actually part of Capybara, so we need Capybara in the Gemfile (gem 'capybara'). And in the spec/rails_helper.rb file, up near the top, we need require 'capybara/rspec'. But have_selector is so useful, and Capybara is useful in its own right, that it's not much of a project burden to include them.

What does this view test do?

First we create our given: the data. We use let to create the on-schedule project and task. The objects need to be in the database so that the Rails associations all work. But there are options here to make the test faster, including creating projects and stubbing the on_schedule? method or using FactoryGirl.build_stubbed to create real objects without having to save them in the database.

In the spec itself, we set the @projects variable. We're testing the view in isolation, so we don't have a controller to set this up for us; we need to create the instance variables that will be given to the view.

Our "when" section is one line, render, which tells RSpec to render the view. Which view? The one specified by the outermost describe block. In our case, that's projects/index—Rails will connect that to the index.html.erb file in the file base. Alternatively, you can explicitly pass the view as an argument, render template: "projects/index". If the view is a partial, you need to specify that: render partial: "projects/data_row. An optional locals argument with key/value pairs specifies local variables to the partial. As with the regular Rails render method, you can use a shortcut of the form render "projects/data_row, project: @project.

All Rails helpers are loaded. If you want to stub one of their values, the helper methods are accessible via a view object, as in view.stub(:current_user).and_return(User.new). You can also use stub_template to stub a partial that you don't want to render; stub_template takes a key/value pair where the key is the exact file name of the partial and the value is the string you want returned in place of rendering the partial.

In the "then" portion of the spec, the rendered text is available via the method rendered. You can then use any RSpec matcher to set expectations on that value. In this test we use have_selector, but you can also use match to do a simple regular-expression match.

The have_selector matcher is defined by Capybara to be used with RSpec and is typically used to make assertions about the existence of a selector pattern in the output rendered by a controller action (though, as we saw in the helper spec, you can pass any string to the matcher).

In this case we're testing for the existence of a selector pattern with a DOM ID #project_#{on_schedule.id} that has a subordinate object containing the DOM class.on_schedule, and a similar selector pattern with the DOM ID #project_#{behind_schedule.id} containing an item with the DOM class .behind_schedule. We're passing the result of the rendered view to the matcher.

The selector syntax that have_selector uses is very similar to jQuery and other DOM selection tools. As in jQuery, the use of two separate selectors means we expect to match an instance of the first selector, which contains an instance of the second. For example, we're looking for an HTML element with the DOM ID of the form project_12, where 12 is the on_schedule project's ID. We also need for that outer HTML element to contain an inner HTML element with a DOM class on_schedule.

The pattern project_12 is exactly what the Rails dom_id helper uses, and we previously put that in the tr element of each project in the index listing. So we're looking for an on_schedule class inside that view.

This test will fail with an error message that looks something like this, showing that the test is looking for a pattern that is not found:

```
Failure/Error: expect(response).to
    have_selector("#project_#{on_schedule.id} .on_schedule")
    expected to find css "#project_980190963 .on_schedule"
    but there were no matches
```

A minor change in our index template gets the test to pass—we change the project name cell to use the name_with_status helper:

```
display/02/gatherer/app/views/projects/index.html.erb
<h1>All Projects</h1>
<table>
  <thead>
    <tr>
      <td>Project Name</td>
      <td>Total Project Size</td>
    </tr>
  </thead>
  <tbody>
    <% @projects.each do |project| %>
      <tr class="project-row" id="<%= dom_id(project) %>">
        <td class="name"><%= name_with_status(project) %></td>
        <td class="total-size"><%= project.total_size %></td>
      </tr>
    <% end %>
  </tbody>
</table>
```

Now the tr field with the appropriate DOM ID has a span element from the helper that contains the expected DOM class.

We can augment have_selector in a number of ways. The selector argument to have_selector can be just an element, as in div, or an element plus a class or ID decoration, as in div.hidden. In the latter case, a matching element must have both the HTML tag and the DOM class or ID. As with other DOM selectors, a dot (.) indicates a DOM class and # indicates a DOM ID. You can also use brackets to indicate arbitrary HTML attributes, as in input[name='email']. The Capybara docs have more details, especially the description of the all method.[2] (You can use XPath in Capybara to represent nodes rather than CSS selectors. I find that syntax awkward, but it could work for you.)

> **Prescription 21** When testing for view elements, try to test for DOM classes that you control rather than text or element names that might be subject to design changes.

---

2. http://rubydoc.info/github/jnicklas/capybara/master/Capybara/Node/Finders#all-instance_method

You can make a more specific match by including an optional text: argument. The value associated with the text is a string or a regular expression. The assertion passes if at least one HTML tag matches the selector and has inner content that matches the argument. String arguments must match the content exactly. Regular-expression arguments must =~ match the contents. In other words, we could make our assertions more specific like this:

```
have_selector("#project_#{on_schedule.id} .on_schedule", text: "On Schedule")
```

In the preceding case, the test passes because On Schedule is the project name and is included in the .on_schedule span tag.

Additionally, you could pass a count: option, which takes an integer. If there is a count:, then the have_selector passes only if the number of matching elements equals the number passed as an argument. (You can pass a range with the between option, and the matcher also supports maximum and minimum.) Therefore, we can verify that there is exactly one on-schedule element on the page with the following:

```
assert_select("#project_#{on_schedule.id} .on_schedule", count: 1)
```

It's often useful to be able to say that an element is not on the page—an edit button for a nonadministrator, for example. Capybara provides a special matcher for this, have_no_selector, which should be used over the normal RSpec .not_to have_selector because it will better deal with asynchronous JavaScript. We have no JavaScript here, but it's good to be in the habit of doing the right thing.

Presenters

Testing helpers is handy, but if you have a lot of logic in your helpers, I recommend moving the logic into presenter objects. This is especially true if you have a series of helpers that take the same argument.

There's nothing complicated about using presenters in Rails; I often roll my own using Ruby's SimpleDelegator class. If you want a little more structure, you can use the draper gem.[3]

We can convert the project helper to a project presenter. This version of the code uses SimpleDelegator and includes a method for converting a list of projects into a list of presenters. In a break from our usual convention, I'll show you the code first:

---

3. https://github.com/drapergem/draper>

```
display/03/gatherer/app/presenters/project_presenter.rb
Line 1  class ProjectPresenter < SimpleDelegator

    def self.from_project_list(*projects)
      projects.flatten.map { |project| ProjectPresenter.new(project) }
  5   end

    def initialize(project)
      super
    end
 10
    def name_with_status
      dom_class = on_schedule? ? 'on_schedule' : 'behind_schedule'
      "<span class='#{dom_class}'>#{name}</span>"
    end
 15
  end
```

The main action here starts on line 7, with our initializer. All we need to do is call super, and SimpleDelegator will take care of the rest: if SimpleDelegator gets a message it doesn't understand, it automatically delegates it to the object passed to the constructor. In practice this delegation means we can treat the presenter as though it were an instance of the original object, plus the presenter includes any new methods we choose to add to the presenter itself.

The name_with_status method in the presenter is simpler than the pre-existing helper method in one way and more complex in another. Since calls to methods like on_schedule? or name are now automatically delegated, there's no need to explicitly have the project as the message receiver, so we can just use on_schedule? rather than project.on_schedule?. However, since we're no longer inside a Rails helper we no longer have access to the content_tag method we used to build the HTML output. Instead we build the output as a string. (There are other options, such as explicitly including the module that content_tag is a part of, but building the string is simplest in this case.)

Finally, at the top of the class, we have a method that takes in a list of Project instances and converts them to presenters. The *projects argument in conjunction with projects.flatten allows the method to be called with either an explicit array, ProjectPresenter.from_project_list([p1, p2]), or an implicit arbitrary list of projects, ProjectPresenter.from_project_list(p1, p2). If we were using presenters more frequently, this kind of method would be easy to abstract to something generic rather than needing to be rewritten for each presenter class.

The test for the presenter is a little simpler than the tests we've seen so far:

display/03/gatherer/spec/presenters/project_presenter_spec.rb

```ruby
require 'rails_helper'

describe ProjectPresenter do
  let(:project) { instance_double(Project, name: "Project Runway") }
  let(:presenter) { ProjectPresenter.new(project) }

  it "handles name with on time status" do
    allow(project).to receive(:on_schedule?).and_return(true)
    expect(presenter.name_with_status).to eq(
        "<span class='on_schedule'>Project Runway</span>")
  end

  it "handles name with behind schedule status" do
    allow(project).to receive(:on_schedule?).and_return(false)
    expect(presenter.name_with_status).to eq(
        "<span class='behind_schedule'>Project Runway</span>")
  end
end
```

Do you see what we've done here? Since our presenter class has no dependencies on Rails, we can write a test class that also has no dependency on Rails. Rather than have the project be an actual project, we've replaced it with a double that responds to the only messages of project that we care about for this test.

We've given up a couple of things. We don't have have_selector, which belongs to controller and view groups (though it'd be possible to add it back in if we really wanted it).

But we've gained something big.

Since this test has no dependencies on Rails, we don't need the Rails environment—with a little bit more work we could replace require rails_helper at the top of the file with require spec_helper. That means we could execute the test without running Rails—which is great because it's potentially much faster not to load Rails than to load it.

Hold that thought; we'll be coming back to it Chapter 15, *Running Tests Faster and Running Faster Tests*, on page 287.

Testing Mailers

Testing Rails mailers involves two separate bits of functionality: specifying whether the email gets sent as a result of some action, and specifying the contents of that email. Specifying whether the email gets sent often starts as part of a controller or integration test, while specifying the content has a lot in common with view testing. The somewhat indirect nature of the Rails ActionMailer makes testing email less obvious than it might be, but it's not hard. We'll also look at a third-party library that makes email testing easier.

Let's say, for example purposes, that we want to send an email in our project system when a task is marked as complete. We don't have a user model yet (we'll talk about users in this system when we get to Chapter 11, *Testing for Security*, on page 205), so we'll assume for the moment that all the emails go to some kind of common audit or monitoring address. (Insert nsa.gov joke of your choosing.)

At this point we have one of those weird, unique-to-book-examples problems. Specifically, we haven't written very much of our task-tracker site—just a project index and new-project page. We don't have a list of tasks on a single project, let alone a way to mark a task as complete. This would be a problem if we were to start with an external integration test using Capybara; that would need to interact with actual web pages.

Rather than walk you through writing a bunch of basically boilerplate web pages or having those pages magically insert themselves in the code repository, we'll focus on the controller action that handles marking a task as complete. If we write tests for just that controller action, we don't need the rest of the application to exist. Everything I write here about dealing with mailers in a controller test also applies to a Capybara integration test.

With that hand-waving out of the way, let's write our controller test. We take a moment to think about what we need:

- Given: We'll need one task that starts off incomplete.

- When: The action of this test is a controller action. In a RESTful Rails interface, that action would be TasksController#update. Let's go with that. (Later, in Chapter 13, *Testing JavaScript*, on page 247, we'll make this an Ajax action.) The controller action has a completed: true parameter.

- Then: The task updates and an email is sent.

There's a simple case to start with, where completed is not set and no email is sent. Writing that test first will let us write the structure of the method.

> **Prescription 22** When testing a Boolean condition, make sure to write a test for both halves of the condition.

display/04/gatherer/spec/controllers/tasks_controller_spec.rb

```
Line 1  require 'rails_helper'

        RSpec.describe TasksController, :type => :controller do
          before(:example) do
5           ActionMailer::Base.deliveries.clear
          end

          describe "PATCH update" do
            let(:task) { Task.create!(title: "Write section on testing mailers", size: 2) }
10          it "does not send an email if a task is not completed" do
              patch :update, id: task.id, task: {size: 3}
              expect(ActionMailer::Base.deliveries.size).to eq(0)
            end
          end
15      end
```

Most of this is a standard controller test for update logic, but two lines are specific to the code we're testing. On line 5 we're using the before(:example) block to clear the ActionMailer::Base.deliveries object. Doing so ensures that the data structure holding the mailings is emptied. Otherwise, emails from other tests will linger and make your test results invalid.

We also need to ensure that in the config/environments/test.rb file we have the line config.action_mailer.delivery_method = :test; this should be done by default, and ensures that mail delivery in tests saves the outgoing email messages to a data object whose behavior we can examine.

In the test, on line 12, we look at the mailer object, ActionMailer::Base.deliveries, and confirm that no emails have been sent.

This test passes with this boilerplate controller method (plus a blank template in app/views/tasks/edit.html.erb):

display/04/gatherer/app/controllers/tasks_controller.rb

```
class TasksController < ApplicationController
  def update
    @task = Task.find(params[:id])
    if @task.update_attributes(params[:task].permit(:size))
      redirect_to @task, notice: "'project was successfully updated.'"
    else
      render action: 'edit'
    end
  end

  def show
    @task = Task.find(params[:id])
  end
end
```

And here's the test with the complete task that specifies email behavior:

```
display/05/gatherer/spec/controllers/tasks_controller_spec.rb
Line 1  it "sends email when task is completed" do
     2    patch :update, id: task.id, task: {size: 3, completed: true}
     3    task.reload
     4    expect(task.completed_at).to be_present
     5    expect(ActionMailer::Base.deliveries.size).to eq(1)
     6    email = ActionMailer::Base.deliveries.first
     7    expect(email.subject).to eq("A task has been completed")
     8    expect(email.to).to eq(["monitor@tasks.com"])
     9    expect(email.body.to_s).to match(/Write section on testing mailers/)
    10  end
```

Again we simulate the call to the update method, this time with a pseudo-attribute completed, which we can assume indicates a check box of some kind. After that, on line 3, we reload the task object to take in the changes from the controller update, and verify that the completed_at attribute has, in fact, been updated.

Then we get to the mailer. We verify that one email has been sent, and then on line 6 we look at the email object, ActionMailer::Base.deliveries.first,[4] and query it for its subject and the list of addresses it's going to. We also check that the body contains the task's title. (Generally the accessors have the names you would expect.)

This task fails. The first failure is the check for the completed_at time, and the mailer will fail too.

The passing controller logic uses the completed param to trigger whether the task is updated and the mailer is sent:

```
display/05/gatherer/app/controllers/tasks_controller.rb
class TasksController < ApplicationController

  def update
    @task = Task.find(params[:id])
    completed = params[:task].delete(:completed)
    params[:task][:completed_at] = Time.current if completed
    if @task.update_attributes(params[:task].permit(:size, :completed_at))
      TaskMailer.task_completed_email(@task).deliver if completed
      redirect_to @task, notice: "'project was successfully updated.'"
    else
      render action: 'edit'
    end
  end
```

---

4. http://guides.rubyonrails.org/action_mailer_basics.html

```
  def show
    @task = Task.find(params[:id])
  end
end
```

Now all we need is the actual mailer. We can build a mailer from the command line using a Rails generator:

```
$ rails generate mailer TaskMailer
create  app/mailers/task_mailer.rb
     invoke  erb
     create      app/views/task_mailer
     invoke  rspec
     create      spec/mailers/task_mailer_spec.rb
```

The mailer itself is straightforward; we need to take the task object and set some mail variables:

display/05/gatherer/app/mailers/task_mailer.rb
```
class TaskMailer < ActionMailer::Base
  default from: "from@example.com"

  def task_completed_email(task)
    @task = task
    mail(to: "monitor@tasks.com", subject: "A task has been completed")
  end
end
```

And we need a template. We'll keep this simple:

display/05/gatherer/app/views/task_mailer/task_completed_email.text.erb
```
The task <%= @task.title %> was completed at <%= @task.completed_at.to_s %>

Thanks,

The Management
```

And the tests pass.

Outside of core Rails, the email-spec library provides a number of very useful helpers. For the most part they are ways of performing the tests we've already examined, but with a slightly cleaner syntax. The library also provides the ability to follow a link in an email back to the site, which is very helpful for acceptance testing of user interactions that include email.[5]

---

5. http://github.com/bmabey/email-spec

Managing Controller and View Tests

Testing controllers and views is a very tricky part of Rails testing. Unlike model testing (which tends to be isolated to the particular model) or integration testing (which explicitly covers the entire stack), controller and view testing have boundaries that are more blurred. Controlling those boundaries is the difference between tests that run quickly and fail only when the logic being tested is incorrect, and tests that are slower and dependent on logic outside the test.

Ideally, controller tests are written so that they have minimal interaction with the model. There are costs to be balanced. A controller action that has minimal contact with the model and can therefore have that interaction stubbed will often run faster and have fewer points of failure. On the other hand, the stubbing and additional classes that may be needed to mediate a controller-and-model interaction may feel overly complex, especially for boilerplate actions.

I'm aggressive about moving controller logic that interacts with the model to some kind of action object that doesn't have Rails dependencies. The controller logic and controller testing then tends to be limited to correctly dispatching successful and failed actions. That said, many Rails developers, notably including David Heinemeier Hansson, find adding an extra layer of objects to be overkill and think that worry about slow tests is misplaced. I recommend you try both ways and see which one best suits you.

Focused view tests are possible in Rails but overlap heavily with helper tests, logic placed in presenter objects, and integration testing.

## CHAPTER 9

Minitest

Some people like the classics.

Some people don't like RSpec's syntax or its metaprogramming.

Some people use Minitest.

Minitest is the standard testing framework in the Ruby 2.0 Standard Library. It is also the default test framework for Rails.

Minitest's design is based on a structure that was originally created by Kent Beck for the SUnit framework in Smalltalk and popularized by Beck and Erich Gamma in JUnit for Java. In Ruby this design was originally implemented in the Test::Unit framework, which Minitest supplanted. Minitest is cleaner and easier to extend; it uses traditional testing terms like "test" and "assert" and defines individual tests as actual Ruby methods. (Although we will be using a Rails add-on that lets us define tests as blocks.)

Getting Started with Minitest

Installing Minitest itself is easy: do nothing.

Minitest is part of core Ruby, and the extensions we'll be covering here are part of core Rails.

A couple of add-on libraries we've come across so far require specific installations for Minitest.

If we want the Capybara features we've been using in our controller and feature tests, we do need to explicitly add a Minitest-Capybara adapter gem to our Gemfile:

```
gem "minitest-rails-capybara", group: :test
```

Minitest's included test-double package, Minitest::Mock, is small and lacks some useful features. We'll demonstrate test doubles using Mocha, which is the package the Rails team uses.

To install Mocha, place the following in the Gemfile:

```
gem "mocha", require: false, group: [:development, :test]
```

Minitest uses the test/test_helper.rb file to store setup. We'll need to load Capybara and Mocha in that file:

```
ENV["RAILS_ENV"] ||= "test"
require File.expand_path('../../config/environment', __FILE__)
require 'rails/test_help'
require "minitest/rails/capybara"
require "mocha/mini_test"
```

And we're off to the races.

Minitest Basics

Our project's test directory contains Minitest equivalents of the RSpec tests we've written thus far.

Here's an example—specifically, the tests for our Task model:

minitest/01/gatherer/test/models/task_test.rb
```
Line 1   require 'test_helper'

         class TaskTest < ActiveSupport::TestCase

     5     test "a completed task is complete" do
             task = Task.new
             refute(task.complete?)
             task.mark_completed
             assert(task.complete?)
    10     end

           test "an uncompleted task does not count toward velocity" do
             task = Task.new(size: 3)
             refute(task.part_of_velocity?)
    15       assert_equal(0, task.points_toward_velocity)
           end

           test "a task completed long ago does not count toward velocity" do
             task = Task.new(size: 3)
    20       task.mark_completed(6.months.ago)
             refute(task.part_of_velocity?)
             assert_equal(0, task.points_toward_velocity)
           end
```

```
25    test "a task completed recently counts toward velocity" do
  -     task = Task.new(size: 3)
  -     task.mark_completed(1.day.ago)
  -     assert(task.part_of_velocity?)
  -     assert_equal(3, task.points_toward_velocity)
30    end
  - end
```

This looks broadly similar to the RSpec we've been looking at, but the syntax has some clear differences. Let's take a look at the main ones.

On line 1 we require the file test_helper, which contains Rails- and application-related setup common to all Minitest files.

In Minitest you can't put a test method just anywhere; tests need to be methods of a subclass of the class Minitest::Test. In standard Minitest, a test method is any method whose name starts with test_, as in test_this_thing_with_a_long_name. However, this test uses a Rails extension that allows you to just say test "some string" followed by a block. Rails uses metaprogramming to convert test "some string" into an actual method called test_some_string, which invokes the block and is, by virtue of the name, executed by Minitest during a test run. I find the test_long_name syntax to be significantly less readable, so we'll be using the shortcut here. (Quick note for RSpec fans: unlike RSpec, the name-munging in Minitest means that two tests in the same class cannot have the same string description—they'd resolve to the same Minitest name.)

Inside our test method we do two things. First, we create a Task instance. Then, on line 9, we make our first assertion—namely, that the method call task.complete? will result in a true value. The assert method is the most basic of Minitest's assertions. It takes one argument, and the assertion passes if the argument is true (for Ruby values of true), and fails if the argument is false.

Minitest defines about a dozen assertion methods and their opposites.[1] (For example, assert passes if the argument is true, whereas refute passes if the argument is false.) Here are the six assertions you probably will use most frequently.

Assertion	Passes if
assert(test)	test is true
assert_block block	associated block returns true
assert_equal(expected, actual)	expected == actual

---

1. http://docs.seattlerb.org/minitest/Minitest/Assertions.html

Assertion	Passes if
assert_includes(collection, object)	collection.include?(object)
assert_match(expected, actual)	expected =~ actual
assert_raises(exception) block	the associated block raises the exception

All Minitest assertions share two useful features.

First, they all take an optional message argument as the last argument. Here's an example:

```
assert_equal("Noel", author.name, "Incorrect author name")
```

If the assertion fails, the message is output to the console. I don't normally use message arguments, because the messages are more overhead and clutter the tests. But if you're in a situation where documentation is particularly important, messages can be useful to describe a test's intent.

Also, every assert method has an opposing refute method: refute_equal, refute_match, and so on. The refute methods pass where the assert methods would fail, so refute_equal passes if the two arguments are not equal. These are occasionally useful, but go light on them; most people find negative logic harder to reason about.

Rails ActiveSupport provides a subclass called ActiveSupport::TestCase that provides a handful of shortcuts and goodies:

- The ability to load data from fixtures before tests
- The declarative test "test name" do syntax described earlier
- The assertions assert_difference, assert_no_difference, assert_blank, and assert_presence
- Support for asserting the existence of Rails deprecations, unlikely to be helpful unless you're working on Rails itself
- Logging support to put the test class and test name in the Rails test.log before each test
- Support for multiple setup and teardown blocks, defined with the method name, similar to Rails callbacks or filters

Note that the assert_valid(foo) test mentioned in this book's previous edition has been deprecated in favor of assert foo.valid?.

Also, For every Minitest refute method, Rails throws in a similar assert_not, as in assert_not_equal. (Weirdly, the method name for refute_match, however, is assert_no_match. My understanding is that somebody on the Rails core team really dislikes the refute syntax.)

Running Minitest

Rails provides some standard Rake tasks for running all or part of the test suite.

The one to use most of the time, which is not the Rails default, is `rake test:all`; it grabs any files ending with `_test.rb` in the test directory or any of its subdirectories and executes them through Minitest. For running a single file, Minitest and Rails use the syntax open `rake test test/models/task_test.rb`. For now we'll assume we're using `rake test:all`. In Chapter 15, *Running Tests Faster and Running Faster Tests*, on page 287, we'll cover better ways to focus test execution.

When you run `rake test:all`, the Rake task identifies any files matching the pattern `test/**/*_test.rb` and passes them all to Minitest. (The related task `rake test:all:db` first resets the database using `db:test:prepare`.) Once Minitest gets the list of matching files, it does the following for each file:

- The Ruby interpreter loads the file. In a Rails context, the line `require test_helper` is important, as the `test_helper` file includes global and Rails-specific setup.

- Inside any subclass of `Minitest::Test`, Minitest identifies test methods in the file—either because the method name starts with `test` or because we're using the ActiveSupport `test` method directly.

That gives Minitest a list of test methods to run. For each of those methods it does the following:

- Loads or resets all fixture data, as discussed in *Fixtures*, on page 95.
- Runs all setup blocks. Setup blocks are defined as `def setup` or, in Rails, `setup do`.
- Runs the test method. The method execution ends when a runtime error or a failed assertion is encountered. Otherwise the test method passes. Yay!
- Runs all teardown blocks. Teardown blocks are declared similarly to setup blocks, but their use is much less common.
- Rolls back or deletes the fixtures as described in the first bullet point. The result of each test is passed back to the test runner for display in the console or IDE window running the test.

The following figure shows the flow.

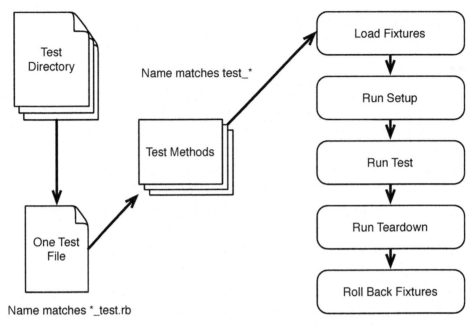

Name matches *_test.rb

You can control fixture loading with a few parameters, which are set in the test/test_helper.rb file. The most important is the fixtures :all method call, which ensures that all your fixture files are loaded in all your tests. This line being written in the file is a little bit of framework archeology. The original default in Rails was to load fixtures for only the class under test. You can still specify particular fixtures to be loaded by passing the model names as symbols to the fixtures method, though I'm not sure there's a good reason for doing so these days.

Minitest and Rails Controllers

Rails provides a different subclass of ActiveSupport::Test for testing controllers. It's called ActionController::TestCase. Controller tests look like this:

minitest/01/gatherer/test/controllers/projects_controller_test.rb
```
Line 1  test "the project method creates a project" do
     2    post :create, project: {name: "Runway", tasks: "start something:2"}
     3    assert_redirected_to projects_path
     4    assert_equal "Runway", assigns[:action].project.name
     5  end
```

This test simulates a call to a controller method, skipping Rails routing, and then allows us to make assertions about what the controller does.

This test's code is very similar to the RSpec controller test we wrote previously. The post method triggers the controller action and takes two arguments: a symbol naming the action to be invoked and a Hash representing the request parameters. As with RSpec, the other HTTP verbs have corresponding test methods, such as get, put, and delete.

Minitest controller tests behave a little differently from RSpec controller tests when it comes to managing the view. The Minitest/Rails testing engine will run the controller action, setting the params hash to the parameters you specify in the test. Rails will parse the associated view but will not execute it unless you specifically make a view assertion.

In other words, a controller test will fail with a parse error if the view contains an incorrect Ruby string such as 1 +. However, if the view contains semantically valid Ruby and you do not specifically make assertions against the view, the test will pass even if that code references values that don't exist. So the view could contain syntactically valid nonsense like banana + cheese * 7, and your test will be fine as long as you do not make an assertion against the view's specifics.

In a Minitest controller test, you have access to the request object as @request, to the controller object as @controller, and to the response object as @response. You can get at the HTTP headers using the hash @request.headers.

Rails defines a couple of custom assertions for controllers. These will seem similar to the RSpec list—in fact, these came first and the RSpec controller matchers are written in terms of these matchers.

Rails provides assert_response to verify the HTTP response code sent back to the browser from Rails. You can pass the same four special symbols in as arguments.

Symbol	HTTP Code Equivalent	Symbol	HTTP Code Equivalent
:success	200–299	:redirect	300–399
:missing	404	:error	500–599

Minitest uses a slightly different list of symbols for more specific responses.[2]

The assert_template assertion determines whether the controller is passing control to the expected view template. The Minitest version is more flexible than the RSpec version. Like the RSpec version, assert_template takes the name of the rendered template as a string or symbol.

There are two optional arguments to assert_template in Minitest. The layout option specifies that the template in question was rendered against a particular Rails

---

2.   http://guides.rubyonrails.org/layouts_and_rendering.html

layout. (You can explicitly assert the no-layout case by passing layout: false or layout: nil.) The common use case here is perhaps using different layouts for mobile or desktop browsers based on request headers.

If you want to make sure a specific partial is rendered along the way, use the :partial option, as in assert_template partial: '_user_data_row'. In this case you're testing whether the specified partial is called when the controller action is rendered. The partial name in the test method must include the leading underscore. Adding the :count option verifies that the specified partial was called a specific number of times, which is potentially useful for a partial that is rendered inside a loop. This is perilously close to view testing, so I wouldn't recommend testing for partials in general. I have had cases where the partial to be rendered was determined dynamically in the view, and testing that the logic is correct was useful in that case.

Minitest provides assert_redirected_to, which compares any Rails URLable object to the redirect target. As with the RSpec version, if you pass an entire URL, in whatever format, the comparison will be made to the entire URL; but if you pass a hash of component pieces, the comparison will be on only those specific components. The assertion fails if the controller does not redirect.

Within the controller method, you have access to instance variables assigned via the assigns hash. Unlike RSpec, it uses hash syntax, assigns[:user], rather than method syntax. The session, cookies, and flash are also available hashes for their data.

Minitest and Views

In Rails and Minitest, view testing takes place inside the controller or integration tests. Here's an example from the projects controller:

```
minitest/01/gatherer/test/controllers/projects_controller_test.rb
test "the index method displays all projects correctly" do
  on_schedule = Project.create!(due_date: 1.year.from_now,
      name: "On Schedule",
      tasks: [Task.create!(completed_at: 1.day.ago, size: 1)])
  behind_schedule = Project.create!(due_date: 1.day.from_now,
      name: "Behind Schedule",
      tasks: [Task.create!(size: 1)])
  get :index
  assert_select("#project_#{on_schedule.id} .on_schedule")
  assert_select("#project_#{behind_schedule.id} .behind_schedule")
end
```

The last two lines of this test use assert_select, which is similar to the Capybara have_selector matcher we've already seen, but is a separate implementation with its own syntax quirks. By default assert_select works against the test's response body.

The selector syntax that assert_select uses is very similar to jQuery and other DOM selection tools, though assert_select uses its own HTML parser. As in jQuery, the use of two separate selectors means we expect to match an instance of the first selector, which contains an instance of the second. For example, we're looking for an HTML element with the DOM ID of the form project_12, where 12 is the ID of the on_schedule project. We also need for that outer HTML element to contain an inner HTML element with a DOM class on_schedule.

There are a number of ways we can augment assert_select. The selector argument to assert_select can be just an element, as in div, or an element plus a class or ID decoration, as in div.hidden. In the latter case, a matching element must have both the HTML tag and the DOM class or ID. As with other DOM selectors, a dot (.) indicates a DOM class and a hash mark (#) indicates a DOM ID. You can also use brackets to indicate arbitrary HTML attributes, as in input[name='email']. The selector is an instance of the ActionView class HTML::Selector; you can find a complete listing of the syntax at http://api.rubyonrails.org/classes/HTML/Selector.html.

You can make a more specific match by including an optional text: argument. The value associated with the text is a string or a regular expression. The assertion passes if at least one HTML tag matches the selector and has inner content that matches the argument. String arguments must match the content exactly. Regular-expression arguments must =~ match the contents.

Additionally, you could pass a count: option, which takes either an integer or a range. If there is a count:, then the assert_select passes only if the number of matching elements either equals the number or is in the range.

When you want to say that an element is not on the page, make the second argument to assert_select false, as in assert_select(selector, false).

Minitest and Routing

The primary method that Rails/Minitest uses for route testing is assert_routing. Here are the Minitest versions of the same standard routes:

minitest/01/gatherer/test/controllers/projects_controller_test.rb
```
test "routing" do
  assert_routing "/projects", controller: "projects", action: "index"
  assert_routing({path: "/projects", method: "post"},
      controller: "projects", action: "create")
```

```
    assert_routing "/projects/new", controller: "projects", action: "new"
    assert_routing "/projects/1", controller: "projects",
        action: "show", id: "1"
    assert_routing "/projects/1/edit", controller: "projects",
        action: "edit", id: "1"
    assert_routing({path: "/projects/1", method: "patch"},
        controller: "projects", action: "update", id: "1")
    assert_routing({path: "/projects/1", method: "delete"},
        controller: "projects", action: "destroy", id: "1")
  end

end
```

The first argument to assert_routing represents the path. As you can see from the preceding examples, this argument is either a string representing the URL, or a hash with a :path key representing the URL and a :method key representing the HTTP method being invoked. If no method is specified, the default is GET.

The second argument is a hash representing any the elements of the route after it is processed by the Rails router, meaning you would expect this argument to specify a :controller, an :action, and any other symbols defined by the route. This second argument does not contain any elements that are expected to be part of the query string as opposed to the base URL.

The third argument is defined as defaults. As far as I can tell, it's essentially merged into the second argument. (The documentation says this parameter is unused, though it's clearly referenced in the source code.) It seems to be safe to leave it as an empty hash if you need the fourth argument. That fourth argument is where you specify key/value pairs for any part of the route you expect to be in the query string.

The assert_routing method validates the routing in both directions. You can also run the routing tests in one direction using assert_generates to go from a string to a hash, and assert_recognizes to go from the hash to the string.

Minitest Helper Tests

Rails provides the ActionView::TestCase class, which is a subclass of ActiveSupport::TestCase specifically designed to load enough of the Rails controller structure to enable helpers to be called and tested. Let's look at the Minitest version of the name_with_status helper tests:

```ruby
require 'test_helper'

class ProjectsHelperTest < ActionView::TestCase

  test "project name with status info" do
    project = Project.new(name: "Project Runway")
    project.stubs(:on_schedule?).returns(true)
    actual = name_with_status(project)
    expected = "<span class='on_schedule'>Project Runway</span>"
    assert_dom_equal expected, actual
  end

  test "project name with status info behind schedule" do
    project = Project.new(name: "Project Runway")
    project.stubs(:on_schedule?).returns(false)
    actual = name_with_status(project)
    expected = "<span class='behind_schedule'>Project Runway</span>"
    assert_dom_equal expected, actual
  end

  test "project name using assert_select" do
    project = Project.new(name: "Project Runway")
    project.stubs(:on_schedule?).returns(false)
    assert_select_string(name_with_status(project), "span.behind_schedule")
  end
end
```

The assert_dom_equal method doesn't have an RSpec equivalent. We use assert_dom_equal to compare the string we expect to the string we actually get from the helper. The assert_dom_equal assertion checks that two strings both resolve to equivalent DOM structures; it tests that attributes have identical values but don't necessarily need to be in the same order. It's nice to have because it spares us some fiddling around with HTML strings in our test.

I wrote the assert_select_string method; it uses an assert_select trick I wanted to mention—the ability to pass a block to assert_select and then have assert_select work on an arbitrary HTML element rather than the entire page output.

If you pass a block to assert_select then asset_select invokes the block with a single argument containing an array of all HTML elements that match your selector, each element is of the Rails class HTML::Node. You can then do whatever you want with that array. A common choice is to iterate over the array and run further assertions, perhaps using assert_select. This is a different way to test for nested elements. Our original assert_select from the controller test, which was "#project_#{on_schedule.id} .on_schedule", could instead be written as follows:

```
assert_select("#project_#{on_schedule.id}") do |matches|
  matches.each do |element|
    assert_select(element, ".on_schedule")
  end
end
```

This may be more explicit in some cases or may allow for more complex logic for the internal selector.

The inner assert_select in that snippet is doing something we haven't seen. The first argument, element, is one of the matching HTML::Node objects. When assert_select is passed an HTML::Node, it searches that HTML for the matching selector rather than the default behavior, which is to use the current HTTP response object.

That HTML::Node first argument is handy for the block syntax, but we can also take advantage of it to use assert_select against arbitrary strings that happen to be valid HTML with a parent root element. All we need is a helper method, which we place in our test_helper.rb file:

minitest/01/gatherer/test/test_helper.rb
```
def assert_select_string(string, *selectors, &block)
  doc_root = HTML::Document.new(string).root
  assert_select(doc_root, *selectors, &block)
end
```

We're using Rails HTML parsing classes, which aren't normally part of a balanced Rails breakfast but allow us to parse a string into an HTML document and take the root element. That root element can then be used as the basis for an assert_select search. We then use this method in our helper test.

Mocha

The Mocha library is the one Rails uses for its own testing, so it seems the natural choice for a test-double library to use with Minitest. Full Mocha docs are available at http://gofreerange.com/mocha/docs/.

Installing Mocha

Mocha needs to be installed after Minitest, which requires a slight indirection to ensure your Rails app does the right thing.

First, in the Gemfile's :test group, add the Mocha gem:

```
gem "mocha", require: false
```

The require: false ensures that Mocha loads in the correct order.

Then, inside the test/test_helper.rb file, you manually require Mocha at any point in the file after the rails/test_help library is loaded:

```
require "mocha/mini_test"
```

At that point we should be good to go. Please see Chapter 7, *Using Test Doubles as Mocks and Stubs*, on page 117, for a full discussion of test doubles. Here we're just going to cover Mocha syntax.

In Mocha you can create a full double that is just a set of stubbed methods by calling stub, which is available throughout your test cases.

```
test "here's a sample stub" do
  stubby = stub(name: "Paul", weight: 100)
  assert_equal("Paul", stubby.name)
end
```

Mocha has a verification syntax for full doubles. In Mocha you use responds_like and responds_like_instance_of to trigger verification that the object matches a given object's API. You might do so like this:

```
stubby = stub(size: 3)
stubby.respond_like(Task.new)
```

Or this:

```
stubby = stub(size: 3)
stubby.respond_like_instance_of(Task)
```

In either case, if you called stubby with a method that is not defined for the Task class—say, stubby.due_date—then Mocha will raise a NoMethodError. Internally this uses the Ruby respond_to? method, so if you're using dynamically generated methods via define_method, method_missing, or something more esoteric, you need to ensure that your respond_to? method works in sync.

Mocha provides stubs, which is mixed in to any Ruby object.

```
minitest/01/gatherer/test/models/project_test.rb
Line 1  test "let's stub an object" do
     2    project = Project.new(name: "Project Greenlight")
     3    project.stubs(:name)
     4    assert_nil(project.name)
     5  end
```

This test passes: line 3 sets up the stub, which intercepts the project.name call in line 4 to return nil and never even gets to the actual project name.

Mocha allows you to specify a return value for the stubbed method:

```
minitest/01/gatherer/test/models/project_test.rb
test "let's stub an object again" do
  project = Project.new(name: "Project Greenlight")
  project.stubs(:name).returns("Fred")
  assert_equal("Fred", project.name)
end
```

The stubs method returns a Mocha Expectation object, which is effectively a proxy to the real object but responds to a number of methods that let you annotate the stub. The returns method is one of those annotation messages that associates the return value with the method. Mocha also provides the shortcut project.stubs(name: "Fred"), allowing you to specify messages and return values as key/value pairs.

As with RSpec, you can stub classes as well as instances:

```
minitest/01/gatherer/test/models/project_test.rb
test "let's stub a class" do
  Project.stubs(:find).returns(Project.new(:name => "Project Greenlight"))
  project = Project.find(1)
  assert_equal("Project Greenlight", project.name)
end
```

And you can stub all instances of a class with the method any_instance, as in this example:

```
Project.any_instance.stubs(:save).returns(false)
```

```
stubby.stubs(:user_count).raises(Exception, "oops")
```

As with stubs, Mocha provides a way to create whole mocks that exist just as mocks, as well as a way to create partial mocks that add expectations to an existing object. The method for whole-mock creation is mock:

```
test "a sample mock" do
  mocky = mock(name: "Paul", weight: 100)
  assert_equal("Paul", mocky.name)
end
```

The method for adding a mock expectation to a message on an existing object is expects. (I know, you'd think they'd have used mocks. But they didn't.)

```
minitest/01/gatherer/test/models/project_test.rb
test "let's mock an object" do
  mock_project = Project.new(:name => "Project Greenlight")
  mock_project.expects(:name).returns("Fred")
  assert_equal("Fred", mock_project.name)
end
```

Mocha has its own set of methods that can be chained to the mock declaration to add specifics:

```
proj = Project.new
proj.expects(:name).once
proj.expects(:name).twice
proj.expects(:name).at_least_once
proj.expects(:name).at_most_once
proj.expects(:name).at_least(3)
proj.expects(:name).at_most(3)
proj.expects(:name).times(5)
proj.expects(:name).times(4..6)
proj.expects(:name).never
```

If you have multiple return values specified, the stubbed method returns them one at a time:

```
minitest/01/gatherer/test/models/project_test.rb
test "stub with multiple returns" do
  stubby = Project.new
  stubby.stubs(:user_count).returns(1, 2)
  assert_equal(1, stubby.user_count)
  assert_equal(2, stubby.user_count)
  assert_equal(2, stubby.user_count)
end
```

As with RSpec, the last value is repeated over and over again.

You can get the same effect with a little more syntactic sugar by using the then method. You can chain together as many of these as you want:

```
stubby.stubs(:user_count).returns(1).then.returns(2)
```

That said, there are two occasionally useful things you can do with with. First off, it can take a block as an argument, in which case the value passed to the method is passed on to the block. If the block returns true, then the expectation is considered matched:

```
proj = Project.new()
proj.expects(:status).with { |value| value % 2 == 0 }
    .returns("Active")
proj.expects(:status).with { |value| value % 3 == 0 }
    .returns("Asleep")
```

If more than one block returns true, the last one declared wins. If none of the blocks return true, we get the same unexpected invocation error listed in the preceding code.

The argument to with can also be one of a series of parameter matchers. Probably the most useful one is instance_of, which we can use to simulate behavior given different types of input:

```
proj = Project.new()
proj.expects(:tasks_before).with(instance_of(Date)).returns(3)
proj.expects(:tasks_before).with(instance_of(String)).raises(Exception)
```

The instance_of matcher or any other Mocha matcher can be negated with the Not method. (Yes, it's capitalized, presumably to avoid weird parse collisions with the keyword not.)

```
proj = Project.new()
proj.expects(:tasks_before).with(Not(instance_of(Date))).returns(3)
```

The only other such specialized matcher I've ever found remotely valuable in practice is has_entry, which works against a hash:

```
proj.expects(:options).with(has_entry(verbose: true))
```

The stub in this snippet will match any hash argument that contains a verbose: true entry, no matter what the other contents of the hash might be. Using the has_entry matcher is occasionally valuable against, say, an ActiveRecord or controller method that expects a hash where we care about only one of the methods.

There's about a dozen more of these matchers, many of which are, shall we say, somewhat lacking in real-world value. Rather than cluttering your head with a bunch of stuff you'll never use, I invite you to check out the Mocha docs at http://gofreerange.com/mocha/docs/ for a full listing if you're interested.

Onward

Minitest has a couple of advantages over RSpec. It's less complex and is often faster in practice. If you really like the spec-style syntax, you might be interested in the version of it called Minitest::Spec that works in Minitest.[3] We're not covering Minitest::Spec here because it's just different enough from RSpec to be confusing.

In the rest of this book I'll describe how every new library is set up for both RSpec and Minitest. Although the examples will primarily be RSpec, the sample-code download has analogous Minitest examples for all of them in the test directory of each successive version of the application.

---

3.   https://github.com/seattlerb/minitest

Integration Testing
with Capybara and Cucumber

An integration test specifies the behavior of multiple parts of your application working together. If a unit test is the main course of your testing meal, then an integration test is the cook preparing that meal, the waiter bringing it to you, and you eating it before paying and leaving a correct tip.

There are three related concepts here. An *integration* test is the generic name for any test that combines more than one unit. In Rails, integration tests are often *end-to-end* tests (or *black box* tests), meaning that they cover the entire system from the outside, making requests just as a user would and validating the output a user would see. An *acceptance* test combines an end-to-end test with the idea that the test is specifying not only the behavior the program expects, but that the behavior is correct from the user or customer perspective. So while every acceptance test is an integration test, not every integration test is an acceptance test.

In this chapter we'll focus on integration tests that are also end-to-end tests, assuming we'll need tools that will simulate HTTP requests and evaluate HTTP responses. For other kinds of integration tests, Minitest and RSpec can do just fine on their own.

What to Test in an Integration Test

We've talked before about the idea of the testing pyramid (see the following figure), where your tests have a relatively large number of unit tests that run quickly and test one small segment of the application, backed by significantly fewer integration tests that run more slowly over the application as a whole.

The pyramid metaphor makes it sound like the integration tests sit passively on top of a foundation of unit tests. It may be more useful to think of integration tests as the frame of a house. Without integration tests, you can't specify how your application works together. Without unit tests there are all kinds of potential holes that bugs can sneak through.

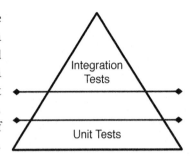

Prescription 23	By far the biggest and easiest trap you can fall into when dealing with integration tests is the temptation to use them like unit tests.

That is to say, don't use integration tests to specify logic that consists largely of internal details of your codebase. One way to tell if your integration test is overly concerned with internal details is to think about what problem in the code would make the test fail. By definition an integration test can fail in many places, but each test you write should have some particular circumstance that only that test protects against. That is, there should be some specific logic failure that would only be caught by that test.

If that unique point of failure concerns the interaction between two objects (or sometimes, the interaction between two methods of the same object), then an integration test is called for. If the unique point of failure is the internal logic of a single object, then that condition is better covered with a unit test.

In a Rails context, the following are fodder for integration tests:

- The interaction between a controller and the model or other objects that provide data
- The interaction between multiple controller actions that comprise a common work flow
- Certain security issues that involve the interaction between a user state and a particular controller action

These things, generally speaking, are *not* integration tests. Use unit tests instead:

- Special cases of business logic, such as what happens if data is nil or has an unexpected value
- Error cases, unless an error case genuinely results in a unique user experience
- Internal implementation details of business logic

Two kinds of problems happen when we use integration testing to cover things that are better done in unit tests. The first is speed. Integration tests are slower—not because the tools themselves are slow, but because the tests are winding their way through the Rails stack to get to the method you're interested in. An entire suite of integration tests is like a house that's all frame: overbuilt.

The second is accuracy. Because the integration test is not making any assertions until after the internal logic has executed, it's often hard to piece together what went wrong. Often the way to deal with this is to have a failing integration test trigger the writing of a unit test.

Rails developers can use many different tools for integration-testing their code. We'll talk about two of them. *Capybara* is a library that allows for easy integration with a web page, and integrates with RSpec and Minitest. *Cucumber* is a higher-level tool that allows you to specify interactions in a natural-language style.

Setting Up Capybara

Capybara allows an automated test to simulate a user interaction with a browser. When simulating this interaction, Capybara works in conjunction with a driver, using the simple Capybara API to determine what elements to interact with and using the driver to manage the actual interaction. By default Capybara uses a native Ruby library that doesn't manage JavaScript interactions, but it can be configured to use a headless browser such as PhantomJS or Selenium to allow JavaScript interactions to be simulated.

Capybara and RSpec

Capybara is designed for use with RSpec, and if you want to use them together, add Capybara to your Gemfile's testing group:

```
gem "capybara"
```

You also need to add the following line to your rails_helper.rb, toward the top:

```
require 'capybara/rails'
```

Capybara and Minitest

The setup for Minitest is similar but uses different gems that bridge the gap between Capybara and Minitest:

```
gem "minitest-rails-capybara"
```

The minitest-rails-capybara gem combines capybara, mintest-rails, minitest-capybara, and a little bit of its own glue. To get all that in our application, put the following line in the test_helper.rb file:

```
require "minitest/rails/capybara"
```

Capybara and Its Own language

At this point we're forced to confront another library syntax decision. Capybara defines its validations mostly as things that look like RSpec matchers. It also defines its own optional integration-test syntax, similar to RSpec but with terms like feature and scenario to drive home the integration testing point.

All of this adds up to a lot of different ways to express the same test. In the interest of minimizing the amount of time we spend talking about syntax, which is the least interesting thing we could be talking about, we'll stick to the same basic RSpec syntax we've been using in most of the book. Keep in mind that the other forms exist; that way when your coworker shows you her Capybara tests, you know how to read them.

Outside-in Testing

The process we'll use to manage our Capybara tests is sometimes called *out-side-in* testing—we start using Capybara to write a test from the outside and use that test to drive our unit tests. In the same way that TDD uses a failing unit test to drive code, outside-in testing uses a failing acceptance test (or a failing line in an acceptance test) to drive the creation of unit tests.

The process follows Figure 1, *Outside-in testing*, on page 181—we're assuming the creation of a new user-facing feature in a Rails application.

Let's walk through the steps.

1. Write the end-to-end test that shows a user interacting with the new feature. This test should specify data, have one or more user interactions, and validate HTML responses to determine that the interactions behaved as expected. This should be the main, error-free, interaction of the feature. Before this process even starts, it's perfectly normal to noodle around with controllers and views trying to figure out exactly how the user interactions look. You may even get a substantive part of the feature done. You need to be willing to rewrite that code once the tests come into play.

2. Start running the tests. In a reasonably mature Rails application, the first few steps will often already pass. You'll frequently be adding a new feature

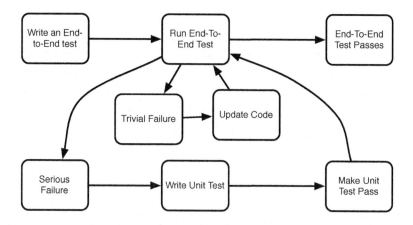

Figure 1—Outside-in testing

to an existing page, so steps where data is prepared, users are logged in, and existing pages are hit might all work.

3. You will come to a test failure. The first failures you see in the integration test are often trivial: attempts to click on links that don't exist and form fields that aren't there yet. These can be quickly dispatched, generally without unit tests, on the theory that adding new stuff to a view isn't normally testable logic.

4. Eventually, though, you cross the chasm. You'll get to the point where you're validating responses and there's a lot of logic missing from the code. Now you have a focused, well-defined task to accomplish in your code, and it's time to drop to unit tests.

5. Exactly what unit tests you need to write depends on the situation. You'll probably have model logic to test, and a controller test or maybe a plain Ruby object managing a transaction. The important thing is that the unit tests may go beyond making the integration test work. They also have some responsibility to cover edge and error cases that integration tests wouldn't cover.

6. When you think the unit tests are done, go back to the integration test. There's a good chance it still fails because you forgot some piece of integration. No problem; that's what the integration test is there for.

7. Finally the integration test passes. Yay! If there's another significant user case in the feature, write that test and start over.

Let's try a sample case and see how this plays out in practice.

Using Capybara

When last we left our application, we allowed for the creation of new projects. Let's follow up on that and add a sequence where we can see a page for an existing project, and add a task to it. To give this a little bit of back-end logic to play with, let's set up a situation where the tasks are ordered and we then want to move one task above the other task.

Writing a Test

That test has a few different parts. Let's take a second to plan the given/when/then of it:

- Given: We'll need one existing project and at least one existing task on that project so that we can test the ordering. We'll probably want two tasks; that way we can verify that the user interface is correct for the first, last, and middle parts of the list.
- When/Then: The user fills out the form for the task and we verify that the new task shows up.
- When/Then: The user moves a test up and we verify that the order changes.

The fact that we have two distinct when/then pairs suggests this is probably really two tests, but for ease of explanation we'll keep it as one. Let's see how it looks:

`integration/01/gatherer/spec/features/add_task_spec.rb`
```ruby
require 'rails_helper'

describe "adding a new task" do
  fixtures :all

  it "can add and reorder a task" do
    visit project_path(projects(:bluebook))
    fill_in "Task", with: "Find UFOs"
    select "2", from: "Size"
    click_on "Add Task"
    expect(current_path).to eq(project_path(projects(:bluebook)))
    within("#task_3") do
      expect(page).to have_selector(".name", text: "Find UFOs")
      expect(page).to have_selector(".size", text: "2")
      expect(page).not_to have_selector("a", text: "Down")
      click_on("Up")
    end
    expect(current_path).to eq(project_path(projects(:bluebook)))
    within("#task_2") do
      expect(page).to have_selector(".name", text: "Find UFOs")
```

```
      end
    end
  end
```

The test is kind of long and rambling. It also doesn't completely test the UI, in the sense that it's not validating that all the "Up" and "Down" links that are supposed to be there are actually there—we might do that in a helper test of some kind. It walks through the interaction, conveniently touching a significant part of the Capybara API.

Let's go through the Capybara API, looking at the Capybara method calls we use in this test and then exploring related methods. Then we'll go through the rest of the process and make the test pass.

The Capybara API: Navigating

Capybara has one method to navigate to arbitrary routes in your system, and it's the first line of our test: visit project_path(projects(:runway)). The visit method takes one argument, which is a string URL (in our case, a Rails routing method that returns a string URL). The route generated by the visit method is always an HTTP GET. If you want to simulate a POST or any other kind of HTTP method, the recommended mechanism in Capybara is to navigate to a link or form button on the web page that triggers the desired interaction.

The Capybara API: Interacting

After our test hits the project_path URL we start to use Capybara methods to interact with the elements on the page. Specifically, we use the fill_in method to place text in a text field, then the select method to choose an option from a select menu, and finally the click_on method to click on a button and submit a form. All told, Capybara has about ten methods for interacting with DOM elements.

Capybara is very flexible in how it allows you to specify the element you want to work with. You can specify any element by its DOM ID. Form elements can also be specified by their name attribute. Form elements that have attached label tags can be specified by the attached label's text. Elements like HTML anchor tags that have internal text can be specified via that text. HTML anchor tags whose body is an image can be located by the image's alt text attribute.

In other words, if you have an HTML snippet like the following:

```
<form>
  <label for="user_email">Email</label>
  <input name="user[email]" id="user_email" />
</form>
```

you can use Capybara to access that form element with any of the following:

```
fill_in("user_email", with: "noel@noelrappin.com")
fill_in("user[email]", with: "noel@noelrappin.com")
fill_in("Email", with: "noel@noelrappin.com")
```

The first one uses the DOM ID, the second uses the form name, and the third uses the label text.

By default Capybara does subset matches, so you could also use "em" as a matcher should you want to. If more than one element matches a locator, Capybara raises an error. (Note: this is the behavior in Capybara version 2.2; older versions behave differently.) If you want an exact match rather than a substring match, pass the option exact: true to any Capybara method that uses a locator.

Which lookup text should you use? It depends on your goals and your context. The label text will usually result in the most readable test. But it's also the most fragile since the user-facing text is most likely to change. In contrast, the DOM ID is probably the most opaque in the test but the least likely to change on a whim.

Here are the Capybara form-interaction methods. First, the ones you'll probably use a lot:

check(locator)
> This asserts that locator finds a check box, and checks it.

choose(locator)
> This is the same as check, but for radio buttons. Other radio buttons in the group are unchecked.

fill_in(locator, with: "TEXT")
> The locator is expected to find a text area or an input text field, and places the value of the with option inside it. Technically the second argument is a generic options hash, but the only option that is unique to this method is with. I have no good reason why the developers chose to create the API with that argument as an option, though I wouldn't be surprised if at some point in the future it became a genuine Ruby 2.0 keyword argument.

select(value, from: locator)
> The method arguments are similar here, in that the second argument is technically an options hash, but the only usable option is from. It looks for a select menu that matches the locator passed to the from argument, and sets its value to the first argument. For what it's worth, the fact that

fill_in takes its locator argument first and select takes the locator second drives me bananas.

click_on(locator)

This finds an anchor link or a button via the locator and simulates a click of it.

Then there are a few methods you will probably use less often:

attach_file(locator, path)

This looks for a form-file upload element that matches the locator, and simulates attaching the file at the given path to the form.

click_button(locator)
click_link(locator)

These are like click_on but work only for a button or a link.

uncheck(locator)

This unchecks a check box specified by the locator.

unselect(value, from: locator)

This method unselects the value from the select box being specified by the locator. This one is most useful for multivalue select boxes. For a single-value select box, all you need to do to unselect a value is select the new value.

The Capybara API: Querying

Capybara has a few methods designed to allow you to query the simulated browser page to check for the existence of various selector patterns in the page. This is one case where the syntax differs slightly between Minitest and RSpec.

We use current_url, which has the current URL as a complete string. That's useful for testing whether your navigation links take you where you're going.

The most common query method in Capybara is written as the matcher have_selector in RSpec, and as assert_selector in Minitest. The two are identical in functionality. By default, Capybara looks for a CSS selector matching the argument to the query method, using # for DOM ID and a dot (.) for DOM class in much the same way we saw in view tests. The assertion passes if the selector is found.

If you want to specify that a given selector does not exist on the page, in RSpec you can use either not_to have_selector or to have_no_selector, which are equivalent. In Minitest, though, you must use assert_no_selector.

Our test first uses have_selector to validate that .name and .size elements exist and match any options given. The Capybara methods all accept options, including the same text and count options as assert_select, meaning that text takes a string or regular expression that matches the content of the selected element, and count matches the number of times the element exists on the page.

Capybara also has a series of methods of the form has_link?, which take locators rather than full CSS selectors and find whether a DOM element of the given type matches the locator. You can find a complete list of those methods at http://rubydoc.info/github/jnicklas/capybara/master/Capybara/Node/Matchers.

Our test also uses the within method, which takes a selector argument and a block. The selector passed to within will find a single element on the page. Inside the block, any Capybara call is scoped to only find or assert against the contents of that element. So, the part of our test that looks like this:

```
within("#task_2") do
  expect(page).to have_selector(".name", text: "Cast the designers")
end
```

will pass only if there is a .name element inside the #task_2 element. This can also be written as expect(page).to have_selector("#task_2 .name", text: "Cast the designers"), though I find that form a little flaky and hard to read.

Finally, the most useful Capybara method when things go wrong is save_and_open_page, which dumps the contents of the Capybara DOM into a temp file and opens the temp file in a browser (opening in a browser requires a gem called launchy). You won't have any CSS or images with relative file names, but it's still usually enough to tell that, say, you're stuck on a login screen because you forgot to set up a logged-in user.

Making the Capybara Test Pass

Let's go through the integration-test process.

Our first error is right on the first line: projects(:bluebook) is a call to a fixture method, but we haven't defined any fixture named bluebook. That's easy enough to fix. We need to add some fixture files to the spec directory:

integration/01/gatherer/spec/fixtures/projects.yml
```
one:
  name: MyString
  due_date: 2013-11-10

two:
  name: MyString
  due_date: 2013-11-10
```

```
bluebook:
  name: Project Blue Book
  due_date: <%= 6.months.from_now %>
```

While we're at it, we'll need two project tasks to make the sorting work. We also must add belongs_to :project in app/models/task.rb:

integration/01/gatherer/spec/fixtures/tasks.yml

```
one:
  project: bluebook
  title: Hunt the aliens
  size: 1
  completed_at:

two:
  project: bluebook
  title: Write a book
  size: 1
  completed_at:
```

I like using fixtures for integration tests because their transactional nature makes them much faster than creating the objects anew for each test. This makes it much more acceptable to have multiple objects in the integration test. (Note, though, that if I use the same "Project Runway" name that is used in test/integration/add_project_test.rb, that test will fail because there will be more tasks than the test expects; you do need to be careful with this global data.)

The next failure is that we don't even have a show method in the ProjectsController. The show method is easy enough, and probably doesn't need additional testing:

integration/01/gatherer/app/controllers/projects_controller.rb

```
def show
  @project = Project.find(params[:id])
end
```

We'll also want a template. We know it's going to need a table for the tasks as well as a form to create a new task. Here's one. It's unstyled, but it's got the table and the form to create a new task:

integration/01/gatherer/app/views/projects/show.html.erb

```
<h2>Project: <%= @project.name %></h2>

<h3>Existing Tasks:</h3>

<table>
  <thead>
    <tr>Name</tr>
    <tr>Size</tr>
  </thead>
```

```erb
  <tbody>
    <% @project.tasks.each do |task| %>
      <tr>
        <td class="name"><%= task.title %></td>
        <td class="size"><%= task.size %></td>
        <td class="completed"><%= task.completed_at.to_s %></td>
      </tr>
    <% end %>
  </tbody>
</table>

<h3>New Task</h3>

<%= form_for Task.new(project_id: @project.id) do |f| %>
  <%= f.hidden_field :project_id %>
  <%= f.label :title, "Task" %>
  <%= f.text_field :title %>
  <%= f.label :size %>
  <%= f.select :size, [1, 2, 3, 4, 5] %>
  <%= f.submit "Add Task" %>
<% end %>
```

At this point we fail because the create task doesn't exist on TasksController. That means we need to create new logic.

This feels like it'll be boilerplate enough not to need additional controller tests. Often, at this point I'll do a mini spike of the controller method to see how much complexity is called for. In this case the controller method is really simple:

integration/01/gatherer/app/controllers/tasks_controller.rb
```ruby
def create
  @task = Task.new(
      params[:task].permit(:project_id, :title, :size))
  redirect_to @task.project
end
```

We don't have any obvious error cases here—Task has no validations. And even if we did have error cases, the remedy would be to go back to the project page anyway. So I'm willing to leave this for now. (In practice, I'd add an error message in the failure case.)

Our next error is Capybara::ElementNotFound: Unable to find css "#task_3".

The actual error here is subtle. In the original Capybara test we're identifying each row by the order of the task, so the three rows will have DOM IDs task_1, task_2, and task_3. Not only don't we have those IDs in the template we just showed; we don't even have a mechanism for ordering the tasks.

This is a good opportunity for some small-scale design. We want a) each task to have an order, b) the project to display the tasks in order, and c) new tasks to come in at the end of the list.

We can handle the first part, giving tasks an order, with a Rails migration:

```
$ rails generate migration add_order_to_tasks
```

I'm calling the new attribute project_order to avoid confusion with the SQL order statement:

```
integration/02/gatherer/db/migrate/20140518182734_add_order_to_tasks.rb
class AddOrderToTasks < ActiveRecord::Migration
  def change
    add_column :tasks, :project_order, :integer
  end
end
```

```
$ rake db:migrate
```

We can make products automatically return tasks in order by using ActiveRecord and changing the declaration of the relationship to

```
has_many :tasks, -> { order "project_order ASC" }
```

We don't need a test because it's part of the framework.

For the tests to work, we also need to add the order to the fixtures in spec/fixtures/tasks.yml. Give the first fixture in the file a project_order: 1 line and the second fixture a project_order: 2.

The part where the project gives new tasks an order adds some logic. There are several ways to do this; here are a few examples. We could make the logic a callback on Task, which would be automatically invoked when the task is saved; we could make it a method on Project to ask the project for the next order; or we could create a Task factory object similar to the CreatesProject object we built earlier.

To keep things simple, I'll make a method on Project that we'll call when creating the Task. We're now in unit-test mode, so I write some unit tests:

```
integration/02/gatherer/spec/models/project_spec.rb
describe "task order" do
  let(:project) { project = Project.create(name: "Project") }

  it "gives me the order of the first task in an empty project" do
    expect(project.next_task_order).to eq(1)
  end
```

```
  it "gives me the order of the next task in a project" do
    project.tasks.create(project_order: 3)
    expect(project.next_task_order).to eq(4)
  end
end
```

This code passes with the following:

integration/02/gatherer/app/models/project.rb
```
def next_task_order
  return 1 if tasks.empty?
  (tasks.last.project_order || tasks.size) + 1
end
```

Now we need to integrate it. First off, we need to call the new method in the controller. I've slightly reorganized the controller logic so that we have a project to query:

integration/02/gatherer/app/controllers/tasks_controller.rb
```
def create
  @project = Project.find(params[:task][:project_id])
  @project.tasks.create(title: params[:task][:title],
      size: params[:task][:size],
      project_order: @project.next_task_order)
  redirect_to @project
end
```

I still don't think the controller logic warrants another test.

Now, in the app/views/projects/show.html.erb template file we replace the table-row line with the following:

```
<tr id="task_<%= task.project_order %>">
```

That gives us our #task_3 selector, at long last.

And that brings us to our next point of failure, Unable to find link or button with text "Up", meaning that the update logic is not yet in place.

What's the logic we want? And how can we write a test for it?

We want an "Up" link for all tasks but the first one, and a "Down" link for all tasks but the last one. That means we need to be able to tell if a task is first or last. That's testable:

integration/02/gatherer/spec/models/task_spec.rb
```
describe "order" do
  let!(:project) { Project.create!(name: "Project") }
  let!(:first) { project.tasks.create!(project_order: 1) }
  let!(:second) { project.tasks.create!(project_order: 2) }
  let!(:third) { project.tasks.create!(project_order: 3) }
```

```
it "finds that a task is first or last" do
  expect(first). to be_first_in_project
  expect(first).not_to be_last_in_project
  expect(second).not_to be_first_in_project
  expect(second).not_to be_last_in_project
  expect(third).not_to be_first_in_project
  expect(third). to be_last_in_project
end
```

That's more assertions than I would normally place in a single test, but they are very closely related, so I think it reads best as a single group.

And the test passes:

integration/02/gatherer/app/models/task.rb
```
def first_in_project?
  return false unless project
  project.tasks.first == self
end

def last_in_project?
  return false unless project
  project.tasks.last == self
end
```

Now we need to place that logic in the view template, which we can do by adding some code inside the loop in app/views/projects/show.html.erb. There's a decision point here, which is whether to send that link to the regular update method for TasksController, which already exists and would need to be changed, or to create new up and down controller actions. It's not strictly RESTful, but this isn't strictly a RESTful action.

Let's go with the non-RESTful controller actions for up and down. We need to define them in the routes file:

integration/02/gatherer/config/routes.rb
```
Gatherer::Application.routes.draw do
  resources :tasks do
    member do
      patch :up
      patch :down
    end
  end

  resources :projects
end
```

Then we'll attach the routes to the template in app/views/projects/show.html.erb:

```
<td>
  <% unless task.first_in_project? %>
    <%= link_to "Up", up_task_path(task.id), method: :patch %>
  <% end %>
  <% unless task.last_in_project? %>
    <%= link_to "Down", down_task_path(task.id), method: :patch %>
  <% end %>
</td>
```

Next we need the ability to swap a task's order with one of its neighbors', which implies the ability to find those neighbors. This would seem to be a model concern, which means we're back writing unit tests.

What do these tests need? The same set of three tasks, presumably, and a move_up and move_down method to test.

Although I wrote and passed these two tests one at a time, let's look at them together:

`integration/02/gatherer/spec/models/task_spec.rb`
```
it "can move up" do
  expect(second.previous_task).to eq(first)
  second.move_up
  expect(first.reload.project_order).to eq(2)
  expect(second.reload.project_order).to eq(1)
end

it "can move down" do
  expect(second.next_task).to eq(third)
  second.move_down
  expect(third.reload.project_order).to eq(2)
  expect(second.reload.project_order).to eq(3)
end
```

And here's one set of task methods that passes the tests and has gone through a refactoring step:

`integration/02/gatherer/app/models/task.rb`
```
def my_place_in_project
  project.tasks.index(self)
end

def previous_task
  project.tasks[my_place_in_project - 1]
end

def next_task
  project.tasks[my_place_in_project + 1]
end
```

```
def swap_order_with(other)
  other.project_order, self.project_order =
      self.project_order, other.project_order
  self.save
  other.save
end

def move_up
  swap_order_with(previous_task)
end

def move_down
  swap_order_with(next_task)
end
```

And now we are really, really close. All we need to do is wire up the controller:

```
integration/02/gatherer/app/controllers/tasks_controller.rb
def up
  @task = Task.find(params[:id])
  @task.move_up
  redirect_to @task.project
end

def down
  @task = Task.find(params[:id])
  @task.move_down
  redirect_to @task.project
end
```

And...now the integration test passes, and all the tests are green and we celebrate.

Retrospective

Let's take a step back and discuss what happened here. We're supposed to be talking about integration tests, and yet we never touched the integration test after we initially wrote it. What good is that? (Full disclosure: in initial writing I did have to go back and clean up the integration test because I had syntax errors and the like. Sometimes I need to fix the assertions after I see what the view looks like.)

The existence of the integration test gives us a few benefits as we write these tests:

- There's a structure; we know what needs to be done next. This is valuable, although given the nature of a lot of server-side development there does tend to be one large gap where the integration test provides the expected outcome but doesn't give much guidance on how to get there.

- The integration test proves that all of our unit tests work together as a cohesive whole (though you really need to test in a browser when you are done). One danger cited for unit tests is that it's easy to see the trees and not the forest. Having an end-to-end test forces you to describe the forest.
- Although the integration test is slow compared to unit tests, it's often lightning-fast compared to manually setting up the browser integration. If you've ever tested a form with dozens of required fields, you can see the benefit here.

Looking back at the original test, I said it was kind of long and unwieldy. I could go back and split out related lines into their own methods.

Or I could try Cucumber.

Trying Cucumber

Cucumber is a tool for writing acceptance tests in plain language. (I almost said in plain English, but that's too limiting—Cucumber speaks a lot of different languages, including LOLCat.) It's designed to allow you to write simple and clear integration and acceptance tests. It can be used to have a nondeveloper client or manager cowrite or sign off on the acceptance tests, though my personal experience with that has been hit-and-miss. Because it adds a level of indirection to acceptance testing, some people feel that Cucumber is more trouble than it's worth.

I like to look at Cucumber as a tool that does two things. First, it allows me to structure integration tests somewhat cleanly. Second, it allows me the option to describe the system's intended behavior without using the code part of my brain at all, which I find helpful.

Setting Up Cucumber

To install Cucumber, we need two gems in the Gemfile:

```
group :development, :test do
  gem 'cucumber-rails', require: false      # The false prevents a warning
  gem 'database_cleaner'
end
```

Then bundle install.

Strictly speaking, database_cleaner isn't required, but it's valuable and gives fixture-like transaction behavior to your nonfixture using tests. The cucumber gem will be installed as a dependency of cucumber-rails. As I write this, we're talking about version 1.3.15 of Cucumber and version 1.4.1 of cucumber_rails.

To install Cucumber, there's a command-line generator:

```
rails generate cucumber:install
```

This creates a config/cucumber.yml file for runtime options, the actual cucumber command-line script, a rake task, a features directory with subdirectories for step_definitions and support, and a features/support/env.rb file (the latter is analogous to test_helper.rb). Also, it modifies the database.yml file to add a cucumber environment that copies the test environment. Cucumber has some additional configuration options; you can type rails generate cucumber:install —help to see them.

Writing Cucumber Features

In Cucumber you write tests as a series of steps using a very minimal language called Gherkin. An individual Cucumber test is called a Scenario, and a group of them is called a Feature.

Let's take the Capybara integration test from the last section and convert it to Cucumber. Cucumber feature files go in the features directory and typically end in .feature. Here is features_add_task.feature:

integration/03/gatherer/features/add_task.feature
```
Feature: Adding a task

  Background:
    Given a project

  Scenario: I can add and change priority of a new task
    When I visit the project page
    And I complete the new task form
    Then I am back on the project page
    And I see the new task is last in the list
    When I click to move the new task up
    Then I am back on the project page
    And the new task is in the middle of the list
```

This file has three parts. The Feature declaration is at the top. Our Cucumber file needs to have one, but the description there is strictly for the humans; we can put anything there that we want. Gherkin is whitespace-sensitive, so anything that goes beyond that top line needs to be indented.

The next section is the Background, which is optional. It might not be clear from the preceding code, but the Background line is indented subordinate to Feature. In Cucumber, Background is like Minitests's setup and RSpec's before, indicating code that is run to initialize each test. In our case, since we have only one Scenario, it's not necessary to have a Background, but if we did have multiple "Add a task" scenarios, they'd likely all share that one common Background.

After the Background comes the Scenario, which is the actual test. Both Background and Scenario are made up of steps. In Cucumber a step usually consists of one of the words Given, When, or Then followed by a sentence. This corresponds to the same basic structure we've been using informally to discuss tests all through the book: Given indicates a precondition to the action. When indicates a user action that changes the state of the application. Then specifies the result of the state change. You can also start a line with And or But (or *, if you must) if it's desirable for readability. Using And or But to start a line means that the line belongs to whichever of Given/When/Then is closest above it.

The distinction between Given, When, and Then is for the humans. Cucumber does not require the steps to be in a particular order. And when it comes time to match each step to its definition the Given/When/Then header is not significant in the match.

This scenario is executable now, using the cucumber command, or we can specify the file with cucumber feature/add_task.feature. The output comes in two parts. The first is a listing of the execution step by step, which starts like this:

```
Background:        # features/add_task.feature:3
  Given a project # features/add_task.feature:4
    Undefined step: "a project" (Cucumber::Undefined)
    features/add_task.feature:4:in `Given a project'

 Scenario: I can add and change priority of a new task
             # features/add_task.feature:6
   When I visit the project page
             # features/add_task.feature:7
     Undefined step: "I visit the project page" (Cucumber::Undefined)
     features/add_task.feature:7:in `When I visit the project page'
```

You can't see this on the page, but all that text other than the Background and Scenario lines will be yellow.

When a scenario is run, Cucumber attempts to run each step by matching it to a step definition and executing that step definition. In this output Cucumber helpfully tells us the line number of each step it tries to execute, and then tells us that the step is undefined. That makes sense because we haven't defined any steps yet.

After it goes through all the steps and reports that we have one scenario with eight steps, of which one scenario and eight steps are undefined, Cucumber adds some extra output to the terminal. It starts like this:

You can implement step definitions for undefined steps with these snippets:

```
Given(/^a project$/) do
  pending # express the regexp above with the code you wish you had
end

When(/^I visit the project page$/) do
  pending # express the regexp above with the code you wish you had
end
```

This output continues for all the undefined steps. Cucumber is doing something really useful here: giving us boilerplate templates for each of the undefined steps that we can paste directly into our editor and then fill out.

Lets do that. I'm taking the whole ball of wax—pasting all eight of those pending blocks into a new file, features/step_definitions/add_task_steps.rb. When I do that and rerun Cucumber...well, a little bit changes:

```
Background:         # features/add_task.feature:3
  Given a project # features/step_definitions/add_task_steps.rb:1
    TODO (Cucumber::Pending)
    ./features/step_definitions/add_task_steps.rb:2:in `/^a project$/'
    features/add_task.feature:4:in `Given a project'

  Scenario: I can add and change priority of a new task
              # features/add_task.feature:6
  When I visit the project page
              # features/step_definitions/add_task_steps.rb:5
  And I complete the new task form
              # features/step_definitions/add_task_steps.rb:9
  Then I am back on the project page
              # features/step_definitions/add_task_steps.rb:13
  And I see the new task is last in the list
              # features/step_definitions/add_task_steps.rb:17
  When I click to move the new task up
              # features/step_definitions/add_task_steps.rb:21
  Then I am back on the project page
              # features/step_definitions/add_task_steps.rb:13
  And the new task is in the middle of the list
              # features/step_definitions/add_task_steps.rb:25
```

The top lines are yellow and the lines under Scenario are light blue. Cucumber is stopping the test at the first pending step and marking each further step as "skipped."

It's time to tell Cucumber what each of those steps should do.

Writing Cucumber Steps

Sadly, it's unrealistic for Cucumber to know what to do just from a step like Given a project. So we must define all the steps so that Cucumber can execute them.

When Cucumber gets a step like Given a project, it searches through all the files in the step definition folder looking for one definition that matches. What does matching mean? Let's look at the boilerplate for that step again:

```
Given(/^a project$/) do
  pending
end
```

The first line of the definition is one of those Given/When/Then words (it doesn't matter which one) followed by a regular expression. Cucumber matches a step to a definition when the end of the step, such as a project, matches the regular expression, such as /^a project$/. We'll see in a little bit why Cucumber uses regular expressions instead of just strings. So, when Cucumber sees the step Given a project, it will run the code inside the block for the matching step definition. If Cucumber finds more than one matching step definition it will raise an error.

Inside a step definition you can write any arbitrary Ruby code. Instance variables declared in one step definition will be available to later step definitions in the same test. Be careful with instance variables; it's not always easy to tell what variables might exist from previous steps, or what state they might be in. Cucumber understands Capybara methods and it understands RSpec matchers (assuming RSpec is installed). Arbitrary methods defined in any step-definition file will be available to any step definition.

By default Cucumber doesn't understand Minitest. If we want to use Minitest assertions, we can place the following file inside features/support:

```
integration/03/gatherer/features/support/minitest.rb
require 'minitest'
module MiniTestAssertions
  def self.extended(base)
    base.extend(MiniTest::Assertions)
    base.assertions = 0
  end

  attr_accessor :assertions
end
World(MiniTestAssertions)
```

The last line here is Cucumber-specific: World is Cucumber's global configuration object. Passing it a module name extends World with that module, triggering the extended method, which injects Minitest assertions into Cucumber. Or you could ignore this entire paragraph and just use RSpec matchers.

Our case here is unusual in that we already have this feature managed as a non-Cucumber integration test, so filling the steps is mostly a question of splitting that test into pieces. My copy looks like this:

```
integration/03/gatherer/features/step_definitions/add_task_steps.rb
Given(/^a project$/) do
  @project = Project.create(name: "Bluebook")
  @project.tasks.create(title: "Hunt the Aliens", size: 1, project_order: 1)
  @project.tasks.create(title: "Write a book", size: 1, project_order: 2)
end

When(/^I visit the project page$/) do
  visit project_path(@project)
end

When(/^I complete the new task form$/) do
  fill_in "Task", with: "Find UFOs"
  select "2", from: "Size"
  click_on "Add Task"
end

Then(/^I am back on the project page$/) do
  expect(current_path).to eq(project_path(@project))
end

Then(/^I see the new task is last in the list$/) do
  within("#task_3") do
    expect(page).to have_selector(".name", text: "Find UFOs")
    expect(page).to have_selector(".size", text: "2")
    expect(page).to have_no_selector("a", text: "Down")
  end
end

When(/^I click to move the new task up$/) do
  within("#task_3") do
    click_on("Up")
  end
end

Then(/^the new task is in the middle of the list$/) do
  within("#task_2") do
    expect(page).to have_selector(".name", text: "Find UFOs")
  end
end
```

There are only a few differences between the Cucumber steps and the original integration test.

In the original integration test we defined the project using fixtures. In the Cucumber test I explicitly create the @project and its tasks in the Given a project step. Cucumber does not use fixtures by default. Although it's possible to get Cucumber to understand fixtures, it's another page of wonky Rails internals, and frankly nobody needs that right now. We do lose the speed benefit of fixtures and database transactions. That change cascades—references to the fixture project are replaced with references to the instance method.

I've split up checking that the new task is last and clicking to move it up, so each needs its own within block. Also, for some reason Cucumber didn't like refute_selector, so I replaced it with the identical assert_no_selector. Other than that the Ruby code is the same, with just a different background structure.

Since we've already written the code once, there's no reason to go through the whole process again. The Cucumber process is very similar to the Capybara-only process: I write a scenario and try to make the steps pass one by one, dropping down to unit tests when I need logic. The biggest difference is that Cucumber makes it easier for me to write the scenario's outline without writing the details of the later steps.

More-Advanced Cucumber

This section should be titled "Things Cucumber lets you do that are bad ideas." Cucumber allows for a lot of flexibility in the way steps match with step definitions. By and large, the Cucumber-using community has come to the conclusion that most of these things should be used sparingly, if at all.

Earlier I alluded to the idea that step definitions were regular expressions and not strings. This allows you to have the same step definition apply to multiple strings. More to the point, you can use regular-expression groups to capture those matches. The parts of the string that are in groups are then passed as block variables to the block part of the step definition. This allows you to use a Cucumber step as a method call with parameters.

In our existing initial step, we hard-code the project name inside the step definition. If, on the other hand, we wanted to be able to specify the name of the project in the Cucumber feature, we could write the step definition as follows:

```
Given /^a project named "(.*)"$/ do |project_name|
  @project = Project.create!(name: project_name)
end
```

That definition would match steps like this:

```
Given a project named "Rails 4 Test Prescriptions"
Given a project named "Evil Master Plan"
```

In each case the step definition would create a project with the given name.

You can go even further in terms of putting data in the Cucumber feature file. Cucumber allows you to append a table of data to a step. It's a very clever feature, and like a lot of very clever features it should be used judiciously.

You use something like Markdown table syntax to create the table. In the feature file it might look something like this:

```
Given the following users:
    | login| email           | password| password_confirmation|
    | alpha| alpha@example.com| alpha1  | alpha1               |
    | beta | beta@example.com | beta12  | beta12               |
```

The step with the table needs to end with a colon. The table uses pipe characters to delimit entries. They don't have to line up, but normally you'll want them too.

When Cucumber matches a step definition to a step that has a table, the table becomes an argument to the step definition's block—if there are other regular-expression matches, the table is the last argument. The argument is a special Cucumber data type, and there are a few different ways you can deal with it. Most commonly you'll deal with it as an array of hashes, where the keys are the first row of the table and every subsequent row provides a set of values, like so:

```
Given /^the following users$/ do |user_data|
  User.create!(user_data.hashes)
end
```

You can do something similar with a large string literal:

```
Given I have typed the following
  """
  some big amount of text
  """
```

That's an indented line, three quotation marks, some text, and then three more quotation marks at the end. The text inside the triple quotes will be passed as the last argument to the step definition's block.

If you really want to have fun, you can combine scenarios and tables to create a loop called a *scenario outline*, like so:

```
Scenario Outline: Users get created
  Given I go to the login page
  When I type <login> in the login field
  And I type <password> in the password field
  Then I am logged in
Examples:
  | login| email             | password| password_confirmation|
  | alpha| alpha@example.com| alpha1  | alpha1               |
  | beta | beta@example.com | beta12  | beta12               |
```

The steps inside the outline are regular Cucumber steps. When the outline runs, it runs once for each data row in the Examples table, with the <login> syntax indicating that a value from that table should be inserted in the row.

All these features give you a tremendous amount of power. I advise you to use it sparingly. It's tempting to use these tools to reduce duplication or make your steps more general. But the flip side is that you are often declaring implementation data explicitly in the Cucumber file rather than implicitly in the step definition.

There are at least three problems with explicit Cucumber steps:

- All the flexibility can make for complicated step definitions. Since Cucumber depends on the step definitions doing exactly what they say they're going to do 100% of the time, complex step definitions are bad because they're more likely to contain errors. Debugging step definitions will make you question your life choices. Keeping step definitions simple makes Cucumber easier to manage.
- Putting a lot of codelike things—including data, attribute names, and CSS selectors—in Cucumber feature files makes them hard to read and parse. Since the point of Cucumber is to be natural-language-like, writing unreadable steps defeats the purpose.
- Similarly, but more subtly, putting data in the feature file robs the feature file of its ability to declare intent. What is the point of the line Given a user that has been on the site for 2 months? It's hard to tell. Given a user that has been on the site long enough to be trusted is much more clear and explains why the step exists. This is a case where specifics imply greater meaning to your somewhat arbitrary data choices than they deserve.

Is Cucumber Worth It?

That depends on what "it" is. Cucumber is a very helpful acceptance-test framework, provided your expectations of it are reasonable. It's a lousy unit-test framework, and if you try to use it for unit testing you will hate it and possibly stop eating salads to avoid cucumbers, which is bad for your health.

I use Cucumber for the relatively minimal goals of a) being able to write my integration tests at the level of user behavior and b) being able to easily separate my slower integration tests from my faster unit tests. For those things, it works great.

You will sometimes hear that Cucumber allows for nondeveloper members of your team to participate in the acceptance-testing process because Cucumber is natural-language-like. My experiences in that regard are mixed. I've had some success with writing Cucumber scenarios on my own and giving them to managers or clients for approval. Going the other direction, the limiting factor in my experience is not the syntax, but rather experience in how to specify requirements. That's tricky for everybody.

Some tips for better cuking:

- Write the scenario in natural language that defines the system's behavior from the user perspective; smooth out details in the step definition.
- Avoid anything in the feature file that looks like code or data—that includes CSS selectors and database attributes.
- Keep step definitions simple.
- Don't worry about duplicating bits of step logic. Prefer multiple simple steps over one big one with complex logic.
- Specify what isn't on the page; that's often as important as specifying what is.
- Worry about implementation details in the unit tests. The suggestions about what is an integration test and what is a unit test also apply here.
- Validate against user-visible pages rather than database internals. (Sometimes this means going to an admin page or similar to validate that a change has taken place.)

Looking Ahead

We'll be talking more about these tools in future chapters.

In Chapter 13, *Testing JavaScript*, on page 247, we'll cover how both Capybara and Cucumber can be attached to drivers that run the tests against a browser engine that executes JavaScript, allowing for client-side actions to be integration-tested. In Chapter 12, *Testing External Services*, on page 229, we'll talk about integration tests that might need to touch a third-party service. And in Chapter 15, *Running Tests Faster and Running Faster Tests*, on page 287, we'll talk about how to optimize the command-line execution of both tools so as to speed up your feedback loop.

## CHAPTER 11

Testing for Security

Web security is a very scary topic. All of our applications depend on cryptography and programming that is beyond our immediate control. Despite that, certain parts of web security *are* in our control—all the logins and access checks and injection errors that happen on our site as a result of programming choices we make.

When it comes to security and testing, there's good news and bad news. The good news is that all kinds of access and injection bugs are amenable to automated developer testing. Sometimes unit testing will do the trick; other times end-to-end testing is the correct tool, but the effects of a security problem are often easily reproducible in a test environment. The bad news is that you need to actively determine where access and injection bugs might lurk in your code. We'll focus on user logins, roles, and using tests to make sure basic user authentication holds in your application.

	Security issues are, at base, just bugs. Most of the practices
Prescription 24	you follow to keep your code bug-free will also help prevent
	and diagnose security issues.

User Authentication and Authorization

We've gotten quite far in our example without adding a user model to it, which we'll rectify now.

We want to get users and passwords in the system without spending too much time in the setup weeds—that way we can focus our attention on the security issues that having users causes. To let us do that, we'll use the Devise gem[1] for basic user authentication and focus on how to use Devise as part of

---

1.   http://devise.plataformatec.com.br

our security and testing goals. (Part of me wants to derive user authentication from first principles, and someday when I publish a book from The Purist Press I'll do that.)

Devise is a big, multifaceted gem, and we'll only be scratching the surface of what it can do. It handles all kinds of login needs, including confirmation emails, changing passwords, "remember me" cookies, and much more. First up, we need to put it in the Gemfile:

```
gem 'devise'
```

As of this writing, the current version of Devise is 3.3.0.

After we install the gem with bundle install, we need to take two generation steps. The first is the general installation of the Devise setup:

```
$ rails generate devise:install
      create  config/initializers/devise.rb
      create  config/locales/devise.en.yml
```

This gives us a devise.rb initializer, containing a lot of setup options that we aren't going to worry about at the moment, and a locale file containing all the static text Devise uses. We won't worry about that file, either.

At the end of the generation process, Devise gives us a useful list of a few tasks we need to do by hand to allow Devise to integrate with the application. The relevant tasks are as follows:

- In config/environments/development.rb, set some default mailer options by adding the suggested default line, config.action_mailer.default_url_options = { host: 'local-host:3000' }. In a real application we'd need that in our other environments as well, with the host pointing to, well, the host URL.
- Our config.routes.rb needs a root route—for example, by adding root to: projects#index, which is the closest thing we have to a root route.
- Devise uses the Rails flash to distribute messages of success and failure. Add the following to app/views/layouts/application.html.erb any place in the file that seems relevant:

```
<p class="notice"><%= notice %></p>
<p class="alert"><%= alert %></p>
```

That's it. If we wanted to copy all of the Devise view code for the dialogs and stuff, we could also run rails generate devise:views from the command line. We'll skip that for now.

Now we need to actually generate a User model compatible with Devise:

```
% rails generate devise User
```

This creates a User model, a migration, a spec or test file, and a factory_girl factory if factory_girl is installed. It also adds a line to the routes.rb file that handles all the login and logout routes.

Our User model has nothing but some Devise commands:

```
security/01/gatherer/app/models/user.rb
class User < ActiveRecord::Base
  # Include default devise modules. Others available are:
  # :confirmable, :lockable, :timeoutable and :omniauthable
  devise :database_authenticatable, :registerable,
         :recoverable, :rememberable, :trackable, :validatable
end
```

Each of those symbols passed to the devise method enables another of Devise's features and assumes a certain set of database columns, the list of which you can see in the generated migration file.

To get these new columns in the database, we need to run the migrations:

```
% rake db:migrate
```

Finally, Devise has some test helpers that we need to include in our controller tests to enable login behavior in tests. At the bottom of our rails_helper.rb file, add the following:

```
security/01/gatherer/spec/rails_helper.rb
config.include Devise::TestHelpers, type: :controller
```

Minitest fans should go into the test_helper.rb file and add the following:

```
security/01/gatherer/test/test_helper.rb
class ActionController::TestCase
  include Devise::TestHelpers
end
```

This line adds the same test helpers. (Minitest fans should also note that from here out the code directory for this book will often have Minitest versions of tests in the text, even though I won't specifically call out all of them in the book.)

Adding Users and Roles

Now that we have Devise installed, let's see how we can use testing to expose security issues.

The most basic security issue is user login. Since our application involves projects that would presumably be limited to a specific, private set of users, it makes sense that you would need to be logged in to access the application.

This is testable logic—a logged-in user can access a page, whereas an ordinary browser who happens along the page cannot.

So here's an integration test for the project index page:

```
security/01/gatherer/spec/features/user_and_role_spec.rb
Line 1  require "rails_helper"

   -    describe "with users and roles" do

   5      def log_in_as(user)
   -        visit new_user_session_path
   -        fill_in("user_email", :with => user.email)
   -        fill_in("user_password", :with => user.password)
   -        click_button("Log in")
   10     end

   -      let(:user) { User.create(email: "test@example.com", password: "password") }

   -      it "allows a logged-in user to view the project index page" do
   15       log_in_as(user)
   -        visit(projects_path)
   -        expect(current_path).to eq(projects_path)
   -      end

   20   end
```

This test uses Capybara, and we've seen most of the component parts before. However, this test does have the first of several answers to the question "How do I simulate a user login in an automated test?" In the helper method log_in_as on line 5, we simulate a user login by actually simulating a user login. The method uses Capybara and the standard Devise login route and login form to simulate heading to the login page, which Devise calls the new_user_session_path, filling in the user's email and password and then clicking a button, for which the default Devise caption is "Log in." (Devise fans note: this is a change in Devise 3.3—for older versions, the caption will be "Sign in.") This method will be boilerplate across projects, depending on the name of the model that controls login or how much you customize the login page itself.

Directly simulating a login has the benefits of exercising the real login page and making sure that Devise is correctly integrated with your application. However, it's an extra page load, so it's kind of slow. We'll see a shortcut in our next example. In practice you should use the real login page at least once in your test suite.

In our test, we create a user and pass it to the log_in_as method. We then visit the project index page, projects_path, and verify that the program got there.

And the test passes as is—which should be a little suspicious.

In our case it means we've done only half the test. We've done the "this is okay" part, but we haven't done the "blocking miscreants" part.

> **Prescription 25** Always do security testing in pairs: the blocked logic and the okay logic.

The test for blocking unauthorized access is just to simulate unauthorized access—or, in other words, just hit the page without logging in.

security/01a/gatherer/spec/features/user_and_role_spec.rb
```
it "does not allow user to see the project page if not logged in" do
  visit(projects_path)
  expect(current_path).to eq(new_user_session_path)
end
```

We're asserting that a user who goes to the project page and is not logged in is redirected to the login page, which is standard Devise behavior.

The test fails. To make it pass, we just add Devise's authenticate behavior to the parent controller, which will make our entire application login-protected:

security/01/gatherer/app/controllers/application_controller.rb
```
class ApplicationController < ActionController::Base
  # Prevent CSRF attacks by raising an exception.
  # For APIs, you may want to use :null_session instead.
  protect_from_forgery with: :exception
  before_action :authenticate_user!
end
```

The line we've added is before_action :authenticate_user!. The before_action part means it will run before any action in the application, and the authenticate_user! part is the Devise check to see if the current session has a logged-in user.

The good news is that both of the new security tests now pass.

Here's the bad news:

```
$ rake test:all
Run options: --seed 16144

# Running:

FF.F.FFF...E.....................EF...........
```

A lot of other tests fail.

When a change in your code breaks multiple tests, that's often a good time to revisit your testing strategy. It's very common for new data or security constraints to break tests that are unaware of new requirements. But multiple tests breaking can be a sign that your tests are too entangled with the internals of classes that are not directly under test.

> **Prescription 26** When a single change in your code breaks multiple tests, consider the idea that your testing strategy is flawed.

The specific test failures are all due to code attempting to hit the site without having a login. It might mean that some of the testing that we are doing at the controller level might better be done at a unit test level against an action object. In our case, it also means we have some spurious tests floating around from the mocks chapter.

We need to simulate a logged-in user for each failing test. We have four failing test areas: the project and task controller tests, and the two other integration tests we have for adding projects and adding tests.

We need a fake user to log in. Since we really don't care about the details of this user, and we'd need to re-create it for each test, this seems like a fine use case for fixtures. Here's a user fixture for our test user:

```
security/01/gatherer/spec/fixtures/users.yml
user:
  email: "test@example.com"
  encrypted_password: <%= User.new.send(:password_digest, 'password') %>
```

The gobbledygook being sent to encrypted_password is there to ensure that our password is being sent to the database encrypted in exactly the way Devise expects so we can match the user on login. If we were creating the user from Rails, we could just use User.create(email: "test@email.com", password: "password"), but since password is not in the database but is instead an accessor mediated by Devise, we don't have access to it from the fixture and must go directly to the encrypted_password column in the database.

The controller tests can then use Devise's methods directly in their setup. You need this snippet of code in both projects_controller_spec.rb and tasks_controller_spec.rb:

```
security/01/gatherer/spec/controllers/projects_controller_spec.rb
before(:example) do
  sign_in User.create!(email: "rspec@example.com", password: "password")
end
```

The sign_in method is provided by Devise's test helpers, and it allows us to sign in a particular user. This user is signed into the test session and appears as the currently logged-in user for the duration of the test, or until you use the

Devise helper method sign_out. Alternatively, you could stub the controller method current_user, which is used by most of the rest of the code to determine if there is an active logged-in user.

For the integration tests, we don't have sign_in available, since it works at the internal Rails level, but there is a different shortcut. We can use a helper provided by Warden, which is the tool that Devise uses for the authentication functionality. Warden works at the Rack layer. Without spending a page or two explaining Rack, suffice to say that we can use Warden to fake a logged-in user from outside the Rails stack, suitable for using within our integration tests.

You'll need the following setup line added in both add_project_spec.rb and add_task_spec.rb:

```
security/01a/gatherer/spec/features/add_project_spec.rb
fixtures :all
include Warden::Test::Helpers

before(:example) do
  login_as users(:user)
end
```

The Warden helpers need to be included in the test class, and then login_as is available for our use. The technical difference between login_as and sign_in is not super relevant for us. (The difference in the two names is, however, irritating.) The practical difference is that login_as comes from outside the Rails stack and can therefore be used in integration tests, whereas sign_in only manipulates Rails internals and can only be used in a test, such as a controller test, that's intended to have access to Rails internals.

With that addition to the controller and integration tests, our suite passes again. (Minitest equivalents are available in the security/01a/gatherer/test directory of the code download.) We have nothing to gain right now from trying to move any of these tests to avoid the additional setup, but I will note that our action tests for creating a project in test/actions/creates_project_test.rb didn't have to be changed.

Restricting Access

Having required a login for our application, we've solved part of our potential security problem. The next problem involves limiting access to only projects that the user is associated with.

We'll start with an integration test. The test needs as its *given* a project, and at least two users—one who has access and one who does not. The *when* action is an attempt to view the project show page, and the *then* specification is the successful or unsuccessful page view.

Here's the pair of tests:

```
security/02/gatherer/spec/features/user_and_role_spec.rb
describe "roles" do
  let(:project) { Project.create(name: "Project Gutenberg") }

  it "allows a user who is part of a project to see that project" do
    project.roles.create(user: user)
    log_in_as(user)
    visit(project_path(project))
    expect(current_path).to eq(project_path(project))
  end

  it "does not allow a user who is not part of a project to see that project" do
    log_in_as(user)
    visit(project_path(project))
    expect(current_path).not_to eq(project_path(project))
  end
end
```

The tests both create a project, log in as a user, and visit the project page. In the first test we also add the user to the project. In the second test we assert that the user goes anywhere but the actual project page.

As with our last pair of security tests, the test that assumes no blocking behavior passes whereas the blocking test does not.

In writing these tests, we have a new concept to represent in the code: the combination of a user and a project. This is a design decision. As we write the test, we're making a claim about how we want the application data to be structured. Often just planning the test will expose the need for new data or new structures, and something as simple as this migration might be done before writing the test. That's fine as long as the larger idea of using the test process to drive the design of the code still holds.

We've added the concept of roles to handle the list of users attached to a project. The test suggests that project has a relationship to roles—in fact, the first point of failure for the test will be that call to project.roles.

We could create a whole round of integration testing to drive the addition of a user interface for adding users to projects and allow the data model to be driven as part of that process. Or we could hand-wave the UI, add a basic data model, and focus on the security aspect.

In a full project, the add-user-to-project story would get full treatment. For our purposes, we can start with just a migration and a new model. We'll assume somebody else did the add-user-to-project story.

Let's create the migration:

```
$ rails generate model role user:references project:references role_name:string
$ rake db:migrate
```

That gives us the following migration:

```
security/02/gatherer/db/migrate/20140617021340_create_roles.rb
class CreateRoles < ActiveRecord::Migration
  def change
    create_table :roles do |t|
      t.references :user, index: true
      t.references :project, index: true
      t.string :role_name

      t.timestamps
    end
  end
end
```

This goes a tiny bit beyond the test by adding a role_name.

We'll also need to add the associations—first, to Project:

```
security/02/gatherer/app/models/project.rb
has_many :roles
has_many :users, through: :roles
```

and then to User:

```
security/02/gatherer/app/models/user.rb
has_many :roles
has_many :projects, through: :roles
```

At this point, the test has the failure we expect, which is that we want to block access to a user who's not part of the project, but we don't.

Time to move to unit tests to drive that logic. But where do the tests go? We have more design decisions to make.

There are two distinct responsibilities in blocking a user. There's the actual logic to determine whether a user can see a project, and there's the logic to redirect the user if the access checker fails. Let's test those responsibilities separately.

Let's deal with the access control first. That method is probably either Project#can_be_viewed_by?(user) or User#can_view?(project). The active voice version in User seems more clear.

Right now we're testing just the access logic, which means that all we need for each test is one user and one project:

```ruby
require 'spec_helper'

describe User do

  it "cannot view a project it is not a part of" do
    user = User.new
    project = Project.new
    expect(user.can_view?(project)).to be_falsy
  end

  it "can view a project it is a part of" do
    user = User.create!(email: "user@example.com", password: "password")
    project = Project.create!(name: "Project Gutenberg")
    user.roles.create(project: project)
    expect(user.can_view?(project)).to be_truthy
  end
end
```

The two cases here are similar to the integration tests: either the user is a member of the project and can see it, or the user isn't a member of the project and can't see it.

The second test has one subtle point about how Rails handles associations. In the first test, where the user is not a member of the project, we don't need to save the user, project, and role to the database to run the test. In the second test we do.

We need to save them all to the database because of how Rails handles associations; specifically has_many through: associations such as the relationship between projects and users in this example. If the associations were just ordinary has_many associations, Rails would be able to manage the two-way relationship in memory without touching the database (at least Rails 4 can; older versions don't do that either). However, when there is a join relationship denoted by has_many: through, Rails internals will always need to have saved objects with IDs to resolve the relationship. Although you can work around this problem (and we'll discuss some workarounds when we talk about fast tests in Chapter 15, *Running Tests Faster and Running Faster Tests*, on page 287), for the moment the workarounds are more complicated and distracting than the straightforward creation of the data.

A user can view a project if the user has a role in that project. This method in User will make the tests pass.

security/02/gatherer/app/models/user.rb
```ruby
def can_view?(project)
  projects.to_a.include?(project)
end
```

Although the unit test passes, the integration test is still fails because we haven't added the access check into the controller. That brings in the second kind of logic we need to test: does the controller successfully block the page if the user doesn't have access. The controller gets two tests, one for the has-access condition and one without:

security/02/gatherer/spec/controllers/projects_controller_spec.rb
```ruby
describe "GET show" do
  let(:project) { Project.create(name: "Project Runway") }

  it "allows a user who is part of the project to see the project" do
    controller.current_user.stubs(can_view?: true)
    get :show, id: project.id
    expect(response).to render_template(:show)
  end

  it "does not allow a user who is not part of the project to see the project" do
    controller.current_user.stubs(can_view?: false)
    get :show, id: project.id
    expect(response).to redirect_to(new_user_session_path)
  end
end
```

See how this pair of tests both stub the current_user.can_view? method? This is a perfect use of mock objects. The details of can_view? are complicated to set up, subject to change, and ultimately irrelevant to the controller's behavior. Stubbing the response eliminates the need for these details, so the stub declaration is clearer when reading the test and figuring out what is happening. The test is also robust against future changes in the can_view? logic.

To make this test pass we need to incorporate the check of can_view? into the controller. We can make this work in a couple of ways—here's one:

security/02/gatherer/app/controllers/projects_controller.rb
```ruby
def show
  @project = Project.find(params[:id])
  unless current_user.can_view?(@project)
    redirect_to new_user_session_path
    return
  end
end
```

This controller method redirects back to the login screen and returns if the user is blocked; otherwise it continues normally.

With this code in place, not only does the controller pass, but the integration test passes as well.

We're all green.

More Access Control Testing

The advantage of splitting responsibility and testing into separate controller and model concerns becomes even clearer as we add another requirement. Let's allow for the possibility of administrative users who can see any project, as well as public projects that can be seen by any user.

We'll want to represent these properties in the database—in this case, we're doing the design work based on planning our test. We'll generate a migration using the command rake generate migration add_public_fields, which gives a skeleton file. Add the following and then run rake db:migrate.

security/03/gatherer/db/migrate/20140621051744_add_public_fields.rb
```ruby
class AddPublicFields < ActiveRecord::Migration
  def change
    add_column :projects, :public, :boolean, default: false
    add_column :users, :admin, :boolean, default: false
  end
end
```

Let's think about where this needs to be tested. The behavior of the User#can_view? method needs to change. But since we've isolated the controller from the details of can_view?, the controller logic doesn't change—it's still *if users can view, let them; redirect otherwise.* We can write this logic as unit tests:

security/03/gatherer/spec/models/user_spec.rb
```ruby
describe "public roles" do
  let(:user) { User.new }
  let(:project) { Project.new }

  it "allows an admin to view a project" do
    user.admin = true
    expect(user.can_view?(project)).to be_truthy
  end

  it "allows a public project to be seen by anyone" do
    project.public = true
    expect(user.can_view?(project)).to be_truthy
  end
end
```

These tests set up the passthrough condition for administrators and public projects—the negative condition is already covered by the "user cannot view an unrelated project" test.

And the test passes with an additional line in the method:

```
security/03/gatherer/app/models/user.rb
def can_view?(project)
  return true if admin? || project.public?
  projects.to_a.include?(project)
end
```

We're at a refactoring step, but we seem pretty clean at the moment.

There's an open question in our testing strategy: whether we should have started the process of adding admin users and public projects with an end-to-end integration test.

The answer to the question depends on the goal of your tests.

From a TDD-integration test perspective, we don't need an integration test because the integration logic didn't change. The code changes we made were localized to a single class, so the behavior of any code that uses that class is unchanged. Although we could write an integration test that would expose this behavior, this test would be slower than the unit tests we just wrote, and it would be harder to diagnose failures.

That said, you may be in a situation where there's value in writing the test strictly as an acceptance test, to verify behavior as part of a set of requirements, rather than to drive development.

 **Prescription 27** Write your test as close as possible to the code logic that's being tested.

Using Roles

Now that we have the concept of users and roles in the system, we need to look at other places where users need access to a project. Two interesting places spring to mind:

- The project index list should be limited to only the projects that the user can see.

- Adding tasks should be limited to only the projects a user can see.

Let's look at the index page. Two places need code here. A User instance needs some way to return the list of projects the user can see, and the controller index action needs to call that method. That argues for an integration test, though only weakly. (Sometimes I'll skip an integration test if the logic is very close to Rails default integration and would very easily be caught manually.)

```
security/04/gatherer/spec/features/user_and_role_spec.rb
it "allows users to only see projects they are a part of on the index page" do
  my_project = Project.create!(name: "My Project")
  my_project.roles.create(user: user)
  not_my_project = Project.create!(name: "Not My Project")
  log_in_as(user)
  visit projects_path
  expect(page).to have_selector("#project_#{my_project.id}")
  expect(page).not_to have_selector("#project_#{not_my_project.id}")
end
```

This tests creates two projects, adding one to our user. On visiting the index page, we expect to see the project we've added and not to see the project we haven't.

This test fails on the last line because we haven't actually implemented the restrictions yet.

On the user side, this functionality must deal with admin users and public projects. The logic is parallel to the can_view? logic.

Here are the unit tests for the User behavior of being able to access a list of projects. Again, I wrote them and passed them one at a time:

```
security/04/gatherer/spec/models/user_spec.rb
describe "visible project listing" do
  let(:user) { User.create!(email: "user@example.com", password: "password") }
  let!(:project_1) { Project.create!(name: "Project 1") }
  let!(:project_2) { Project.create!(name: "Project 2") }

  before(:context) do
    Project.delete_all
  end

  it "allows a user to see their projects" do
    user.projects << project_1
    expect(user.visible_projects).to eq([project_1])
  end

  it "allows an admin to see all projects" do
    user.admin = true
    expect(user.visible_projects).to eq([project_1, project_2])
  end
```

```
it "allows a user to see public projects" do
  user.projects << project_1
  project_2.update_attributes(public: true)
  expect(user.visible_projects).to eq([project_1, project_2])
end

it "has no dupes in project list" do
  user.projects << project_1
  project_1.update_attributes(public: true)
  expect(user.visible_projects).to eq([project_1])
end
end
```

The last test is the direct result of realizing that the code as I left it following the test before would duplicate an entry if a project was both public and had the user as a member.

The setup here is a little tricky. The projects need to be created using let! because they're not referred to before the assertion, so they wouldn't otherwise be lazily created. Also, we need that Project.delete_all in the setup method to clear out the projects defined in the fixtures. Without that line, the admin test would fail because Project.all would return not just the two projects created for the test, but also all the projects created by the fixtures. It also has to be in a before(:context) block, because if it is a before(:example) block, it would be executed after the let! calls, deleting the projects we just created.

Here's the "fast to green" passing code:

security/04/gatherer/app/models/user.rb
```
  def visible_projects
    return Project.all.to_a if admin?
    (projects.to_a + Project.where(public: true).to_a).uniq.sort_by(&:id)
  end
end
```

First off in our refactor, let's move the Project logic to its own class method:

security/04/gatherer/app/models/project.rb
```
def self.all_public
  where(public: true)
end
```

This makes the visible_projects method look like this:

security/05/gatherer/app/models/user.rb
```
  def visible_projects
    return Project.all.to_a if admin?
    (projects.to_a + Project.all_public).uniq.sort_by(&:id)
  end
end
```

The User code has a larger problem. It now has two methods, can_view? and visible_projects, that duplicate the logic of whether a user can view a project. One possible solution would be to rewrite can_view? in terms of visible_projects:

security/05/gatherer/app/models/user.rb

```ruby
def can_view?(project)
  visible_projects.include?(project)
end
```

If we do that, we get some test failures—our tests that didn't save a project to the database now need to. Actually, we have a test refactoring here—two sets of tests covering the same logic. Let's combine them to make it even more clear that the two methods are in parallel:

security/05/gatherer/spec/models/user_spec.rb

```ruby
require 'rails_helper'
describe User do
  RSpec::Matchers.define :be_able_to_see do |*projects|
    match do |user|
      expect(user.visible_projects).to eq(projects)
      projects.all? { |p| expect(user.can_view?(p)).to be_truthy }
      (all_projects - projects).all? { |p| expect(user.can_view?(p)).to be_falsy }
    end
  end

  describe "visibility" do
    let(:user) { User.create!(email: "user@example.com", password: "password") }
    let(:project_1) { Project.create!(name: "Project 1") }
    let(:project_2) { Project.create!(name: "Project 2") }
    let(:all_projects) { [project_1, project_2] }

    before(:example) do
      Project.delete_all
    end

    it "a user can see their projects" do
      user.projects << project_1
      expect(user).to be_able_to_see(project_1)
    end

    it "an admin can see all projects" do
      user.admin = true
      expect(user).to be_able_to_see(project_1, project_2)
    end

    it "a user can see public projects" do
      user.projects << project_1
      project_2.update_attributes(public: true)
      expect(user).to be_able_to_see(project_1, project_2)
    end
```

```
    it "no dupes in project list" do
      user.projects << project_1
      project_1.update_attributes(public: true)
      expect(user).to be_able_to_see(project_1)
    end
  end
end
```

We've created a custom matcher, be_able_to_see, which takes in a list of projects and validates the can_view? and visible_projects in parallel, thereby asserting that the two methods stay in synch. It also validates that projects that aren't specified are not visible—we get around the fixture data by explicitly specifying the universe of all_projects. (In Minitest I'd use a custom assertion; you can see an example in the sample code at code/security/05/gatherer/test/models/user_test.rb.)

At this point our original integration test is still failing because we still haven't integrated the controller with the new model function. We already have a controller index test that we'll need to adapt. We need to focus on specifying the behavior that's unique to the controller, which is that it calls the visible_projects method of the current user:

```
security/05/gatherer/spec/controllers/projects_controller_spec.rb
describe "GET index" do
  it "displays all projects correctly" do
    user = User.new
    project = Project.new(:name => "Project Greenlight")
    controller.expects(:current_user).returns(user)
    user.expects(:visible_projects).returns([project])
    get :index
    assert_equal assigns[:projects].map(&:__getobj__), [project]
  end
end
```

This test sets up a user, uses a Mocha expectation to ensure that the user is the Devise current_user, and then sets a Mocha expectation that visible_projects is called on that user. This test is simpler than the previous index test—since the integration test is managing the expected response, we no longer need to handle the view logic in this test. All we need to do is verify that the controller is calling the correct model method and passing expected values to the view. The last line of the test describes the contract with the model—the expected list of projects as returned by the visible_projects stub is passed to assigns[:projects], plus a little bit of manipulation because we're using a decorator wrapped around the project objects.

The test fails because the controller method still calls Project.all, but we can fix that:

security/05/gatherer/app/controllers/projects_controller.rb

```
def index
  @projects = ProjectPresenter.from_project_list(current_user.visible_projects)
end
```

At this point the new integration test also passes, but we have an interesting regression failure:

```
1) Failure:
AddProjectTest#test_a_user_can_add_a_a_project_and_give_it_tasks
 [gatherer/test/integration/add_project_test.rb:20]:
expected to find css "#project_980190963 .name"
with text "Project Runway" but there were no matches
```

After investigating, we find that the test in question is an integration test that creates a new project using CreatesProject and then goes to view the page. The test is failing because the user isn't added as a member of the new project and therefore can't see the project page.

Fixing this involves changing the CreatesProject action to take a user (or users) and add them to the project when the project is created. Since CreatesProject is an action, we can isolate the test and just make sure that a passed user is applied to the project—or in this case, we set the API to take an array of users:

security/05/gatherer/spec/actions/creates_project_spec.rb

```
it "adds users to the project" do
  user = User.new
  creator = CreatesProject.new(name: "Project Runway", users: [user])
  creator.build
  expect(creator.project.users).to eq([user])
end
```

Then we need to add the new keyword argument to the action and use the value when creating the new project:

security/05/gatherer/app/actions/creates_project.rb

```
attr_accessor :name, :task_string, :project, :users

def initialize(name: "", task_string: "", users: [])
  @name = name
  @task_string = task_string
  @users = users
end

def build
  self.project = Project.new(name: name)
  project.tasks = convert_string_to_tasks
  project.users = users
  project
end
```

Then we need to update the controller method to pass the user to the action:

security/05/gatherer/app/controllers/projects_controller.rb
```ruby
def create
  @action = CreatesProject.new(
    name: params[:project][:name],
    task_string: params[:project][:tasks] || "",
    users: [current_user])
  success = @action.create
  if success
    redirect_to projects_path
  else
    @project = @action.project
    render :new
  end
end
```

That breaks the mock we use in the controller test to bypass the action—which I admit is more fumbling in the codebase than I thought we were going to have to do when I started this example:

security/05/gatherer/spec/controllers/projects_controller_spec.rb
```ruby
it "creates a project (mock version)" do
  fake_action = instance_double(CreatesProject, create: true)
  expect(CreatesProject).to receive(:new)
      .with(name: "Runway", task_string: "Start something:2", users: [user])
      .and_return(fake_action)
  post :create, project: {name: "Runway", tasks: "Start something:2"}
  expect(response).to redirect_to(projects_path)
  expect(assigns(:action)).not_to be_nil
end
```

After all that, we have basic user and role authentication in the system. Now we need to protect against a couple of attacks that require the user to not use our application's UI directly.

> **Prescription 28** Adding user authentication can be very disruptive to existing tests. Try to get the basic infrastructure in place early.

Protection Against Form Modification

We have at least one blind spot in our user and role protection. The project show page has a form that submits a new task. That form is submitted to the TasksController, which doesn't handle any user-access control. The use case here is a malicious user not going through the web UI but creating his own HTTP request and pointing it at the server.

There are two important issues here, at least from my perspective as Rails Testing Author Guy. First is the habit of noticing when you're using a resource that's being accessed as a result of a user request as opposed to being stored server-side. This is even true when the resource is protected indirectly, as in this case, where we're accessing a Task that belongs to the actual Project, which is where the access control is attached. Second, we need to discuss how to test such a case.

We have two similar cases to deal with—task creation from the project form via TaskController#create and any of the update and move task methods in the controller.

Let's plan our create test. For the *given* we need a user, a project that the user belongs to, and a project the user doesn't belong to. The *when* is the creation of the task; the *then* is whether the task is created or not.

The design question before us is where to put the access check, and by extension where to write the test. We're at a slight disadvantage; since the potentially malicious request is coming from outside the UI, Capybara isn't going to be effective in crafting an integration test. The code logic for creating tasks is in the TaskController, and that seems the most likely place for an access control test (though if we'd moved the creation logic to an action item, the way that we did with CreatesProject, then we could've put the access logic there).

We just need a small change to the setup for the test to allow us access to the User object in question:

security/05/gatherer/spec/controllers/tasks_controller_spec.rb
```ruby
let(:user) { User.create!(email: "rspec@example.com", password: "password") }

before(:example) do
  sign_in(user)
  ActionMailer::Base.deliveries.clear
end
```

Then all we need to do is create a project and see what happens:

security/05/gatherer/spec/controllers/tasks_controller_spec.rb
```ruby
describe "POST create" do
  fixtures :all
  let(:project) { Project.create!(name: "Project Runway") }

  it "allows a user to create a task for a project they belong to" do
    user.projects << project
    user.save!
    post :create, task: {project_id: project.id, title: "just do it", size: "1" }
    expect(project.reload.tasks.first.title).to eq("just do it")
  end
```

```
it "does not allow a user to create a task for a project without access" do
  post :create, task: {project_id: project.id, title: "just do it", size: "1" }
  expect(project.reload.tasks.size).to eq(0)
end
end
```

The trickiest part in this test is remembering that you need to reload the project to see if the controller has added any tasks to it, since the controller will create a local ActiveRecord instance backed by the same database row and will update the database row without changing the ActiveRecord instance that is local to the test.

To make the test pass we just need to add a bit of logic to the controller action:

security/05/gatherer/app/controllers/tasks_controller.rb
```
def create
  @project = Project.find(params[:task][:project_id])
  unless current_user.can_view?(@project)
    redirect_to new_user_session_path
    return
  end
  @project.tasks.create(title: params[:task][:title],
      size: params[:task][:size],
      project_order: @project.next_task_order)
  redirect_to @project
end
```

The new part is the unless statement, which checks to see if the current_user can actually see the project in question. We can trust the current_user value because it is not dependent on any data coming from the user; it's managed by the Rails session.

There are a lot of possibilities from here. We could extract the current controller method to a CreatesTask action item, which would make it easier to separate the access logic from the rest of the code. We could also add similar protection to the update, up, and down methods, which involves the design question of modeling access control from the task's perspective.

Mass Assignment Testing

Mass assignment is a common Rails security issue, caused by Rails's ability to save an arbitrary hash of attribute names and values to an instance by sending an entire hash as a parameter, as in new(params[:user]), create(params[:user]), or update_attributes(params[:user]). The security issue happens when somebody hacks a request and adds unexpected attributes to the incoming parameters, typically an attribute that you wouldn't want an arbitrary user to be able to change, such as User#admin or Project#public. (GitHub was famously hacked via this vector by a user who added himself as a committer to the Rails repo.)

Rails 4 provides the concept of *strong parameters* to allow you to identify parts of the parameter hash from an incoming request as required or permissible. To be used in a mass assignment, the attributes need to be identified using the require or permit methods of the Rails parameter object. Attributes that aren't whitelisted aren't passed on to the ActiveRecord object, and they are helpfully listed in the Rails log as a warning and to make debugging these issues easier.

Our Gatherer application currently uses strong parameters in one location, TasksController#update, where we have this line:

```
@task.update_attributes(params[:task].permit(:size, :completed_at))
```

We manage the strong parameters issue in other ways. The TasksController#create method explicitly lists the items that are being passed to create:

```
@project.tasks.create(title: params[:task][:title],
        size: params[:task][:size],
        project_order: @project.next_task_order)
```

In ProjectsController, the create method similarly lists the attributes that are passed to the CreatesProject action object, which explicitly assigns the one attribute it uses when building the project.

As with other features the framework provides, the important part from the testing framework is the behavior—preventing the user from setting a particular attribute—rather than the implementation.

 Prescription 29 Test for mass assignment any time you have an attribute that needs to be secure and a controller method that touches that class based on user input.

As it happens, we have ProjectsController#update sitting in the Gatherer code. It has no strong parameter protection; we it added solely to illustrate mock objects. This means the parameters have never been tested.

I wonder if a user could maliciously make a project public?

`security/05/gatherer/spec/controllers/projects_controller_spec.rb`
```
it "does not allow user to make a project public if it is not theirs" do
  sample = Project.create!(name: "Test Project", public: false)
  patch :update, id: sample.id, project: {public: true}
  expect(sample.reload.public).to be_falsy
end
```

Turns out the answer is no:

```
1) Error:
ProjectsControllerTest#test_a_user_can_make_a_project_public:
ActiveModel::ForbiddenAttributesError: ActiveModel::ForbiddenAttributesError
```

But it's not because none of the attributes are permitted. ForbiddenAttributesError means that the params object is being used without any attempt to set permitted attributes—meaning that nobody could make a project public via this method even if they had access.

To make the test pass, we just need to change one line in the project controller to add the permit call:

```
security/05/gatherer/app/controllers/projects_controller.rb
def update
  @project = Project.find(params[:id])
  if @project.update_attributes(params[:project].permit(:name))
    redirect_to @project, notice: "'project was successfully updated.'"
  else
    render action: 'edit'
  end
end
```

That's fine, but what if the mass assignment takes place outside the controller?

We don't do this in the current version of Gatherer, but if we had passed the entire params object to the CreatesProject action, we could easily have something like this:

```
class CreatesProject

  attr_accessor :params, :project, :users

  def initialize(params: {}, users: [])
    @params = params
    @users = users
  end

  def build
    self.project = Project.new(params.permit(:name))
    project.users = users
    project
  end
end
```

This code has a mass assignment, params.permit(:name), which is fine; but if you try to test this code by passing a regular hash to CreatesProject, the test will error at params.permit because ordinary hashes don't have a permit method.

The workaround is to create the underlying Rails object directly:

```
CreatesProject.new(ActionController::Parameters.new(name: "Project"))
```

Rails provides the class ActionController::Parameters, which wraps the hash and allows for the permit and require behavior needed to support strong parameters.

Other Security Resources

There's a limit to what you can test with security using TDD. It's a good idea to use a static analysis tool to look for security issues. Two options are Brakeman, which you would run yourself, and CodeClimate, which automatically runs Brakeman on each commit.[2] Brakeman looks for a variety of security issues and provides some tips on working around them.

Prescription 30	Use an automatic security scanner to check for common security issues.

The Open Web Application Security Project has all kinds of useful information on security risks.[3] Of particular interest is WebGoat, a deliberately insecure application designed to allow you to hack and test solutions. The Rails version is called RailsGoat.[4]

---

2.   http://brakemanscanner.org, http://www.codeclimate.com
3.   https://www.owasp.org/
4.   https://github.com/OWASP/railsgoat

## CHAPTER 12

Testing External Services

We've decided the one thing our project-management tool really needs is a bit of graphical spark. Specifically, we've been asked to have users' Twitter avatars show up on the site attached to tasks they have completed. (Handily, Twitter has a Ruby gem that's not to hard to set up.) Since this is *Rails 4 Test Prescriptions* and not *Rails 4 Connecting to Twitter Prescriptions*, we'd like to be able to test our interaction with the Twitter API.

Unfortunately, interacting with a third-party web service introduces a lot of complexity to our testing. Connecting to a web service is slow—even slower than the database connections we've already tried to avoid. Plus, connection to a web service requires an Internet connection, and we'd like our test suite to be able to run on the train, on a boat, or during a network outage. Some external services are public—we don't want to post an update to Twitter every time we run our tests, let alone post a credit-card payment to PayPal. Some services have rate limits, some cost money to access, some actually deal with money, and some require API keys and authentication.

The point is, we'd really, really like to be able to write and execute tests without hitting the service more than strictly necessary.

The strategies we've developed so far for test isolation and for using mocks to limit the scope of tests will help us successfully test an external service. We'll be able to test it on a train and test it on a boat and test it in the rain and test it on a goat.

External Testing Strategy

Our external-service testing story has two main characters:

- The *client*, the part of our application code that uses the external API, either because it needs data accessible via the API or because it is sending data to the API to be used by somebody else. In either case, we're dealing with a request and a response, even if the response is just a status code.

- The *server*, which for our purposes is outside our application and reachable via some kind of network request (though many of the strategies in this chapter also apply even if the service isn't separated by the network).

We also introduce two characters to the story for design and testing purposes:

- A *fake server*, which intercepts HTTP requests during a test and returns a canned response object. We'll be using the VCR gem to manage our fake server (more about VCR shortly).

- An *adapter*, which is an object that sits between the client and the server to mediate access between them.

The following diagram shows the relationship between these objects and the tests we'll write using them:

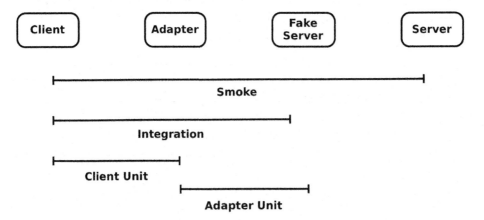

There are several test types that relate different combinations of these objects:

- A *smoke test*, which goes from the client all the way to the real server. In other words, it's a full end-to-end test of the entire interaction. We don't want to do this often, for all the reasons listed earlier, but it's useful to be able to guard against changes in the server API.

- An *integration test*, which goes from the client to the fake server. This tests the entire end-to-end functionality of our application but uses a stubbed response from the server. This will be our go-to strategy for integration-testing the external server.

- A *client unit test*, which starts on the client and ends in the adapter. The adapter's responses are stubbed, meaning that the adapter isn't even making fake server calls. This allows us to unit-test our client completely separate from the server API.

- An *adapter unit test*, which starts in the adapter and ends in the fake server. These tests are the final piece of the chain and allow us to validate the behavior of the adapter separate from any client or the actual server.

Prescription 31	Mediating interaction to an external server through an adapter that is part of your code makes the interaction easier to test and to use.

Our Service Integration Test

We'll use the Twitter gem to interface with Twitter.[1] We'll put that in the Gemfile. We're also going to need the VCR and Webmock gems in our test environment:

```
gem 'twitter'
gem 'vcr', group: :test
gem 'webmock', group: :test
```

We'll also have to reinstall the bundle with bundle install.

We need a Twitter API key and secret key. In Rails 4, those get placed in the secrets.yml file, which typically is not stored in your code repository, though I've put it in our sample code for ease of setup:

external/01/gatherer/config/secrets.yml
```
development:
  secret_key_base: |
    9cbb1cdd81bd1e79999d8f91ec57b0ced0e59ec961f9af56e77a5e514acf7cc9f646e83aedd
    5293f44685c47e717eade8677fca153d9c65ffb441d4fdff33052

test:
  secret_key_base: |
    9cbb1cdd81bd1e79999d8f91ec57b0ced0e59ec961f9af56e77a5e514acf7cc9f646e83aedd
    5293f44685c47e717eade8677fca153d9c65ffb441d4fdff33052
  twitter_api: "IVCwuly8UuymHROaIwsJ4IcgK"
  twitter_secret: "ZzfZNLEF72ELnELH3jsRG41AY0cLfP2QfAyKMpChxNfJOmloqw"


production:
  secret_key_base: <%= ENV["SECRET_KEY_BASE"] %>
```

---

1.   https://github.com/sferik/twitter

We'll use those keys when we connect to the Twitter API. By the way, those keys will have long since been changed by the time you read this. The existing tests might work because they'll have been stubbed via VCR. But you also might want to go to https://apps.twitter.com and generate your own application and set of keys.

We want to attach the current user to a task when the task is completed and then show the user's Twitter avatar next to that task on the project page. As has been our fashion so far, we're going to hand-wave over some UI functionality that doesn't relate to our focus. In this case we're going to pretend that the pair down the hall has already covered the ability to connect a user to a task, and we're just going to add the data migration. This migration includes the connection between a user and a task, and adds the user's Twitter handle, which we need to access the person's avatar via the Twitter API:

```
external/01/gatherer/db/migrate/20140629211718_add_user_to_task.rb
class AddUserToTask < ActiveRecord::Migration
  def change
    add_column :tasks, :user_id, :integer
    add_column :users, :twitter_handle, :string
  end
end
```

Don't forget to run the migration. No, really—don't forget. As I was writing this chapter I added the migration and then started running tests without ever running the migration—which doesn't work.

```
$ rake db:migrate
```

We need to add the association, in app/models/task.rb:

```
belongs_to :user
```

and, for completeness's sake, in app/models/user.rb:

```
has_many :tasks
```

With that bit of setup out of the way, we can write an integration test. In this case we'll integrate our code with Twitter:

```
external/01/gatherer/spec/features/shows_twitter_avatar_spec.rb
require 'rails_helper'

include Warden::Test::Helpers

describe "task display" do

  fixtures :all
```

```
before(:example) do
  projects(:bluebook).roles.create(user: users(:user))
  users(:user).update_attributes(twitter_handle: "noelrap")
  tasks(:one).update_attributes(user_id: users(:user).id,
      completed_at: 1.hour.ago)
  login_as users(:user)
end

it "shows a gravatar", :vcr do
  visit project_path(projects(:bluebook))
  url = "http://pbs.twimg.com/profile_images/40008602/head_shot_bigger.jpg"
  within("#task_1") do
    expect(page).to have_selector(".completed", text: users(:user).email)
    expect(page).to have_selector("img[src='#{url}']")
  end
end

end
```

With one exception, this test is a simplified version of the integration test we wrote in Chapter 10, *Integration Testing with Capybara and Cucumber*, on page 177. Our *given* here is the project, user, and task, which are already defined in our fixtures, along with a simulated login. Our *when* is visiting the show page for the project, and *then* we validate that the user associated with the task is displayed, by both the user's email and Twitter avatar. I've seeded this test with a known Twitter avatar—mine—by setting the user's Twitter handle and then setting the expected image source to my known Twitter-profile URL.

You've probably noticed that the test has an unusual piece of metadata: :vcr. Since I've mentioned VCR a couple of times in this chapter, you may have further assumed that, in this context, VCR has more to do with external service testing than it does with that Blockbuster store that closed seven years ago.

Introducing VCR

VCR is one of my favorite testing tools. The concept is simple. When VCR is enabled, it intercepts any third-party HTTP request. By default, the first time the request is made VCR allows the request to proceed normally. However, VCR saves the response and associated metadata to a YAML file, which VCR calls a *cassette*. When the test is run again, VCR intercepts the request. Rather than actually making the request as a network call, VCR converts the cassette back into a response object and returns that response object. By default, if you then make an HTTP request that the VCR cassette doesn't know about, the test will fail.

VCR has many great features. Because the data that VCR stores is based on a real request, it's real data, meaning your tests are not running on some slapdash mock object you put together. This makes the tests have greater fidelity to the runtime environment, which makes them more trustworthy. VCR is super-simple to use and almost always just works. (Sometimes when you change a test, you need to manually force VCR to re-record data, though.) You can even set VCR to automatically regenerate the cassette on an arbitrary time frame to protect against changes in the API.

Prescription 32	Use the VCR gem to allow your integration tests to run against server response data.

VCR is very configurable, allowing you to specify URLs or patterns that should be allowed to pass through without VCR caring (a common one being localhost). You can also do some pattern matching as to what constitutes the same URL for VCR purposes—many APIs have some kind of timestamp parameter that you'd want VCR to overlook for the purposes of returning stubbed output.

VCR and RSpec

You can use RSpec metadata to specify that any RSpec it or describe block uses a VCR cassette. The configuration goes into the rails_helper.rb file:

```
external/01/gatherer/spec/rails_helper.rb
VCR.configure do |c|
  c.cassette_library_dir = 'spec/cassettes'
  c.hook_into :webmock
  c.configure_rspec_metadata!
end
```

We are specifying three options to start: first, the directory where VCR is going to place its cassette files (which can be anything you want, but something like spec/cassettes is customary).

The second option involves the HTTP stub library. VCR handles the creation and use of the cassette files, but it subcontracts the actual stubbing of HTTP calls to another library. You can specify which HTTP library is used; we're using webmock, but that's an implementation detail and this is the last time we're going to talk about webmock.

Finally, it'll probably come as no surprise that the line c.configure_rspec_metadata! configures the RSpec metadata.

Then we can specify VCR as a metadata option in the spec, as we just saw.

When we declare the test, we also declare :vcr as metadata. The cassette is automatically named using the names of the describe blocks as directory names and the name of the it block as a file name. If you wanted to pass options to the VCR call, change the metadata declaration from :vcr to vcr: {options}.

Within a spec with VCR declared, VCR will behave in one of two ways.

It may think that the cassette needs to be recorded. This will most commonly be because the cassette doesn't exist yet, but there are ways to tell VCR to overwrite an existing cassette. If VCR is trying to record a cassette, it'll allow all HTTP requests to happen but save all the requests and responses in a single file—which it'll store in the directory specified in the config, and with the file name specified by the spec name or by an option passed to the metadata.

If VCR doesn't believe the cassette needs to be recorded, it'll act in play mode. In play mode any HTTP request that matches a request in the cassette file will be intercepted, and its response will be crafted by the data on the cassette. Any HTTP request that doesn't match a request in the cassette file will trigger an error and a test failure. You can also make VCR fail if a request in the cassette file isn't matched during the test; in this case VCR is behaving like a mock expectation, including the option allow_unused_http_interactions: false to the spec metadata. If multiple requests in the cassette file match, VCR will use them one at a time in sequence as long as there are further requests to the same URL during the test.

Alternatively, you can use the method call VCR.use_cassette inside RSpec specs just as you would in Minitest, which I'll explain next.

VCR and Minitest

To make VCR work in our Minitest environment, we need to add some configuration to the test_helper.rb file:

```
external/01/gatherer/test/test_helper.rb
VCR.configure do |c|
  c.cassette_library_dir = 'test/vcr'
  c.hook_into :webmock
end
```

To use a cassette in Minitest, we surround some code with the method VCR.use_cassette, which takes a string argument and a block. The argument is the name of the cassette file, so it needs to be unique, and the block is the body of the test that is being recorded by that cassette. We can pass options to the use_cassette method—we'll get to those in a bit.

```
external/01/gatherer/test/integration/shows_twitter_avatar_test.rb
require "test_helper"

class TaskShowsTwitterAvatar < Capybara::Rails::TestCase

  include Warden::Test::Helpers

  setup do
    projects(:bluebook).roles.create(user: users(:user))
    users(:user).update_attributes(twitter_handle: "noelrap")
    tasks(:one).update_attributes(user_id: users(:user).id,
        completed_at: 1.hour.ago)
    login_as users(:user)
  end

  test "I see a gravatar" do
    VCR.use_cassette("loading_twitter") do
      visit project_path(projects(:bluebook))
      url = "http://pbs.twimg.com/profile_images/40008602/head_shot_bigger.jpg"
      within("#task_1") do
        assert_selector(".completed", text: users(:user).email)
        assert_selector("img[src='#{url}']")
      end
    end
  end
end
```

Inside the block, VCR behaves exactly as it would in an RSpec spec that was
defined with the :vcr metadata.

VCR and Cucumber

To use VCR with Cucumber, first place the same configuration code in a file
somewhere in the Cucumber features/support directory. Once that's done, you
have two options: you can put VCR.use_cassette calls inside step definitions or
you can use Cucumber tags.

To use tags, you need to define them by writing additional configuration code,
presumably in the same file where you put the basic configuration. The tag
configuration will look like this:

```
VCR.cucumber_tags do |t|
  t.tag '@vcr', use_scenario_name: true
  t.tags '@twitter', '@facebook'
end
```

Any options you would pass to use_cassette can be passed as key/value pairs
after the tag name. If you want to define multiple tags at once, you can use
the tags method.

The tags can then be used like normal Cucumber tags:

```
@vcr
Scenario: Get the user's Twitter avatar
  Given a logged-in user
  When that user has completed a task
  And I view the project page
  Then I should see the user's Twitter avatar
```

When a VCR-related tag is used for a Cucumber scenario, VCR is activated for the duration of the scenario. The resulting cassette file is named after the tag unless the use_scenario_name: option is true, in which case VCR generates a name based on the feature and scenario names, similar to how it generates a name when using RSpec metadata.

Client Unit Tests

VCR is set up; now let's make the Twitter integration work. As it stands, the test fails because the user data is not in the view at all. The test suggests that the user email and the Twitter avatar should be in the view, so let's add them to the view file.

We have a design decision to make about how our application should interact with Twitter. We have many options, ranging from calling the gem and service directly from the view to placing the interaction within the User class.

My design here tends toward more objects and structure on the grounds that we're using this avatar to stand in for a more complex third-party integration. The set of classes might feel like overkill, but I want to demonstrate what this is like with all the moving parts.

With that throat-clearing out of the way, let's write some tests. It seems like getting the Twitter avatar-image URL is a User responsibility.

The relevant view code looks like this in app/views/projects/show.html.erb:

```
<td class="completed">
  <% if task.complete? %>
    <%= task.user.email %>
    <%= task.completed_at.to_s %>
    <img src="<%= task.user.avatar_url %>" />
  <% end %>
</td>
```

If I were being stricter, I'd argue that the avatar_url is only a view-level responsibility—which would imply a decorator, the same way we have one already in the codebase for the ProjectsController#index action. We'll hold that thought for a possible refactoring.

The test now fails because user.avatar_url doesn't exist. Let's write tests for it. These are client unit tests, which assume the existence of an adapter. In this testing plan, the adapter is frequently stubbed in the client unit test. We can use this test as a place to design the adapter's interface with the rest of the application. In this case, the logic from the user object's perspective is simple. We pass the user's email to the adapter and expect to call a method on the adapter that returns the avatar URL.

The test looks like this:

```
external/01/gatherer/spec/models/user_spec.rb
describe "avatars" do
  let(:user) { User.new(email: "test@example.com") }
  let(:fake_adapter) { instance_double(AvatarAdapter) }

  it "can get a twitter avatar URL" do
    allow(fake_adapter).to receive(:image_url).and_return("fake_url")
    allow(AvatarAdapter).to receive(:new).with(user).and_return(fake_adapter)
    user.avatar_url
    expect(fake_adapter).to have_received(:image_url)
    expect(AvatarAdapter).to have_received(:new)
  end
end
```

This test does not depend in any way on the actual HTTP request; instead it defines the API of the adapter. The test creates a User instance, and then creates a fake adapter using RSpec's instance_double method to ensure that any method we stub actually exists in the AvatarAdapter class. Then we use spies to set the expectation that the avatar will receive the image_url method.

> **Prescription 33** Use the adapter to test client behavior without being dependent on the server API.

The "when" part of this test is the last line: the call to the user.avatar_url method. At this point we've set up the following expectations for what happens next.

- The AvatarAdapter class will be sent the new method with the user instance as an argument.
- The resulting instance of AvatarAdapter will be sent the image_url method.

To make this test pass, we need a method in User:

```
external/01/gatherer/app/models/user.rb
def avatar_url
  adapter = AvatarAdapter.new(self)
  adapter.image_url
end
```

And we need a new AvatarAdapter class:

```
external/01/gatherer/app/models/avatar_adapter.rb
class AvatarAdapter
  def initialize(user)
  end
  def image_url
  end
end
```

Right now the AvatarAdapter class is just a skeleton, which is all we needed to make the unit tests pass.

Now it's time to get that adapter done.

Why an Adapter?

Using an adapter class to mediate interaction with the external service is a good idea even when, like Twitter, the external service already has a Ruby gem. The adapter encapsulates logic that is specific to the interaction between your application and the service.

An adapter is useful if your code has any or all of the following qualities:

- The external service will be accessed from multiple points in your code.
- The interaction with the external service has logic of its own, such as authentication or type changing or common sets of options.
- There's a mismatch between the language or metaphor of the API and the domain terms and structures of your code.

Our Twitter example doesn't have the first one, at least not yet. We do have the second feature: the adapter needs to manage a Twitter client object that nothing else in the application needs to care about or be aware of. It also manages an argument to the Twitter API: the :bigger argument, which specifies the size of the image we want to download.

Whether we have a mismatch between the API and our code is a matter of interpretation, but I think we do. At the very least, the Twitter client exposes a lot of data that our application doesn't care about, so limiting access to the full set of Twitter data seems like a good idea.

My experience with adapters like the one we've written is that they tend to attract functionality as you use them, with the side effect that it's much easier for a full range of complexity to be available at each use. For example, if we allow the adapter to take an argument to image_url to represent the size, then that ability automatically is available whenever the adapter is used. This ability is especially valuable for security and error handling, which are easy to leave off when you're creating each connection separately.

Adapter Tests

The adapter tests work between the adapter and the server, using VCR as a medium:

```
external/02/gatherer/spec/models/avatar_adapter_spec.rb
require 'rails_helper'

describe AvatarAdapter do
  it "accurately receives image url", :vcr do
    user = double(twitter_handle: "noelrap")
    adapter = AvatarAdapter.new(user)
    url = "http://pbs.twimg.com/profile_images/40008602/head_shot_bigger.jpg"
    expect(adapter.image_url).to eq(url)
  end
end
```

This test has no dependency on the client, which we show by passing in a double rather than an actual User instance. Using a VCR cassette, we create a new adapter and assert that the adapter provides the expected URL when queried. The test also doesn't have a particular dependency on the Twitter gem, beyond the specific URL value being from Twitter's asset storage. This is a test of the adapter's behavior, not of the implementation.

The passing code requires a bit of Twitter connection setup:

```
external/02/gatherer/app/models/avatar_adapter.rb
class AvatarAdapter
  attr_accessor :user, :client

  def initialize(user)
    @user = user
  end

  def client
    @client ||= Twitter::REST::Client.new(
        consumer_key: Rails.application.secrets.twitter_api,
        consumer_secret: Rails.application.secrets.twitter_secret)
  end

  def image_url
    client.user(user.twitter_handle).profile_image_uri(:bigger).to_s
  end
end
```

The Twitter gem requires a client to be created using the API keys we put in the secrets.yml file. Our adapter lazily creates that client as needed.

Once the client is created, it calls the user method on the client with the Twitter handle and then grabs the profile_image_uri property. The gem uses the :bigger argument to determine the size of the resulting image, and we need to call to_s, because the actual property is an internal class of the Twitter gem and all we want is the URL. All of these are features of the interaction with the Twitter API that the rest of our application doesn't need to care about because the adapter is managing that information.

At this point, our adapter test passes. Even better, all the parts of the interaction have now been written and connected, so our integration test passes as well.

If we go to the spec/vcr directory, we now see two cassette files, one for each test. They are both about 150 lines long, so I'm not putting them in the book. The first few lines look like this:

```
---
http_interactions:
- request:
    method: post
    uri: <big long URI to twitter>
    body:
      encoding: UTF-8
      string: grant_type=client_credentials
    headers:
      Accept:
      - "*/*"
      User-Agent:
      - Twitter Ruby Gem 5.11.0
      Content-Type:
      - application/x-www-form-urlencoded; charset=UTF-8
      Accept-Encoding:
      - gzip;q=1.0,deflate;q=0.6,identity;q=0.3
  response:
    status:
      code: 200
      message: OK
```

Each cassette file chronicles two HTTP requests to the Twitter API: one for authentication of our API key and one to get the user data. If you delete the files and try again, you'll hopefully notice that the first test run is slow because the HTTP requests are being made. Once the VCR cassette is in place, the test speeds up. (On my machine, the suite went from 2.2 to 0.8 seconds.)

Testing for Error Cases

Our application design allows us multiple ways to simulate errors for testing purposes:

- We can make an API call to the actual service that results in an error and capture the result using VCR. We can use this approach in an integration or adapter test.
- We can stub a method that's internal to the adapter. For example, we can stub the client method to return a double that simulates an API error. We'd use this in an adapter test.
- We can stub the adapter to return an unexpected value in a client test.

Which approach you choose depends on the details of the library you're working with. Often, stubbing the external service makes sense for the same reason that stubbing ActiveRecord methods does—crafting a call that will reliably return an error is not always possible. If you can, try to stub methods of your adapter rather than methods of the third-party gem; it's generally a good idea to stub only code you control.

Keeping tests consistent with the location of the logic being tested is still a good policy. Use adapter tests to ensure that the adapter behaves gracefully when it gets weird responses from the server. (Normally, server or gem exceptions shouldn't leak out of the adapter.) Use unit tests to make sure that the clients are able to handle whatever the adapter does in response to unexpected input.

> **Prescription 34** Test the error code based on which object in the system needs to respond to the error.

Smoke Tests and VCR Options

So far we've used VCR to record an interaction once and preserve it for all time. VCR provides other options. These options are passed as key/value arguments to VCR.use_cassette(re_record_interval: 7.days) or, if you're using RSpec metadata, as the value part of the metadata, as in vcr: {re_record_interval: 7.days}.

That re_record_interval that we just used as an example allows you to use the same VCR test as both an integration and a smoke test. The re_record_interval is an amount of time. If the requests on the associated cassette are older than the interval, then VCR will attempt to reconnect to the HTTP server and re-record the cassette. If the server is unavailable, VCR will just use the existing cassette.

This allows you to protect your application against API changes in the server. If the server API changes, eventually your VCR cassette will pick up the change and your test will fail. This can be a useful feature. It can also be a little on the opaque side when a test randomly fails, but it's better in testing than production.

VCR lets you set different record modes with the :record option. The default, which we've been using so far, is :once, which records new interactions if they don't exist but raises an error for new interactions if the cassette already exists.

Here are all the VCR recording options:

Option	Description
:all	Always connect to HTTP and re-record. Useful for forcing cassette updates.
:new_episodes	Replays a request that is already on the cassette. New requests are made via HTTP and added to the cassette.
:none	Only replay existing cassettes; never make an actual request.
:once	Replay existing cassettes; record new requests if the cassette doesn't exist. Raise an error on new requests if it does.

If you want to specify the recording options for all cassettes at once, you can do so in the configuration with the default_cassette_options method:

```
VCR.configure do |c|
  # existing configuration
  c.default_cassette_options = { record: :all }
end
```

By occasionally adding the previous line to the configuration for one test run, you get one run of smoke tests as all the VCR cassettes go back to their servers for data.

Let's look at a couple of other important configuration options.

Sometimes you want VCR to not deal with specific requests. The c.ignore_localhost = true property handles one common case, where you don't want VCR to touch requests back to the actual application being tested, such as Ajax requests or callbacks for authentication information. The method c.ignore_hosts takes an optional list of hostnames to ignore, and the method ignore_request {|req| CODE} ignores any request for which the associated block returns true.

By default, VCR looks for an exact match on the URI being requested when attempting to match a cassette request to a new HTTP request from the code, including query strings and HTTP methods. However, some services never have the exact same URI twice. For example, the Amazon API calls contain a timestamp. In other cases, additional headers may be relevant to how the request is processed. VCR provides the match_requests_on configuration option to manage the matching between cassette and request.

You use match_requests_on as an option to a VCR call or as a default. The argument is an array of elements that you want to use in the match. Valid values are :method, :uri, :host, :path, :query, :body, :headers, and :body_as_json. You can also use the method uri_without_params as a substitute for uri where there are parameters in the query string that are not important for the match.

For example, the following configuration was used to match all the dynamic elements in an application that used the Amazon API:

```
VCR.configure do |c|
  c.cassette_library_dir = 'test/vcr'
  c.hook_into :webmock
  c.ignore_localhost = true
  c.default_cassette_options = {
    :match_requests_on => [:method,
      VCR.request_matchers.uri_without_params(
        "Timestamp", "Signature", "AWSAccessKeyId", "AssociateTag")]
  }
end
```

The match_requests_on option is used to match on the combination of HTTP method and URI but with several parameters to the URI ignored.

The filter_sensitive_data option lets you keep passwords and the like from appearing in your VCR cassette. It allows you to use a block to grab the sensitive text from the HTTP response and replace it with a custom dummy string.

VCR has other options for more elaborate use. You can see the full list in the documentation at https://relishapp.com/vcr/vcr/v/2-9-2/docs.

The World Is a Service

Once you get used to the idea of having adapters mediate access between your application and external services, it's not that far a leap to have adapters internally to mediate between different parts of your application. This approach is sometimes called *hexagonal architecture*, and there are many, many resources online describing hexagonal architecture as it applies to Rails (such as http://victorsavkin.com/post/42542190528/hexagonal-architecture-for-rails-developers). At the same time you can find many, many resources online saying that hexagonal architecture is an awful idea. (David Heinemeier Hansson is a particularly vocal critic.)

We've taken baby steps in this direction by creating action objects such as CreatesProject, which are somewhat like adapters between the controller and model. Many web frameworks use adapters between model objects and the database. Rails does not, but the pattern is not uncommon.

In the next chapter, as we test JavaScript, we'll also explore the interaction between our application and the browser DOM as another possible site for a service-and-adapter relationship.

## CHAPTER 13

Testing JavaScript

Testing JavaScript is a big subject. JavaScript's development tools, which for years lagged behind the tools for languages like Ruby and Python, have been improving by leaps and bounds. Not only do you have really powerful client-side frameworks like Angular and Ember; you also have really good debugging tools, especially when running Chrome. Multiple testing frameworks are building ecosystems and support. There are multiple mock libraries and pure assertion matcher libraries. Entire books could be and have been written on the topic.

We've got one chapter. So we need to focus.

We'll deal with two different JavaScript needs. We'll talk about unit-testing JavaScript using the Jasmine test library. And we're going to talk about acceptance-testing an interaction that contains JavaScript by running Capybara or Cucumber through a headless browser tool that will run JavaScript.

More specifically, we'll assume a Rails application that is mostly a server-side application, but with some interactions managed by JavaScript. While some of the techniques described here are also applicable to a single-page app using a framework like Angular or Ember, testing in those frameworks involves specialized framework setup and knowledge that is outside our scope here.

I'm assuming a few things about you for this chapter. Specifically, I'm assuming that you know enough JavaScript and jQuery to be dangerous. If you need a refresher, I humbly recommend my own *Master Space and Time with JavaScript.*[1] The free book will cover most of what you need.

---

1. http://www.noelrappin.com/mstwjs

Unit-Testing JavaScript

We are lucky enough to already have an interaction in our application that can be converted to JavaScript without much trouble and without being wildly implausible. We'll go back to the project show page and convert those up and down buttons to JavaScript-enabled buttons that respond to clicks by rearranging the two rows in question and sending an Ajax notification of the change back to the server.

Setting Up Jasmine

We'll be using Jasmine 2.0 as our primary JavaScript testing engine. Complete Jasmine documentation is at http://jasmine.github.io/2.0/introduction.html, and will cover any corners of the framework that we don't get to here.

I like Jasmine because of its RSpec-like syntax, and it has historically been relatively easy to set up with Rails. That said, several of the test runners that integrate with Jasmine and Rails have not upgraded to Jasmine 2.0 yet. We'll be using the jasmine-rails gem from Justin Searls, which is a name you'll see again before this chapter is out.

One of the challenges of JavaScript testing has been just getting the testing tools set up, especially within a Rails environment. Our setup starts with installing the jasmine-rails gem in the :test, :development group of the Gemfile:

```
gem 'jasmine-rails'
```

And then there's an installer script:

```
$ rails generate jasmine_rails:install
```

The generator creates a settings file in spec/javascripts/support/jasmine.yml. The settings have a lot to do with where Jasmine looks for files. By and large, it looks for files in the same place as your Rails asset pipeline does, and we won't mess with that file much.

Jasmine-rails also adds a line to the routes.rb file:

```
mount JasmineRails::Engine => '/specs' if defined?(JasmineRails)
```

This line makes the /specs route in your Rails application run your Jasmine specs in the browser.

Let's kick the tires and write a simple Jasmine test. Place this file in the spec/javascripts directory:

javascript/01/gatherer/spec/javascripts/basic_spec.js

```
describe('This is how jasmine works', function() {
  it("can do basic math", function() {
    expect(1 + 1).toEqual(2);
  });

  it("also knows when math is wrong", function() {
    expect(1 + 1).not.toEqual(3);
  });
});
```

Jasmine's syntax is heavily inspired by RSpec, with JavaScript function objects taking the place of Ruby blocks. Like RSpec test suites, Jasmine test suites start with describe. In Jasmine, describe is a method that takes two arguments: a string and a function. The function defines the behavior of an entire test suite.

Inside the describe function argument, individual specs are defined by calls to the function it, which also takes a string description argument and a function argument. The function argument to it is the actual spec.

Inside the spec individual expectations are denoted with the expect method. That method takes an argument, which should be the actual value from the test. The return value of expect is an object that Jasmine calls an *expectation*. The expectation can then be called with one of several matchers, such as toEqual. The matchers typically take an argument, which is the predetermined expected value. Hence expect(1 + 1).toEqual(2).

We can run our example by starting the Rails application with rails server and then hitting the URL localhost:3000/specs, which jasmine-rails intercepts before starting a Jasmine run. The browser output looks like this:

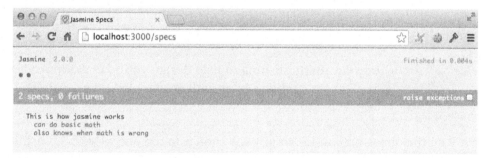

We can also run our Jasmine specs from the command line. For this to work, you need PhantomJS installed on your development machine; see http://phantomjs.org/download.html for complete download instructions. If you're on a Mac and have Homebrew installed, then you can just install PhantomJS with this:

```
$ brew update && brew install phantomjs
```

The command-line invocation looks like this:

```
$ RAILS_ENV=test bundle exec rake spec:javascript
Running [A LONG SET OF FILES]
Starting...

Finished
----------------
2 specs, 0 failures in 0.004s.

ConsoleReporter finished
```

When we ran the Jasmine suite, each it block is executed in turn. In the first block expect(1 + 1) results in an expectation object with an actual value of 2. The matcher toEqual is called with an expected value of 2, and the matcher passes. In the second spec the same calls happen, except that a call to not is chained in. The not tells the expectation to reverse the result of any matcher that is called. The 3 passed to the matcher does not equal 2, so the matcher would fail, but the not call reverses the failure so the test as a whole passes.

Whether you run the command-line or browser version of Jasmine is a matter of preference. The command line is easier to use with a continuous integration system or a local tool like Guard. The browser tool allows you access to the browser debugger and inspect tools, which can be very helpful.

Our Real Jasmine Project

One common problem in testing JavaScript is splitting the functionality and code into testable units. If you're not working within the structure of a client framework, and are instead doing something more like the traditional bowl of jQuery spaghetti, you'll need to adjust your coding to allow for testable units.

> **Prescription 35** Use JavaScript testing to help design your JavaScript code to allow for modular items with few tangled interdependencies.

We'll do this using an outside-in process similar to the one we've been using server-side, just with different boundaries. For JavaScript purposes we'll be using integration tests to be black-box tests of the client interaction. In other words, the integration tests will assume a certain set of DOM structures, simulate user clicks, and verify the result against the DOM. Unit tests will then specify the behavior of specific parts of the JavaScript code.

Integration Tests, Client Side–Style

Let's follow the process and think about what this integration test needs:

- *Given:* A DOM structure that parallels the structure that appears on our project show page when we display the list of tests. Specifically, this is a table with one row for each task. We'll need to add a couple of markers in the view for the JavaScript code to attach to.

- *When:* The user clicks up on a task. Or down.

- *Then:* The DOM elements are in a different order.

Here's a Jasmine test that does just that:

```
javascript/02/gatherer/spec/javascripts/task_move_spec.js
describe("with a list of tasks", function() {

  beforeEach(function() {
    table = affix("table");
    table.affix("tr.task#task_1 a.up");
    table.affix("tr.task#task_2 a.up+a.down");
    table.affix("tr.task#task_3 a.up");
  });

  it("correctly processes an up click", function() {
    $("#task_2 .up").click();
    expect($.map($("tr"), function(item) { return $(item).attr("id") }))
        .toEqual(["task_2", "task_1", "task_3"]);
  });

});
```

We need one add-on library to make this test work. In the beforeEach method, we need to create our DOM elements. You'll notice a method called affix, which comes from a very helpful library called *jasmine-fixture*, by Justin Searls.[2]

The jasmine-fixture library solves the problem of succinctly creating DOM elements inside our Jasmine browser and then automatically cleaning them up when each test is over. The library defines the affix method, which takes one argument: a jQuery selector. It then creates the exact sequence of DOM elements that would match that selector, and returns the first element of that set as a jQuery object. If the affix method is called on its own, it injects the resulting DOM elements into the Jasmine browser at the end of the body. If the affix method is called on a jQuery object, the created DOM elements are inserted inside the receiving object.

---

2. https://github.com/searls/jasmine-fixture

Our test starts with table = affix("table");, which creates the DOM element <table></table> and puts it in the DOM. The three subsequent lines each create individual rows using slightly more complex jQuery selectors. The next line has the selector tr.task#task_1 a.up, which creates the following HTML, more or less:

```
<tr class="task", id="task_1>
  <a class="up"/>
</tr>
```

At the end we've set up three rows, all of which have the DOM class task and individual DOM IDs. Each row has an up link and/or a down link, depending on its placement in the table, also denoted by a DOM class.

Not all of those DOM class markers are in our Rails view output, which we'll need to take care of at some point.

We have a minimal skeleton of the DOM created by the project page, but one that contains all the elements we need to determine if the JavaScript code changes the order of the elements.

> **Prescription 36** Create only as many DOM elements or data as needed for the test to run.

In the test itself, we simulate a click on the middle element's up button, first by identifying it as #task_2 .up or the element with a DOM class of up (which is contained by an element with a DOM ID of task_2). Then we call click to simulate the actual click, and we gather the DOM IDs of the table rows with $.map($("tr"), function(item) { return $(item).attr("id") }), and compare it against our expectation that moving the middle element up puts it on top.

Unit Tests, Jasmine-Style

Now it's time to write some unit-level tests. This is an opportunity to think about how we want to structure this code. As I see it, the very small functional bits of the "move up" feature are as follows:

- Attaching all the "up" links to a click handler

- Identifying the clicked element's row and its predecessor

- Swapping the two elements—which might be easier to do if we think of it as removing the clicked element and reinserting it before its predecessor

For now we'll keep the server-side code relatively unchanged. The project show page will still send out HTML, and we're going to just do DOM manipulation on the client. Later we may change the interaction so that the DOM sends out just JSON data and the view and all semantic manipulation is done in the client.

Here's a set of unit tests that cover this behavior. As in other test suites, I wrote the tests one at a time but I'm showing you the suite all at once. I think you can see the progression as the unit tests build on each other:

```
javascript/02/gatherer/spec/javascripts/task_move_unit_spec.js
describe("with a list of tasks", function() {

  beforeEach(function() {
    table = affix("table");
    table.affix("tr.task#task_1 a.up");
    table.affix("tr.task#task_2 a.up+a.down");
    table.affix("tr.task#task_3 a.up");
  });

  it("identifies row from target", function() {
    expect(Project.taskFromAnchor($("#task_2 .up"))).toHaveId("task_2")
  });

  it("identifies predecessor if it exists", function() {
    expect(Project.previousTask($("#task_2"))).toHaveId("task_1");
  });

  it("returns null as a predecessor if there is none", function() {
    expect(Project.previousTask($("#task_1"))).toBeNull();
  });

  it("can swap two rows", function() {
    Project.swapRows($("#task_1"), $("#task_2"));
    expect($.map($("tr"), function(item) { return $(item).attr("id") }))
        .toEqual(["task_2", "task_1", "task_3"]);
  });

  it("can handle up click", function() {
    Project.upClickOn($("#task_2 .up"));
    expect($.map($("tr"), function(item) { return $(item).attr("id") }))
        .toEqual(["task_2", "task_1", "task_3"]);
  });

});
```

These tests use the toHaveId matcher, which is defined by the jasmine-jquery library.[3] I downloaded the main file and placed it in the spec/javascripts/helpers directory.

---

3.   https://github.com/velesin/jasmine-jquery

Since we're not storing any client-side data besides the DOM, the setup for the unit tests is exactly the same DOM fixture that the integration test was using. The difference is that the integration test is simulating a user click, whereas these tests are directly calling the component functions that make up that behavior. If we were storing client-side behavior and creating more data-heavy JavaScript classes, I would unit-test those classes with just the data they need, which ideally would not require the creation of the entire DOM structure.

We've structured the code so that all the functions are inside a global Project object, which is a very quick and dirty way to namespace the code, since we don't need separate instances. (We're also kind of assuming that there's only one project table on the page.)

The unit tests here go step by step. First we take in the jQuery object for the actual event target anchor and convert that into the jQuery object for the entire task row. Then we search for the row previous to that row, checking that code handles the case where there is no previous row.

Once we can get the previous row, we test to see that the code can swap two rows. The passing condition here is exactly the same that we used for the integration test. We add one more test for the function that is called by the click handler.

And here's the passing code:

```
javascript/02/gatherer/app/assets/javascripts/projects.js
var Project = {

  taskFromAnchor: function(anchor_element) {
    return anchor_element.parents("tr");
  },

  previousTask: function(task_row) {
    result = task_row.prev();
    if(result.length > 0) {
      return result;
    } else {
      return null;
    }
  },

  swapRows: function(first_row, second_row) {
    second_row.detach();
    second_row.insertBefore(first_row);
  },
```

```
upClickOn: function(anchor_element) {
  row = Project.taskFromAnchor(anchor_element);
  previousRow = Project.previousTask(row);
  if(previousRow == null) { return };
  Project.swapRows(previousRow, row);
}

}

$(function() {
  $(document).on("click", ".up", function(event) {
    event.preventDefault();
    Project.upClickOn($(this));
  });
})
```

All our functions are implemented inside that Project object, plus we have a jQuery "document ready" function at the end of the file; it associates the click-handler function to the DOM elements with class .up.

Most of these functions are slight wrappers around the jQuery API, with names that relate them directly to our application logic rather than jQuery's more generic logic. One great feature about having this functionality captured in unit tests is that it's actually much faster to work through jQuery's API to figure out, say, a way to swap rows when you can automate the setup, than it is when you're manually testing in a browser.

Two notes about the jQuery click handler at the end of the file: We're defining the click handler as a jQuery dynamic handler, using the syntax $(document).on("click", ".up", ...). In jQuery terms this means that when a click happens, the document object does a new lookup for any elements that match the .up selector to determine if the click handler applies. This is in contrast to the static lookup that we would have gotten with the syntax $(".up").on("click", ...), which would have bound the click handler only to the .up elements that existed at the time the file was loaded.

The dynamic behavior is useful in general because it makes the click handler robust against elements being added to the page. Specifically in our testing context, the test fixtures added in the beforeEach function of the test are added *after* the project.js file is loaded—meaning the dynamic behavior ensures that the click handlers will attach to those affixed elements. Without the dynamic behavior added, the .up elements in the test will not be attached to the click handler; nothing will happen when you simulate a click, and you'll have a very hard time trying to figure out why.

Also, the tests define an API from the click handler where the upClickOn method expects a jQuery object and not a raw DOM element. The click handler needs to play along by wrapping the event target in the jQuery function before passing it along, as in $(this).

Making a "down" click work is very similar to making "up" work, so I'm not going to walk through the whole process again. If you want to see the working code for "down," check out the downloadable code at code/javascript/04/.

Jasmine Matchers

So far we've only seen toEqual and toBeNull as core Jasmine matchers, but Jasmine defines quite a few. The built-in ones are as follows:

Matcher	Passes if
toBe(actual)	expected === actual (JavaScript triple equal).
toBeCloseTo(actual, precision)	The floating point value of actual is within precision amount of the expected value.
toBeGreaterThan(actual)	expected > actual.
toBeFalsy()	The expected value is a JavaScript falsy value.
toBeLessThan(actual)	expected < actual.
toBeNull()	The expected value is null.
toBeTruthy()	The expected value is a JavaScript truthy value.
toBeUndefined()	The expected value is undefined; no actual argument needed.
toContain(actual)	expected is an array that contains the actual value.
toEqual(actual)	expected and actual are equal values. Exactly what that means depends on their type.
toMatch(actual)	expected is a string that matches the actual regular expression.
toThrow()	expected is a function that throws an exception when called.

To elaborate slightly, toEqual is based on a (no kidding) 120-line method in Jasmine that uses slightly different criteria for each built-in type and does a deep property comparison of JavaScript objects. Long story short, it tends to do what you'd expect.

You can also create your own matchers in Jasmine; the jasmine-jquery library creates quite a few.

Let's say we wanted to change that somewhat awkward expectation in our tests that takes a jQuery object and compares it against a list of DOM IDs. To turn that into a custom matcher in Jasmine, we need to define a custom matcher object to mix into our Jasmine tests.

If you put the matcher definition in a file in the javascripts/helpers directory, then it will be available to all of your Jasmine test files:

```
javascript/04/gatherer/spec/javascripts/helpers/custom_matchers.js
customMatchers = {
  toMatchDomIds: function(util, customEqualityTesters) {
    return {
      compare: function(actual, expected) {
        var result = {};
        actualIds = $.map($("tr"), function(item) { return $(item).attr("id") });
        result.pass = util.equals(actualIds, expected, customEqualityTesters);
        if (result.pass) {
          result.message = "Expected " + actual + " not to have DOM Ids" +
              expected + ". Instead it had " + actualIds
        } else {
          result.message = "Expected " + actual + " to have DOM Ids " +
              expected + ". Instead it had " + actualIds
        }
        return result;
      }
    }
  }
}
```

There are a couple of nested object layers in the custom matcher definition, so let's untangle them.

The customMatchers group object is a JavaScript object. Each custom matcher to be defined is a property of that object. In this case we've defined one custom matcher, toMatchDomIds.

Each individual custom matcher is a JavaScript function, which takes two arguments, util and customEqualityTesters, both of which are managed internally by Jasmine and which we don't need to worry about too much.

The custom matcher function is expected to return an object with a specific property: compare. The compare property is a function. In fact, it's the function invoked by Jasmine when the matcher is used. The compare function takes two arguments: actual and expected. It returns a result object, which also has a few expected properties. The most important property is pass, which should be true if the matcher passes. Optionally, you can include a message property, which Jasmine uses to define the message displayed when the matcher fails.

Our toMatchDomIds matcher conforms to this structure. Inside the compare function, we've relocated the $.map call that we used to convert the jQuery object to a list of DOM IDs. We then compare the actual IDs to the expected array using Jasmine's util.equals method. The util.equals method is the 120-line equality monster I alluded to earlier. Using it here ensures that our matcher will have the same array-equality semantics that it did when we were using toBeEqual. The result.pass property is set to the result of that comparison.

We set the message in one of two ways, depending on whether result.pass is true or false. This might seem a little weird. Why would we need a failure message if result.pass is true? We need a failure message in the "passing" case because of the way Jasmine handles the not case.

If our matcher is chained using not, then Jasmine will consider the test a failure if the matcher passes. Having two failure messages allows for this eventuality. In other words, our matcher helpfully generates a message even if the matcher passes; this is for Jasmine's use in the case where the matcher is expected to fail. (If we really wanted the negative behavior to be different, we could define a negativeCompare property as a peer to compare. If it's there, it'll get called when the matcher is chained with not.)

To use the matcher we need to mix it in to Jasmine, which is often done in the beforeEach method. Here's what our integration test looks like with the matcher included:

```
javascript/04/gatherer/spec/javascripts/task_move_spec.js
describe("with a list of tasks", function() {

  beforeEach(function() {
    jasmine.addMatchers(customMatchers);
    table = affix("table");
    table.affix("tr.task#task_1 a.up");
    table.affix("tr.task#task_2 a.up+a.down");
    table.affix("tr.task#task_3 a.up");
  });

  it("correctly processes an up click", function() {
    $("#task_2 .up").click();
    expect($("tr")).toMatchDomIds(["task_2", "task_1", "task_3"]);
  });

  it("correctly processes a down click", function() {
    $("#task_2 .down").click();
    expect($("tr")).toMatchDomIds(["task_1", "task_3", "task_2"]);
  });

});
```

We've added one line to the beforeEach function—jasmine.addMatchers(customMatchers);—which adds the customMatchers object into Jasmine. Inside our test, on the last line, we use the matcher just like any other matcher. The actual value is wrapped in an expect clause, and the expected value is passed to the matcher. Internally, Jasmine grabs both the expected and actual values and passes them along to the matcher's compare method. And everything still passes.

Jasmine Mocks and Spies

Jasmine has its own test-double functionality, which is heavily spy-based, meaning that in Jasmine you declare that you're interested in a particular method, and then you make testable expectations about the application's behavior in calling or not calling that method.

The main spy method in Jasmine is spyOn, which takes two arguments: an object and the string name of a property of that object, typically a property whose value is a function. Jasmine replaces that property with a spy object. Unless you specify otherwise, calls to that property are then blocked and null is returned.

> **Prescription 37** Jasmine spies replace a function object with a spy object that keeps track of how often the function is called.

Jasmine's spy objects keep track of how many times they have been called and with what arguments. You can then specify testable expectations on those methods using the Jasmine matchers toHaveBeenCalled and toHaveBeenCalledWith.

For example, in our test suite as it currently stands, all the later methods depend on the earlier methods. In particular, the upClickOn method depends on all the other methods working. If we wanted to isolate that method from some or all of the other methods, we could do that with a Jasmine spy:

```
javascript/04/gatherer/spec/javascripts/task_move_unit_spec.js
it("can handle up click with spy", function() {
  spyOn(Project, 'taskFromAnchor').and.returnValue($("#task_2"))
  Project.upClickOn($("#task_2 .up"));
  expect($("tr")).toMatchDomIds(["task_2", "task_1", "task_3"]);
  expect(Project.taskFromAnchor).toHaveBeenCalled();
});
```

On the first line of the spec, we declare a Jasmine spy on the taskFromAnchor property of the Project object. We chain the and.returnValue methods to specify that the spy should return a particular value (in this case, the same value it would have returned anyway, so this may not be the best practical example of mocks). In the last line we've added the expectation that the spy is called.

While the spy is declared using a string property name spyOn(Project, 'taskFromAnchor'), the expectation is set using the property value itself: expect(Project.taskFromAnchor). This is a common Jasmine spy gotcha—if you're used to more standard Minitest and RSpec behavior, you may expect the spyOn method to define a failable expectation by itself.

In addition to and.returnValue, there are a few other methods you can chain onto a Jasmine spy to define the behavior of the spy when called:

Specifier	Behavior
and.callFake(func)	Calls the given function argument rather than the original function
and.callThrough()	Calls the original function as if there were no spy, but now counts whether the function has been called
and.returnValue(value)	Returns the given value without calling the original function
and.throwError(value)	Throws an error with the given value

The toHaveBeenCalled() matcher looks at the calls property of the spy object. The calls object maintains a lot of tracking information about the spy, including calls.count() (which returns the number of times the spy has been called) and calls.argsFor(index) (which returns the argument list for a given call to the spy). Some other, less generally useful options are available, as well.[4]

You can use the calls property directly in your expectations:

```
expect(Project.taskFromAnchor.calls.count()).toEqual(1);
```

When to Spy in Jasmine

The basic rules of stubbing still apply to JavaScript client testing:

- Stub expensive or dangerous calls. We'll cover Ajax testing and faking the server in the next section.

- Stub to avoid having to do complex or fragile setup. This often includes stubbing DOM structures that your front-end code expects.

---

4. http://jasmine.github.io/2.0/introduction.html

- Stub what you own—which is to say that your expensive, dangerous, complex, or fragile behaviors should be wrapped in an object or function that allows the behavior to be easily stubbed.

One side effect of all this mocking, stubbing, and structure is that it will tend to separate the parts of your JavaScript that directly interact with the DOM from the rest of your code. This is a good thing.

Among the positive benefits of separating the DOM is that DOM interactions are wrapped in methods with meaningful names. In our code sample, we have taskFromAnchor, which is just a wrapper around a jQuery parents call, but which gives the call meaning in our context. Also, it makes the JavaScript code more robust against changes to the DOM structure and allows the code to more easily adapt to being used again.

 Prescription 38 Treating the DOM as an external service that you relate to via an adapter can lead to very maintainable JavaScript code.

Testing Ajax Calls

Our JavaScript up/down functionality has one more piece: we need to notify the server that the up or down has taken place. That involves making an Ajax call to the server. We probably want to notify the user of success or failure (or at least of failure).

Typically we stub Ajax calls to the server because they're slow and because they might otherwise require server-side setup to return useful data. We could use plain Jasmine spies for this, or Jasmine's Ajax framework. Instead I'm going to bring in a different tool that has a slightly higher-level API for managing Ajax.

The tool is called Sinon.[5] It is actually a framework-independent mock-object library, but we're not going to discuss its generic library, just its fake server.

To set up, I downloaded Sinon from http://sinonjs.org and placed the file in the spec/javascripts/helper directory. Now we can add a fake server to our Jasmine test. Let's start by adding to our integration test. There are two steps. First we want to add the fake server to the setup and teardown, as shown in the following code.

---

5.   http://sinonjs.org

```
javascript/05/gatherer/spec/javascripts/task_move_spec.js
beforeEach(function() {
  jasmine.addMatchers(customMatchers);
  table = affix("table");
  table.affix("tr.task#task_1 a.up");
  table.affix("tr.task#task_2 a.up+a.down");
  table.affix("tr.task#task_3 a.up");
  this.server = sinon.fakeServer.create();
  this.server.fakeHTTPMethods = true;
});

afterEach(function() {
  this.server.restore;
});
```

In the beforeEach setup function, we set a variable server to the value sinon.fake-Server.create(). The actual name of the variable is not important; we just need to be able to hold onto the value so that we can remove the fake server when the test is over. Calling fakeServer.create() stubs the internal XMLHttpRequest to ensure that all Ajax calls go through the Sinon fake server.

We've placed this call at the top of the file so that the beforeEach applies to all our tests, not just the ones where Ajax behavior is specified. Once the Ajax behavior exists, we want all our tests to be able to run without making real Ajax calls. The setting server.fakeHTTPMethods allows the Sinon server to mimic Rails behavior by looking for a _method parameter in POST calls to fake things like PUT and PATCH HTTP methods.

At the end of the test, Jasmine calls afterEach and we tear down the server by calling restore on our this.server variable. This removes the fake XMLHttpRequest and allows the rest of the suite to make Ajax calls or set up their own fake servers.

By default the server responds to Ajax calls with a status code of 404 and an empty string. That's rarely what we want, so we can tell Sinon to respond to specific URLs with specific responses.

Here's a Jasmine describe call (nested inside the parent describe we were just looking at) that tells Sinon more details about how to respond:

```
javascript/05/gatherer/spec/javascripts/task_move_spec.js
describe("with a successful Ajax call", function() {
  beforeEach(function() {
    this.server.respondWith("PATCH", "/tasks/2/up.js",
        "{'task_id: 2, new_order: 1}");
  });
});
```

```
    it("invokes a callback on success", function() {
      spyOn(Project, "successfulUpdate").and.callThrough();
      $("#task_2 .up").click();
      this.server.respond()
      expect(Project.successfulUpdate).toHaveBeenCalled();
    });
  });
});
```

In the beforeEach of this inner describe, we call the respondWith method of the Sinon fake server. There are a few different forms to respondWith; the one we're using passes three arguments: an HTTP method, a URL, and a response string. When the fake server intercepts an HTTP method and URL that matches, it simulates the response. So, since we expect the up click to trigger a Rails update on a task with an ID of 2, we trap PATCH methods to the appropriate URL, /tasks/2/up.js.

We can make the fake server more general by leaving off the HTTP method (in which case any method matches) or by leaving off both the HTTP method and the URL (in which case any Ajax call matches). We can also make the response body more elaborate: instead of returning a string, we can return an array where the first item is the return status code (200 is the default), the second element is a JavaScript object representing any header key/value pairs we want the response to have, and the third element is the body of the response. Alternatively, the response can be a functional object, which takes the request object as an argument.

In the actual test all we really care about at this point is that the Ajax call is made successfully; our code doesn't need to do much in response at this point. So, we're going to define a callback method successfulUpdate and assert that it gets called. We're expecting the click on the #task_2 item to trigger the Ajax call, receiving the successful response defined in the fake server and triggering the successful callback.

By default the Sinon fake server holds onto a request until it is explicitly directed to respond via the server.respond method. This allows us to test any functionality that might be limited to the time slice when the Ajax call is in flight—an in-progress signifier or an in-flight status on an object. We can force an immediate response by setting server.autoRespond = true, which you would normally do in the beforeEach method. You can also set a timed response with server.autoRespondAfter = [time in milliseconds].

For this test to pass, we must make the Ajax call and tie the successful response to the method in question. (Strictly speaking, the Sinon server does not have mock behavior, meaning the test won't fail if the Ajax request isn't made, but I recommend acting as though it does.)

```
javascript/05/gatherer/app/assets/javascripts/projects.js
upClickOn: function(anchorElement) {
  row = Project.taskFromAnchor(anchorElement);
  previousRow = Project.previousTask(row);
  if(previousRow == null) { return };
  Project.swapRows(previousRow, row);
  Project.ajaxCall(row.attr("id"), "up");
},

downClickOn: function(anchorElement) {
  row = Project.taskFromAnchor(anchorElement);
  nextRow = Project.nextTask(row);
  if(previousRow == null) { return };
  Project.swapRows(row, nextRow);
  Project.ajaxCall(row.attr("id"), "down");
},

ajaxCall: function(domId, upOrDown) {
  taskId = domId.split("_")[1];
  $.ajax({
    url: "/tasks/" + taskId + "/" + upOrDown + ".js",
    data: { "_method": "PATCH"},
    type: "POST"
  }).done(function(data) {
    Project.successfulUpdate(data)
  }).fail(function(data) {
    Project.failedUpdate(data);
  });
},

successfulUpdate: function(data) {
},

failedUpdate: function(data) {
}
```

This is mostly standard jQuery, making the $.ajax call to the URL that the Rails server will expect—we need to extract the ID from the DOM ID, which is of the form task_1, and then we capture success or failure and pass it along. This is a slight change in the behavior of the original view—when we first wrote the view the DOM ID was the order of the task within the project, not the task's ID. We'll clean that up when we get to the integration test and deal with the actual Rails view.

We haven't specified any behavior on success or failure, so I haven't written any—in a real project something would happen there, of course.

The $.ajax call is wrapped in its own ajaxCall function, which has benefits for our unit testing. Most of our unit tests don't even need to be aware of it, and the click test that does need to be aware of the call can take care of it with a simple spyOn(Project, 'ajaxCall');. If we want to test the successful and unsuccessful behavior, we can unit-test those functions in isolation.

Simulating an unsuccessful Ajax call in the integration test is really easy. If we don't care what the failure status or returned data is, we can just set up the server but not set up any respondWith methods. The Sinon server will interpret calls that it doesn't know about as 404 errors.

If we do care about the error code or data, then we just need to use the version of respondWith that returns an array with the following error code:

javascript/05/gatherer/spec/javascripts/task_move_spec.js
```javascript
describe("with an unsuccessful Ajax call", function() {

  beforeEach(function() {
    this.server.respondWith("PATCH", "/tasks/2/up.js",
        [500, {}, ""]);
  });

  it("invokes a callback on failure", function() {
    spyOn(Project, "failedUpdate").and.callThrough();
    $("#task_2 .up").click();
    this.server.respond()
    expect(Project.failedUpdate).toHaveBeenCalled();
  });
});
```

Since we added failedUpdate when we wrote the unit test, this test passes as is.

Integration Testing with Capybara and JavaScript

At this point I thought I would be able to say, "Well, we've gotten the up and down behavior to work with JavaScript, but we've probably broken the Ruby behavior" and use that to launch a discussion of integration testing of Ajax calls. However...

```
$ rake test:all
# Running tests:

..........................................................

Finished tests in 0.917242s, 71.9548 tests/s, 151.5413 assertions/s.

66 tests, 139 assertions, 0 failures, 0 errors, 0 skips
```

The Ruby tests are not failing.

The code still works because we haven't taken out the server-side links from the up-down tags on the app/views/projects/show.html.erb. If we remove the URL and the method attribute, and add the DOM class that the JavaScript expects, those links look like this:

```
<tr id="task_<%= task.id %>" class="task">
  //OTHER CELLS
  <td>
    <% unless task.first_in_project? %>
      <%= link_to "Up", "#", class: "up" %>
    <% end %>
    <% unless task.last_in_project? %>
      <%= link_to "Down", "#", class: "down" %>
    <% end %>
  </td>
</tr>
```

We might make this change if we were truly confident that the JavaScript would handle the behavior. With the change made, we get an error in the "I can add and reorder a task" test, which suggests that the rows are no longer being swapped.

The failure is because the Capybara tests take place inside the default Capybara driver, RackTest, which does not have a JavaScript interpreter. Happily, we can change that for our single test to use the Poltergeist driver, which integrates with a headless browser engine called PhantomJS.

Installing PhantomJS and Poltergeist

Full instructions for installing PhantomJS are available at http://phantomjs.org/download.html. Here's the nutshell version:

- If you're on a recent Mac OS X system, Homebrew is recommended: brew update && brew install phantomjs.

- If you're on a recent Linux system, download the tarfile at http://phantomjs.org/download.html.

- If you're on Windows, get the binary installer at the same URL: http://phantomjs.org/download.html.

To install Poltergeist, add it to the group :development, :test do block of your Gemfile.

```
gem "poltergeist"
```

Then, of course, run bundle install.

In your test-setup file—meaning the test_helper.rb file for Minitest, the rails_helper.rb file for RSpec, or some file in the Cucumber features/support folder—you need to require 'capybara/poltergeist'. Then you need the following snippet (in most cases only the first line). In our particular case we'll require some other incantations:

```
javascript/06/gatherer/spec/rails_helper.rb
Capybara.javascript_driver = :poltergeist

class ActiveRecord::Base
  mattr_accessor :shared_connection
  @@shared_connection = nil

  def self.connection
    @@shared_connection || retrieve_connection
  end
end

ActiveRecord::Base.shared_connection = ActiveRecord::Base.connection
```

The first line here, Capybara.javascript_driver = :poltergeist, is the important one. The rest has to do with unfortunate specifics of our setup and the way Capybara handles its JavaScript drivers. Please ignore that stuff for the moment; we'll get to it soon.

Now we need to tell our one individual test to use the JavaScript driver.

Using Poltergeist with RSpec

We need to make a few changes in our existing integration test for it to work with Capybara:

- We need to tell Capybara to use the JavaScript driver.

- We need to change the test slightly to adjust for the new behavior. The old test assumed the entire page was redrawn DOM IDs based on the order of the row. The new test moves the same DOM ID around without redrawing the whole page. This means the DOM ID of the row we care about no longer changes, so we need different acceptance criteria.

In RSpec we can set the JavaScript driver for a single test using metadata, in much the same way we did for VCR in Chapter 12, *Testing External Services*, on page 229. The :js metadata is enough to have Capybara switch to the JavaScript driver for the duration of the spec and then switch back at the end.

The entire test looks like the following:

```
javascript/06/gatherer/spec/features/add_task_spec.rb
require 'rails_helper'
include Warden::Test::Helpers

describe "adding a new task" do
  fixtures :all
  include Warden::Test::Helpers

  before(:example) do
    projects(:bluebook).roles.create(user: users(:user))
    login_as users(:user)
  end

  it "can add and reorder a task", :js do
    visit project_path(projects(:bluebook))
    fill_in "Task", with: "Find UFOs"
    select "2", from: "Size"
    click_on "Add Task"
    expect(current_path).to eq(project_path(projects(:bluebook)))
    added_task = Task.last
    within("#task_#{added_task.id}") do
      expect(page).to have_selector(".name", text: "Find UFOs")
      expect(page).to have_selector(".size", text: "2")
      expect(page).not_to have_selector("a", text: "Down")
      click_on("Up")
    end
    expect(current_path).to eq(project_path(projects(:bluebook)))
    expect(page).to have_selector("tbody:nth-child(2) .name", text: "Find UFOs")
  end
end
```

In the body of the test, since we can no longer test based on the DOM ID of the row changing, we explicitly look for the second element in the list—the task we changed was third and last in the list, then we clicked the "up" button—using the tbody:nth-child(2) selector.

The shows_twitter_avatar_spec.rb test also has a within block that depends on the old file and needs to be changed to within("#task_#{tasks(:one).id}").

Using Poltergeist with Minitest

In Minitest we don't have the :js metadata, so we need to explicitly set the JavaScript driver:

```
javascript/06/gatherer/test/integration/add_task_test.rb
require "test_helper"

class AddTaskTest < Capybara::Rails::TestCase
  include Warden::Test::Helpers
```

```ruby
setup do
  Capybara.current_driver = Capybara.javascript_driver
  projects(:bluebook).roles.create(user: users(:user))
  login_as users(:user)
end

teardown do
  Capybara.current_driver = Capybara.default_driver
end

test "i can add and reorder a task" do
  visit project_path(projects(:bluebook))
  fill_in "Task", with: "Find UFOs"
  select "2", from: "Size"
  click_on "Add Task"
  assert_equal project_path(projects(:bluebook)), current_path
  added_task = Task.last
  within("#task_#{added_task.id}") do
    assert_selector(".name", text: "Find UFOs")
    assert_selector(".size", text: "2")
    refute_selector("a", text: "Down")
    click_on("Up")
  end
  assert_equal project_path(projects(:bluebook)), current_path
  assert_selector("tbody:nth-child(2) .name", text: "Find UFOs")
end
end
```

The most relevant lines are in the setup and teardown, where we set the Capy-bara.current_driver. In the setup we change it to Capyabara.javascript_driver, which we had previously set to Poltergeist. In the teardown, we change it back to the Capybara.default_driver.

Using Poltergeist with Cucumber

In Cucumber all you need to do to get the JavaScript driver for a specific scenario is prefix the scenario with the @javascript tag:

```
@javascript
Scenario: We can change the order of tasks
```

Making the Test Pass

Because we've already written the JavaScript code here, the test should pass. The only things keeping this test from passing are some grubby and rather annoying setup issues that are worth bouncing through because they may help you when you try to use Poltergeist in your own test.

When we run the specs the first thing that happens is a VCR failure:

```
An HTTP request has been made that VCR does not know how to handle:
  GET http://127.0.0.1:52253/__identify__
```

This is a request made by Capybara during setup, which we can work around by making VCR ignore localhost requests.

`javascript/06/gatherer/spec/rails_helper.rb`
```ruby
VCR.configure do |c|
  c.cassette_library_dir = 'spec/cassettes'
  c.hook_into :webmock
  c.configure_rspec_metadata!
  c.ignore_localhost = true
end
```

At this point, if you run the tests with the setup given, there's a very good chance you'll get an error claiming the SQLite database you're using is locked.

We have a general Capybara and JavaScript problem and a specific SQLite problem here.

The general problem is that when Capybara runs its JavaScript drivers, they run in a separate thread from the test itself. This becomes a problem if you are using the Rails default behavior of keeping every test in a database transaction. Transactions aren't shared across threads, so any data created in the test—including fixtures and test setup—is not visible to the Capybara driver. That means data that you might be expecting to see in your test is not there, which is very frustrating and can easily lead to a long session of trying to figure out what's wrong.

You can use a gem called database_cleaner to override Rails defaults and explicitly truncate the database before JavaScript tests. A full discussion is a little outside our scope at the moment, but Avdi Grimm has a great collection of useful settings.[6]

However, database_cleaner would not solve all of our problem because SQLite is not threaded, and therefore locks all access when it is read. I'm not sure about the exact mechanism, but having the Ajax call happen while another read is in progress is what's causing the test to block.

That leads to the half dozen or so lines of code that I referred to as an incantation earlier. Let's run that again:

```ruby
class ActiveRecord::Base
  mattr_accessor :shared_connection
  @@shared_connection = nil
```

---

6. http://devblog.avdi.org/2012/08/31/configuring-database_cleaner-with-rails-rspec-capybara-and-selenium/

```
  def self.connection
    @@shared_connection || retrieve_connection
  end
end
ActiveRecord::Base.shared_connection = ActiveRecord::Base.connection
```

This code is overwriting ActiveRecord internals to force multiple threads to use the same database connection and therefore share threaded data. The Capybara documentation warns that this approach "may have thread safety implications and could cause strange failures," but we're not doing anything super complicated, so it works for us here. (In a real project I'd move off of SQLite, but it's very easy to set up for educational purposes.)

If you're getting the sense that using JavaScript drivers with Capybara is flaky, brittle, and frustrating, the only thing I can say is that you left out *slow*. I recommend using them sparingly. You should try to handle testing client interactions in JavaScript to the extent possible, and using server-side testing to specify what data is sent to the client.

 **Prescription 39** Use Capybara's JavaScript integration-testing capabilities sparingly lest you be very, very annoyed. Test as much as possible within each layer, separate from the others.

JavaScript Fiddle

This chapter has presented the basics of testing in JavaScript, but it only scratches the surface. In particular, if you're using Rails to serve data to one of the JavaScript frameworks, you'll need familiarity with the testing tools designed for that framework.

As for our Rails journey, this chapter is the last one that covers testing specific facets of a Rails application. Now we'll spend a few chapters on topics that will help all of your Rails tests, starting with troubleshooting and debugging.

## CHAPTER 14

Troubleshooting and Debugging

Dot, dot, dot, dot, dot.

Tests are passing; looks like it's time for lunch.

Dot, dot, dot, dot, F.

F? F?

But the code works. I know it does.

I think it does.

Why is my test failing?

One of the most frustrating moments in the life of a TDD developer is when a test is failing and it's not clear why.

General Principles

This may be the most obvious piece of advice in the book:

> **Prescription 40** When a formerly passing test fails, something has changed.

Obvious or not, it's worth repeating, mantralike, when confronted with a bad bug. When a formerly passing test fails, it means something changed.

It may be in the code, the system, or the test. But it's probably not sunspots, and it's probably not evil spirits possessing your MacBook (unless you're living in one of Charles Stross's Laundry novels).

The Humble Print Statement

My initial troubleshooting tool of choice is a plucky little Ruby method called p. Perhaps you've heard of it.

I realize that to many of you, debugging with the p statement sounds like trying to fix your television by kicking it. In the p method's defense, it's dirt-simple, works anywhere, and is infinitely adaptable to your current troubleshooting needs. An elegant weapon for a more civilized age, so to speak.

The p method calls inspect on its argument and then outputs it to STDOUT using Ruby's even-more-primitive puts. I prefer p to puts because the extra call to inspect generally results in more readable output. (Though in poking around, it looks like puts does a better job with mixed data these days than it did back in the Ruby 1.8.7 era.)

You can use a couple of other methods that are particularly good at displaying structured data. Ruby defines the method y, which takes its argument and outputs it to STDOUT in YAML format. This is valuable in direct proportion to your ability to read complicated YAML formats.

I like the Awesome Print gem, available with gem install awesome_print and with lots of examples and docs at https://github.com/michaeldv/awesome_print. Including Awesome Print gives you the ap method, which awesomely prints things. Even nicer, you get the logger helper method Rails.logger.ap, which awesomely prints to the Rails log (by default, at the debug level). Awesome Print also has a number of options to customize output, but I have never used them.

One minor downside to Awesome Print is that because it is often loaded into just the development and test groups in the Gemfile, it's not available on staging or production. That sounds great until you accidentally leave an ap statement in the code and it goes to staging and causes a 500 error. With the other methods, which are core Ruby, the worst that happens is STDOUT spew.

Here's a comparison from a Rails console with awesome_print in the Gemfile. This comparison uses a couple of collections, a hash with an array value, and a plain array. This output is lightly edited from a Rails console session:

```
> x = {1 => ['a', 'b'], 2 => 'c'}
> y = ["a", "b"]

> puts x
{1=>["a", "b"], 2=>"c"}
> puts y
a
b

> p x
{1=>["a", "b"], 2=>"c"}
> p y
["a", "b"]
```

```
> y x
---
1:
- a
- b
2: c

 > ap x
{
    1 => [
        [0] "a",
        [1] "b"
    ],
    2 => "c"
}
```

This gives the flavor of how Awesome Print and y create somewhat easier-to-read output for structured data.

One more quick comparison using an Active Record object, again from an edited Rails console:

```
p = Project.new(name: "Project Runway", due_date: 1.month.from_now)

> puts p
#<Project:0x00000102ff3568>

> p p
#<Project id: nil, name: "Project Runway", due_date: "2014-08-16",
    created_at: nil, updated_at: nil, public: false>

> y p
--- !ruby/object:Project
attributes:
  id:
  name: Project Runway
  due_date: 2014-08-16
  created_at:
  updated_at:
  public: false

> ap p
#<Project:0x00000102ff3568> {
             :id => nil,
           :name => "Project Runway",
       :due_date => Sat, 16 Aug 2014,
     :created_at => nil,
     :updated_at => nil,
         :public => false
}
```

There's a nice progression here, from puts just giving the class name, to p giving a class name and key/value pairs, to y putting each key/value on a different line, to Awesome Print lining up the values for readability. The Awesome Print output is also a syntactically correct Ruby hash, should you feel the need for copy and paste.

> **Prescription 41** Using p and various related methods is a quick and easy way to get a sense of why a test is behaving badly.

Using these print statements in a successful troubleshooting section is a tug-of-war between finding interesting data and not overwhelming yourself.

One catch to keep in mind: all these kernel method calls work fine from a test console or in the server log if you run Rails via rails server. If you use a development server, such as unicorn, that does not output STDOUT to the terminal, then you need to use the Rails logger to see printed output. The Rails logger is available anywhere in your application with Rails.logger, which then takes one of several methods, such as Rails.logger.error, all of which take an argument that gets printed to the log or a block whose final value gets printed to the log.

It's highly recommended that when you're troubleshooting with print statements, you use one of the techniques in Chapter 15, *Running Tests Faster and Running Faster Tests*, on page 287, to run just one test at a time for clarity. Fast tests help a lot here, because the quicker you can get data on the screen, the faster you can iterate, and using print statements for test troubleshooting is definitely a rapid-iteration process.

Here are some ways to use print statements in troubleshooting:

You are here: Print little "you are here messages" as a cheap alternative to program traces. (Ruby does have a program tracer, called tracer, but it's going to be wild overkill for most debugging purposes.) I usually go with a simple p "here" and, if I need a second one, p "there". It's a fast way to determine if the method you're looking at is even called during the test invocation.

For the most part I use these as one-and-done quick checks to see what's going on. It's not uncommon for a check like this to save me significant time banging my head against the code looking at a method that isn't even being called.

Also helpful here is the Putsinator gem, which annotates every p and puts with the line number that generated them.[1] This is helpful in tracking down that one line of output in the test suite that you can't otherwise trace.

You may ask yourself, "How did I get here?": At any point in Ruby, you can determine the name of the method that called the method you're in by using the cryptic incantation caller_locations(1,1)[0].label. caller_locations is a kernel method that returns the call stack as an array of objects. The two arguments are index and length, with index 0 being the current method, and index 1 being the immediate caller. So, we have an array of length 1, returning the first element via [0] and then taking that object's label attributes, which is the method name. You are encouraged to tweak the call a bit to see what other data is around; see http://www.ruby-doc.org/core-2.1.1/Kernel.html#method-i-caller_locations for official docs.

I recommend you keep this one on speed dial, in the form of a helper method in your test_helper or rails_helper file.

Print a value: You'll naturally want to use p and the related methods to print values from specific points in the app. Some techniques that are useful here:

- Print the arguments to a method call.
- Print an ActiveRecord object before and after an update.
- Print both sides of a compound Boolean separately.

And so on. If you are particularly industrious, use Ruby string interpolation to give a label—p "user name: #{user.name}"—but for most quick uses you don't need to bother.

Deface a gem: You are not limited to your own application when inserting print statements. It's easy and fun to insert code into a gem (just remember to undo it).

Bundler has two commands: bundle show and bundle open. The bundle show command returns the complete path to the version of the gem that Bundler is using. If you want to go one step further, bundle open will open the gem directory in your default editor.

Add print or log statements to taste. This can be useful when first interacting with a new gem.

When you're done, use the command gem pristine <gemname> to return the gem to its original state. Or reinstall the bundle.

---

1.   https://github.com/tobytripp/Putsinator

Show a page: It is especially important to see what's going on inside an integration test that uses Capybara or Cucumber. Capybara has the helper method save_and_open_page, which does exactly what it says. It dumps the current Capybara DOM to a temp file and opens the file in your default browser.

The resulting browser window will look a little strange. Any relative files or assets won't be displayed, meaning no CSS and only some images. But the text is usually enough to see if your integration test is even looking at the page you expect, and not, say, looking at the login page because you forgot to log in.

Git Bisect

git bisect is the kind of tool you will use about once every six months, but when you use it, you will be totally thrilled that it exists.

git bisect is indicated when something has gone wrong in your code, and you believe it to be the result of a code change but you cannot isolate which change resulted in the problem. git bisect's goal is to isolate the commit where the change occurred.

> **Prescription 42** Use git bisect to track down mysterious failures in your code when you have no idea how they were inserted.

You start using git bisect with two commands:

```
$ git bisect start
$ git bisect bad
```

The first command puts Git into what we'll call *bisect mode*, and the second command says that the current Git snapshot is bad, meaning it contains the behavior we're trying to fix.

You then switch the Git snapshot to the secure hash algorithm of a previous commit that you believe is good because it does not have the behavior. And you tell Git that branch is good. For example, I'd use this if I've determined that SHA 34ace43 is good:

```
$ git checkout 34ace43
$ git bisect good
```

You can combine those into one command, git bisect good 34ace43.

Git now does something really neat. It derives a straight line of commits between the good one and the bad one, picks the middle of that line, and checks itself into that commit. You'll see some commentary on the console explaining how many commits are in the line and roughly how many steps Git expects the bisect to take.

Your job is to do whatever you need to in the newly entered commit to determine if it is "good" or "bad" based on whether the incorrect behavior exists. Based on that, you enter either git bisect good or git bisect bad. (If you really can't tell, you can do git bisect skip.)

Git now has enough information to know that the bad change was in one half of the commits. If you said the commit was bad, then the change was in the first half of the commits; if you said it was good, then the change had to come after. Git splits the narrowed-down list of commits in half and checks out the middle commit.

You repeat your checks until eventually you can isolate two changes where the first one is good and the second one is bad. Ideally, inspecting the commit list of the second commit will give you a hint as to what is causing the behavior, since one of those changes is likely the cause. This process can save you hours.

Furthermore, if you can encapsulate whatever test you're running against your codebase in a script that follows the Unix convention of returning a nonzero value on failure, you can pass that script to git bisect and Git will automatically do the good/bad thing for you based on the result of the script. The syntax is of the following form:

```
$ git bisect run my_script
```

I note in passing that whichever tool you're using to run your tests has this behavior, so git bisect run rspec should work, though it'll probably be a little on the slow side.

For the full git bisect effect, a few things need to be true:

- The problem needs to have been caused by a code change, not a change in your environment.
- You need to be able to reliably trigger the problem.
- It helps if your commits are relatively small and if the system is in a loadable and executable state after each one.

That said, when this works, it can work big.

Pry

Once upon a time, I was a big fan of development environments that had big fancy symbolic debuggers that let you set breakpoints and watch variables and step through the code.

What can I say? I was young and programming in Java.

When I started using TDD, I largely stopped using debuggers. Having small, focused tests eliminates most of the need to walk through code in a step debugger. That said, it's sometimes nice to be able to stop a test in progress and peer inside the Ruby virtual machine to see what's going on.

Enter Pry.

Pry is technically a Ruby console—a souped-up replacement for irb, but with some add-on gems. It makes an excellent debugger. You can even coax it to reload code changes and rerun specs from inside Pry, which is as close as you can get in Ruby to programming inside a Smalltalk image.

Pry improves on irb in many ways. It offers much more powerful examination of live Ruby objects. It also has some niceties that makes it easier to enter code in the console.

We'll load Pry and a couple of extras by including them in the :development, :test group of our Gemfile:

```
gem 'pry-rails'
gem 'pry-byebug'
gem 'pry-stack_explorer'
gem 'pry-rescue'
gem 'better_errors'
```

The pry-rails gem allows Pry to replace irb as the console when you run rails console and adds a couple of handy commands that provide Rails info inside Pry. The other two gems both provide additional useful behavior: pry-byebug allows you to step through the code, and pry-stack-explorer allows you to go up and down the stack trace. The better_errors gem gives you a much prettier and more useful error page for 500 errors in development, which includes a live Pry session in your browser.

A quickish bundle install, and we're on our way.

Basic Pry Consoling

There's a lot of great stuff in Pry and we're not going to cover it all. Full docs are at https://github.com/pry/pry/wiki.

We've set Pry up as our Rails console, so we can access it with a simple rails console:

```
$ rails c
Loading development environment (Rails 4.1.2)

Frame number: 0/21
[1] pry(main)> 1 + 1
=> 2
[2] pry(main)> project = Project.new(name: "Project Runway")
=> #<Project id: nil, name: "Project Runway", due_date: nil,
      created_at: nil, updated_at: nil, public: false>
```

Pry allows you to closely examine the current object under scope, which you can determine with the self command. Right now the current object is main.

```
[3] pry(main)> self
=> main
[4] pry(main)> ls
Rails::ConsoleMethods#methods: app  controller  helper  new_session  reload!
self.methods: inspect  to_s
locals: _  __  _dir_  _ex_  _file_  _in_  _out_  _pry_  project
```

Pry uses the metaphor of Unix directory navigation to work through object trees (which, honestly, I find kind of weird). So, just as typing ls in a regular Unix terminal gives us a list of files, typing ls for Pry gives us a list of all kinds of stuff about the current namespace by introspecting on the object, including the available methods on the current object and local variables. (See https://github.com/pry/pry/wiki/State-navigation for full details.)

You can see that the list of locals contains a bunch of preexisting special variables and then the project variable that we created at the start of the sessions.

Just like you can type ls for a listing, you can type cd to change scopes. Let's go into the scope of our project object.

```
[5] pry(main)> cd project
[6] pry(#<Project>):1> self
=> #<Project id: nil, name: "Project Runway", due_date: nil,
     created_at: nil, updated_at: nil, public: false>
[7] pry(#<Project>):1> ls
==> A BUNCH OF STUFF
```

We use the cd command to change scopes. As with Unix, cd .. will take us back up a level, and there are other syntax quirks to move through multiple levels in a single command.

The bunch of stuff after we type ls includes all the methods that project can respond to. As you might imagine, that's rather a lot. All output in Pry goes through a paginator, though, so you can just type q to get back to the command line rather than wading through the entire listing.

If you start a command with a dot (.), Pry will consider that to be a shell command, so you can keep a Pry terminal open but still interact with, say, your Git repo.

And that's not all.

You can use the show-source command to display, in the Pry console, the source code of any method. You can request methods of the object in scope:

```
[1] pry(main)> project = Project.new(name: "Project Runway")
=> #<Project id: nil, name: "Project Runway", due_date: nil,
        created_at: nil, updated_at: nil, public: false>
[2] pry(main)> cd project
[3] pry(#<Project>):1> show-source on_schedule?

From: /gatherer/app/models/project.rb @ line 59:
Owner: Project
Visibility: public
Number of lines: 4

def on_schedule?
  return false if undefined_rate?
  (Date.today + projected_days_remaining) <= due_date
end
```

You can't see it here, but the method is syntax-colored in the console. You can do this for any method in the system using the ClassName#method_name syntax. Similarly, you can use the show-doc and ri methods to see just the documentation for a method you're interested in, which is particularly useful for Rails methods.

Pry has a couple of special variables that are always available. Like irb, the _ variable always refers to the result of the most recent expression evaluated. The variable _ex_ is the most recently raised exception, even if you have moved out of the exception scope. You can use cat —ex to view the code that caused the exception, and you can see the stack trace with _ex_.backtrace.

Using Pry to Troubleshoot Test Failures

Pry is really a wonderful console, but again, this is *Rails 4 Test Prescriptions* not *Rails 4 Console Prescriptions*. Luckily, you can invoke Pry directly from inside a test.

If you add the line binding.pry to your code, then when the code execution reaches that line a Pry session will start.

Let's see how this works. I'll put a binding.pry in one of the tests in the action test file creates_project_test.rb. Can you guess which line from this session trace contains binding.pry?

```
$ rake test:all
# Running tests:

.........................................................
Frame number: 0/25
From: gatherer/test/actions/creates_project_test.rb @ line 8
CreatesProjectTest#test_creates_a_project_given_a_name:

    5: test "creates a project given a name" do
    6:   creator = CreatesProject.new(name: "Project Runway")
    7:   creator.build
 => 8:   binding.pry
    9:   assert_equal "Project Runway", creator.project.name
   10: end


[1] pry(#<CreatesProjectTest>)>
```

Pry not only opens a session; it displays the test where it stopped, and it sets the Pry scope to the test class (again, this is syntax-highlighted).

We can use the cd notation to see what's going on:

```
[1] pry(#<CreatesProjectTest>)> cd creator
[2] pry(#<CreatesProject>):1> ls
CreatesProject#methods: build  convert_string_to_tasks  create
name  name=  project  project=  save  task_string  task_string=
users  users=
self.methods: __pry__
instance variables: @name  @project  @task_string  @users
locals: _  __  _dir_  _ex_  _file_  _in_  _out_  _pry_
[3] pry(#<CreatesProject>):1> cd project
[6] pry(#<Project>):2> name
=> "Project Runway"
```

And then, if you use <control>-c to exit Pry, the tests just continue on their merry way.

There's nothing special about binding as the receiver of the pry message. It's handy because it's available anywhere and gives you the entire local scope—and Pry will display the surrounding code when you drop into it. You can, however, send pry to anything. We could have used creator.pry in the same test, and we would have been dropped into Pry with the creator local variable as the top-level scope.

The pry-byebug and pry-stack_explorer gems have some commands that are useful in a debugging session.

From pry-byebug we get four commands: continue, finish, next, and step. If you've done much with interactive debuggers, these will be familiar. The step and next commands take you one command forward, with next keeping you in the same frame but step sending you into a frame. The finish command executes until the end of the current frame, and continue ends the Pry session entirely.

The pry-stack_explorer gem allows you to see the entire current stack trace with the show-stack command. You can then use the up and down methods to navigate the trace.

We can also invoke our editor directly from the Pry console using the edit command. Using just edit -c will open the editor to the file where the original binding.pry was located. Using edit ClassName#method_name will open the editor at the file where the given class and method are defined. Similarly, edit with any instance variable as an argument will open the file where that instance's class is defined.

The Pry session will wait while the edit is happening. Closing the edit window will reload that file in the Pry session and allow you to keep going.

We can be even more interactive with the pry-rescue gem. The pry-rescue gem provides a regular terminal command rescue that is prefixed to a different command. If that command raises an exception, then Pry is automatically invoked at the point of the exception. If you run rescue before your test command, Pry will also be invoked on test failure.

In RSpec pry-rescue just works with a rescue rspec command. In Minitest you need to put the following lines in the test_helper.rb first:

```
require 'minitest/autorun'
require 'pry-rescue/minitest'
```

Remember how we said that editing files from Pry causes the file to be reloaded? Wouldn't it be great if you could rerun the failing test inside Pry? The command for doing just that is try-again.

Using these tools together can give you a very interactive workflow. Run the tests via rescue, drop into Pry on failure, keep editing and trying again until that test passes, and keep going. For a slightly more extreme version, check out Joel Turnbull's talk from RailsConf 2014.[2]

---

2. http://www.confreaks.com/videos/3365-railsconf-debugger-driven-developement-with-pry

Really Common Rails Gotchas

The following patterns in Rails lead to relatively silent test failure. I stumble over them all the time.

- ActiveRecord models not saving when I expect them to. The most common cause is that the creation of the object fails a validation. Often this causes a test failure down the line because a record that was supposed to be found in the database isn't there—because it didn't save. Using a factory tool helps with this, as does using save! and create! in test setup to have the failure happen at the point of the code problem and not further down the line.

- In versions of Rails that use attr_accessible, Rails silently ignores inaccessible parameters in mass assignment. Rails 4 will still ignore parameters not specified in a strong parameter permit command, but it will at least log them. This can lead to hours of fun as you try to figure out why that attribute, which is clearly part of the method call, is not part of the resulting object.

- In integration tests, it's common to forget to log in when required. This normally means anything you expect to be on the resulting page fails to show up. The save_and_open_page command is invaluable here since it's sometimes hard to tease out what happened from the log. But save_and_open_page will clearly show you that you're not logged in.

Troubleshooting is only one way to improve you test experience. You can also make your test setup better in a more general way, as we'll discuss in the next chapter.

Running Tests Faster
and Running Faster Tests

Over the course of the book we've talked about how important rapid feedback is to getting the full benefit of the TDD process.

You can make your TDD feedback happen faster in several ways. You can run a focused subset of your test suite so that you see only the tests relating to the code you're working on. You can have tests run automatically when code changes. You can make the loading of the Rails application happen in the background or you can bypass Rails altogether. And, of course, you can just avoid doing really slow things.

Let's look at the many ways to speed up tests.

Running Smaller Groups of Tests

Running just some of your tests at once is often useful when debugging. For one thing, you often just care about one or two tests when debugging. Also, if you're being verbose about printing output to the terminal, then only running one test will spare you from potentially having to wade through a lot of spurious output.

Each tool has its own way to allow you to run one file or one set of tests at once. Also, your editor or IDE probably has a built-in feature or common extension that allows you to run your entire test suite or just some tests directly from the editor.

Running Groups of Examples in RSpec

I recommend using the rspec command directly rather than going through any rake tasks that RSpec defines, because it's a bit faster.

The rspec command can take one or more arguments—files, directories, or file globs. For file globs, all matching files are run:

```
$ rspec spec/models/project_spec.rb spec/models/task_spec.rb
```

RSpec makes it easy to run a single spec. All you need to do is add the line number to the file along with a colon:

```
$ spec/models/task_spec.rb:5
```

When RSpec's default formatter runs, at the end of the output RSpec will place the file name and line number of each failing test, suitable for easy copy-and-paste back to the command line to run the test in isolation. You'll find this quite useful.

If you want to run a set of RSpec specs that isn't quite a single test or a set of files, you can use the RSpec metadata system to mark the tests in question. Or you can simply tag the specs:

```
it "should run when I ask for focused tests", :focus do
end

it "should not run when I ask for focused tests" do
end
```

The top spec here has been tagged with the :focus metadata tag, which is equivalent to focus: true. You can also specify a spec or example group as focused by prefixing its name with f, as in fit, fdescribe, and fcontext.

You can then run all specs with a given tag:

```
$ rspec --tag focus
```

If you want to exclude tags, you prefix the tag name with a tilde:

```
$ rspec --tag ~focus
```

RSpec's default spec_helper file contains a commented-out line that applies the :focus filter automatically.

Minitest

If you're invoking Minitest through the rake tasks that Rails provides, then it's easy to run a single file's worth of output just by passing the file name at the command line:

```
$ rake test test/models/task_test.rb
```

The argument can be an individual file or a directory. You can have more than one file or directory if they're separated by spaces.

This behavior is relatively new to Rails. If you've been using Rails for a while you may know that it provides a number of testing subtasks, such as rake test:models, that wrap the expected directories and run all the tests in that directory. Since Rails has been nice enough to add the directory behavior separately, I recommend using the actual directories rather than trying to remember the names of all the rake tasks.

It's a bit more involved if you want to run a single individual test rather than an entire file. As far as I can tell, there's no way to do that directly from the Rails rake task, so you need to drop down to the Ruby command line. The invocation looks like this:

```
$ ruby -Ilib:test test/models/task_test.rb -n test_a_completed_task_is_complete
```

```
Running tests:
.
Finished tests in 0.019890s, 50.2765 tests/s, 100.5530 assertions/s.
1 tests, 2 assertions, 0 failures, 0 errors, 0 skips
```

In this command, we're running ruby with the capitol I option, which specifies directories to add to the load path. Specifically, we need the lib and test directories so that we can find the test_helper file our test is going to require. (You may be able to get away with not adding lib.) Next we have the name of the file, and then the -n option, which is being passed to Minitest and is the name of the individual test method we want to run. This is the test name after ActiveSupport::TestCase is done munging it, so what's in our file as test "a completed task is complete" is on the command line as test_a_completed_task_is_complete—with the word test prepended to the name and all the spaces turned into underscores.

If that seems like a lot of annoying typing, I can help a tiny bit. The minitest-line gem adds a different switch to the command line: -l,[1] which takes the line number of the test, changing our command line to this relatively brief one:

```
$ ruby -Ilib:test test/models/task_test.rb -l 5
```

The line number doesn't have to be the first line of the test. If you pick an intermediate line, it will run the test that contains that line.

---

1. https://github.com/judofyr/minitest-line

> **Prescription 43**
>
> If you specify a test by line number, be sure not to add lines to the file. Added lines could make it so you aren't running the test you think you're running.

Cucumber

Cucumber's set of options is almost identical to RSpec's. Again, I recommend using the cucumber command line directly rather than going through rake. You can specify one or more files, append line numbers with a colon, and allow or deny tags with the -t or --tag option. (The main difference is that Cucumber tags start with an @, which you must include in the command line.)

Cucumber privileges one special tag, @wip, which is short for "work in progress." Cucumber scenarios tagged with @wip will not count as failures in a test run (much like RSpec's pending). Cucumber also has the separate -w or --wip, which runs Cucumber in reverse and fails if there are any passing scenarios.

Guard

Another way to get test feedback quickly is to allow the tests to run automatically when your code changes. In Ruby, the Guard gem allows you to trigger arbitrary events when files change. It's a powerful system, and running tests is only a fraction of what it can do. We're just going to manage basic setup here; full documentation is available online.[2] [3] [4] Mac users should check out the Mac-specific wiki page to make sure Guard receives file events correctly.[5]

Guard is a generic system for triggering events, and it has separate libraries that make it easy to trigger specific kinds of events, such as starting a test.

To set Guard up, add the Guard gem and any of the dependent libraries to the Gemfile:

```
group :development do
  gem 'guard'
  gem 'guard-minitest'
  gem 'guard-rspec'
  gem 'guard-cucumber'
end
```

---

2. https://github.com/guard/guard
3. https://github.com/guard/guard-minitest
4. https://github.com/guard/guard-rspec
5. https://github.com/guard/guard/wiki/Add-Readline-support-to-Ruby-on-Mac-OS-X

Then, from the command line, run the following:

```
$ bundle exec guard init
```

This gives us a new file, Guardfile, that contains Guard commands for each of the tools we've added.

Here's what the Guardfile portion for RSpec might look like. This is an edited version of what the Guard plugin provides by default; among other things, I've changed the default command to be Spring-aware:

```
guard :rspec, cmd: 'spring rspec' do
  watch(%r{^spec/.+_spec\.rb$})
  watch(%r{^app/(.+)\.rb$})   { |m| "spec/#{m[1]}_spec.rb" }
  watch('spec/spec_helper.rb')  { "spec" }
  watch('spec/rails_helper.rb') { "spec" }
end
```

The guard method takes the name of one of the Guard plugins, some optional arguments (depending on the plugin), and then a block. Inside the Guard block, watched files are sent to that plugin to be processed. Right now we're showing the rspec plugin, which sends changed files to RSpec to be run.

The basic idea behind Guard is this watch command, which takes a string or regular expression and an optional block argument.

The watch command is triggered when the name of a file being changed matches the string or regular-expression argument. That file name is then sent on to the plugin. If there's a block argument, you can modify the file name arbitrarily. The match data from the regular expression is the argument to the block and the result of the block is what's sent to the plugin.

In this basic snippet, we see the first line matches any file in our test suite. If the file is changed, then Guard will run that file. The last lines specifically watch for changes to our spec_helper.rb or rails_helper.rb file and run the entire test suite by just passing spec to the plugin.

The middle pattern is more dynamic. It matches any change to our app directory, changes the directory to spec, and runs the associated file. In other words, if app/models/project.rb is changed, then spec/models/project_spec.rb is run. Typically you'd add some other patterns to cover changes in other parts of the app or to run integration tests if views change.

The Minitest file is similar. Here it is with the Spring option added. I slightly edited the file because the default naming conventions that Guard expects don't match what we've been doing.

```
guard :minitest, spring: true do
  watch(%r{^test/(.*)_test\.rb$})
  watch(%r{^app/(.+)\.rb$}) { |m| "test/#{m[1]}_test.rb" }
  watch(%r{^test/test_helper\.rb$}) { 'test' }
end
```

The watch commands here have the same meaning. If a test file is changed, run that file. If a file in the app directory changes, run the associated test file. If the test_helper.rb changes, run the whole suite.

To run Guard, type the following:

```
$ bundle exec guard
10:39:33 - INFO - Guard is using TerminalTitle to send notifications.
10:39:33 - INFO - Running all features
Disabling profiles...
```

Guard will then run your tests or specs, depending on which plugin you're running. We have both plugins enabled, so Guard rather weirdly runs both our Minitests and RSpec specs. Then it waits with a command prompt—actually a Pry console, which is useful (though it's not, by default, a Rails console). You can run a few custom commands at the prompt; the most valuable are exit, which quits Guard, and all, which runs all the plugins.

If I then make some kind of change in my program—say I change something in task.rb—Guard springs into action, running the Minitests and specs related to task. (I edited this output to remove actual test results.)

```
10:47:07 - INFO - Running: test/models/task_test.rb
10:47:10 - INFO - Running: spec/models/task_spec.rb
..
Finished in 0.01441 seconds (files took 2.56 seconds to load)
2 examples, 0 failures
```

My experience with Guard and related automatic test tools is that they can be useful for focused unit tests but not so useful for integration tests. It's tricky to have specific files know which integration tests they might be a part of without rerunning the entire integration-test suite on every file change. If you're willing to put a little effort into tweaking the Guardfile, though, you won't have to do anything to get the tests you're working on to continue running.

Running Rails in the Background

One difference between TDD in a Rails context and TDD in SUnit's original Smalltalk environment is that testing a Rails program typically requires that Ruby be started from the command line and that the Rails environment be loaded. Starting from the command line can take quite a bit of time on even a moderate-sized Rails project. If you're trying to run, say, a single file's worth of tests that you expect to take about a second, having the Rails startup take more than a minute can break your flow. In contrast, the Smalltalk tests reside inside the same live process as the code and can therefore start instantly.

One way to simulate the Smalltalk behavior in Rails is to not restart the Rails application on every test. A way to avoid restarting the Rails application is to have it already running in a background task and use the existing background application. Over the years a number of tools have attempted to manage this process, and most of them required a fair amount of fiddling to work. But Rails 4.1 and Spring have made this task much easier to manage.

Installing Spring

In Rails 4.1, the Rails core team specified an official background preloader, Spring.[6] It is admirably nonfiddly. It usually just works.

Spring is a gem, and you'll want it in your Gemfile. If you want RSpec to be fully Springified, you need the spring-commands-rspec gem as well:

```
gem "spring", group: :development
gem spring-commands-rspec
```

If you start a fresh Rails 4.1 application with rails new, the first line will already be there.

At this point we can see what all the fuss is about:

```
$ spring status
Spring is not running.
```

That was exciting. Let's try something else:

```
$ spring help
Version: 1.1.3

Usage: spring COMMAND [ARGS]

Commands for spring itself:

  binstub        Generate spring based binstubs.
Use --all to generate a binstub for all known commands.
  help           Print available commands.
  status         Show current status.
  stop           Stop all spring processes for this project.
```

---

6.   https://github.com/rails/spring

```
Commands for your application:

  rails          Run a rails command.
The following sub commands will use spring: console, runner, generate, destroy.
  rake           Runs the rake command
  rspec          Runs the rspec command
```

The last command is there only because we added the spring-commands-rspec gem.

Using Spring

Spring defines a half dozen or so subcommands that can all be called with syntax like bundle exec spring <whatever>. Let's try one:

```
$ bundle exec spring rspec
.............................................................
Finished in 3.76 seconds (files took 1 minute 41.26 seconds to load)
74 examples, 0 failures
```

After I run the tests, I can check the status of Spring again:

```
$ spring status
Spring is running:

41337 spring server | gatherer | started 10 secs ago
41338 spring app    | gatherer | started 10 secs ago | test mode
```

After I run my tests, Spring stays running in the background, as confirmed by the spring status update. If I then enter the Rails console or Rails server, Spring will start up another instance in the development environment and hold onto both of them in the background.

If I then run my tests again with another spring rspec, the tests will start noticeably faster—but sadly, not in a way I can show you by running another set of commands. Since the part that is sped up is the part before Ruby starts timing the tests, the elapsed time shown in the terminal won't change. Trust me, though: depending on your setup you'll see a difference of 5 to 10 seconds. Given that our tests take less than a second to run, that's a significant change in how fast you can get feedback. It's the difference between being able to run tests without losing focus, and not being able to do so.

Spring is a little bit more aggressive about reloading than Rails is in development mode; for instance, it restarts itself when a file changes in the config/initializer directory. However, you will need to restart Spring if you add files or update gems, and I'm normally prepared to restart Spring any time things look the slightest bit strange.

You don't actually need to restart Spring; you can stop it with the command spring stop. Spring will automatically start back up the next time it is invoked.

Spring and Rails ship with commands for rails and rake. There are additional gems, including spring-commands-rspec and spring-commands-cucumber, that extend Spring to allow those tools to be aware of the Spring background applications.

Alternatively, you can connect Spring and Bundler by attaching Spring to Bundler's binstubs. Binstubs are small scripts that are placed in your application's bin directory and automatically invoke the command in the context of a bundle exec to ensure that all the correct gems are in the path and keep you from typing bundle exec before each spring command.

To integrate Spring and Bundler, run one command:

```
$ bundle exec spring binstub --all
```

This command will create new binstubs for executables that Bundler knows about, and it will augment the existing binstubs to be Spring-aware. The upshot is that after this command is created, we have at least three things:

- A bin/spring script that will start Spring.
- Springified versions of bin/rake and bin/rails that use the existing Spring setup. (Spring tweaks Rails' existing rake and rails scripts.)
- A new bin/rspec that uses the Spring setup to run RSpec.

All of these scripts are Bundler-aware—that's the point of having these bin/ versions of each script. If you have other executables known to Spring, you may have grown another bin script or two.

Once Spring is installed, you can invoke the binstubs directly as, for example, bin/rspec, and the Springified version will be invoked. (I have command-line aliases called brake, brails, and bspec. You could also tweak your PATH to look at a local bin directory first, though this is a potential security issue on projects you don't know.)

It Don't Mean a Thing If It Ain't Got That Spring

How useful all this is depends on what you're trying to do.

Essentially, Spring is useful to the extent that startup time is swamping your test runtime. This normally happens in one of the following cases:

- Your test suite runtime is less than your application startup time.
- Your test suite is slow, but you are willing to run just a small subset of your tests during much of your TDD development.
- Any port in a storm—it can't hurt to have a preloader, right?

I'll pause at this point to mention that I use Spring as part of my regular test practice. Pre–4.1 Rails, I used a similar tool, Zeus. So whatever else I say in the rest of this section, I do think that Spring is valuable in a lot of cases.

Spring is, however, one of those tools that best helps you when you're already helping yourself. If your test suite takes 20 minutes to run, you're already sunk and the 15 extra seconds to load Rails isn't going to help much.

Spring can also hide problems in a test suite by letting you run individual pieces of the suite much faster; it can reduce the pressure you might feel to speed up each individual test file. There's a Spring "uncanny valley": if an individual file takes 30 seconds, that's both fast enough for Spring to feel like a win and slow enough for it to be a serious drain on the entire project suite as you continue to add up 30-second files. You don't want to be there. It'll feel like your suite isn't getting any worse, but trust me—it is.

That said, if you're already stuck in a bad situation because you inherited it (or for whatever reason), Spring can be great and can allow you to have fast TDD feedback on the new stuff you're building without being tied to poor decisions of the past. Just don't keep making the same poor decisions.

Writing Faster Tests by Bypassing Rails

The other way to run tests without loading the entire Rails framework is to write tests that don't require the entire Rails framework.

That sounds crazy, I know, since we're writing a Rails application. Bear with me.

The tests we've written so far mostly fall into five groups:

- End-to-end tests. These tests require the entire Rails stack since we're testing the entire stack.
- Tests that use only ActiveRecord and need the database. Right now this group includes tests for ActiveRecord finder methods, and our action object tests that save to the database.
- Controller tests that require ActionPack and may or may not require ActiveRecord and may or may not touch the database.
- Tests that use ActiveRecord objects but don't touch the database.
- Tests that use no Rails-specific classes at all.

The topmost category will, broadly speaking, be slowest, and each step down should be a faster set of tests. Right now we don't have any tests in the bottom category. How do we move tests to the lower and faster categories in this list? And why is removing Rails helpful?

	Rails is not your application; it is a framework on which you build your application. Unless you work at Basecamp and actually develop Rails.
Prescription 44	

I'm indebted to Corey Haines and Gary Bernhardt for the ideas in this section, which have influenced me greatly. I particularly recommend you check out Corey's blog post "Speeding Up ActiveRecord Tests" and his book *Understanding the Four Rules of Simple Design*, as well as Gary's posts "Test Isolation Is About Avoiding Mocks" and "TDD, Straw Men, and Rhetoric."[7] [8] [9] [10]

Why Speed Is Important

Before I explain how we'll use this information to speed up our tests, let me make a pitch for the idea of being a little obsessive about test speed.

You're going to run your tests a lot.

If you're doing the kind of rapid-feedback TDD that we've been discussing up until now, you'll be running at least some of your tests nearly continuously, multiple times an hour. (Any exact number that I put here is going to seem shockingly high to people who aren't used to super-fast test feedback and shockingly low to those who are.) And you are probably not the only developer on your team. And it's likely that your entire test suite runs when you commit code to your repository via some kind of continuous build system.

That's thousands of runs. Tens of thousands. Hundreds of thousands if the project is big. The difference between a 10-second suite and a 1-minute suite (both of which are still relatively fast) becomes a big deal when you're trying to run the tests as often as you can.

The difference between a 1-second suite and a 10-second suite is still important. A 1-second suite allows you get feedback without breaking focus. 10-seconds, and you start to get tempted to check email or Twitter. If you've ever been able to work in an environment with near-instantaneous test feedback, you know it's an entirely different level of dealing with tests.

Worse, there's a slow acclimation that comes with a gradually increasing test suite. You'll add only a little bit of time to the test suite every day—practically nothing. But weeks and months of practically nothing lead you not to notice

---

7.   http://articles.coreyhaines.com/posts/active-record-spec-helper/
8.   https://leanpub.com/4rulesofsimpledesign
9.   https://www.destroyallsoftware.com/blog/2014/test-isolation-is-about-avoiding-mocks
10. https://www.destroyallsoftware.com/blog/2014/tdd-straw-men-and-rhetoric

that suddenly you have time to go get coffee during your test run. Preventing this gradual time creep takes vigilance.

> **Prescription 45** If you have enough time to break focus while your tests run, you aren't getting the full value of the TDD process.

Why Separation from Rails Is Important

The primary advantage of writing your tests to avoid Rails is that doing so encourages you to structure your code to better manage increasing complexity and change over time. Super-fast tests are just a side benefit.

Here are some of the advantages, which are related to the idea that there is a minimum of coupling between any two parts of the code:

- It's easier to change one element of the code if the impact of that change is limited in how it affects other parts of the code. Limiting the access that code has to the internals of other sections makes it easier to change those internals. In Rails terms, ActiveRecord associations and attributes often qualify as internals since they're based on an implementation detail—the naming convention of the underlying database. Putting lots of logic in Rails controllers and models encourages intertwining potentially unrelated functionality.
- The framework imposes generic names on common actions, whereas it is usually valuable to name specific items in your application after domain concepts. For example, order("year ASC") is less meaningful than chronological.
- The fewer details you need to worry about at once, the easier it is to understand code. It's easier to focus on the logic for allowing users access to a specific project if it's not thrown together in the same file with code for finding users, code to display full names, and code to list a user's undone tasks.

It's possible to overdo isolation to the point where the pieces of code are so small that your cognitive load goes back up as you try to put the pieces together. You probably aren't near that boundary yet.

Isolating in a Rails application like this is often mischaracterized as setting up your application to switch away from Rails. That's not the point. If you do need to switch from Rails, you're probably looking at significant code changes no matter how you organize your code. The point is to make your application best able to handle both the complexity in the current application and the inevitable changes over time.

That said, Rails itself does change. And it's even been known to throw in changes that are not backward compatible. When that happens, the less intertwined your application logic is with Rails logic, the easier your upgrade path.

However, the odds that this approach will cause the founder of Rails to call you an architecture astronaut remain pretty high.

> **Prescription 46** This is your regular reminder that software is complex and there are multiple paths to success.

Rails Test Prescriptions, Hold the Rails

The basic idea is isolation: isolating your objects from each other and isolating your code from Rails functionality that would require Rails to be loaded. Isolation means that different objects interact with each other over as small a set of methods as possible. It means objects, ideally, know nothing about the internal structure of other objects in the system.

This doesn't have to be all that complicated. We've been writing tests with reasonably good habits so far. To isolate our Project tests from anything other than ActiveRecord, all we need to do is change the header. We remove the require rails_helper call and replace it:

environment/01/gatherer/test/models/project_test.rb
```
require_relative '../active_record_test_helper'
require_relative '../../app/models/project'
require_relative '../../app/models/task'
```

Where once we had a single require, now we have three.

The first one is the most important; we've replaced our rails_helper (which loads the Rails environment) with an active_record_spec_helper (which only loads ActiveRecord). After that, since we're not loading Rails, we don't have access to Rails autoloading. As a result, we need to explicitly load the model files referenced in this test file—namely, Project and Task.

Let's take a closer look at active_record_spec_helper:

environment/01/gatherer/spec/active_record_spec_helper.rb
```
Line 1  require 'spec_helper'
     -  require 'active_record'
     -  require 'yaml'

     5  connection_info = YAML.load_file("config/database.yml")["test"]
     -  ActiveRecord::Base.establish_connection(connection_info)
```

```
   RSpec.configure do |config|
     config.around do |example|
10     ActiveRecord::Base.transaction do
         example.run
         raise ActiveRecord::Rollback
       end
     end
15 end
```

This code is based on Corey Haines's spec helper.[11]

First, we require a number of things. The critical part of this section is what is *not* there—namely, loading the Rails config/environment, which brings in the entire Rails system. We're loading ActiveRecord and YAML.

The next two lines, starting with line 5, load our test database information from the Rails database.yml and then dig into ActiveRecord to set up a connection to that database. This will enable our tests to save to and read from the same database setup we've been using, but again, without loading the entire Rails stack.

Finally, on line 10, we have to handle database cleanup. RSpec has a global around method that takes a block and allows you to insert code both before and after each spec. In this case we surround the spec with an ActiveRecord transaction, then execute the test with example.run, then roll back the database to its pretest state. If you need more-sophisticated database management, look at the DatabaseCleaner gem.[12]

With this helper and the additional requirement of our project and task files, we have all we need to run this test file directly from the command line without using the rake task provided by Rails:

```
% rspec spec/models/project_spec.rb
.................

Finished in 0.06155 seconds (files took 0.4728 seconds to load)
17 examples, 0 failures
```

We run rspec spec/models/project_spec.rb all by itself and it works, bypassing the Rails environment. RSpec 3's command line reports how long the file load takes preceding the test, so I can confidently tell you that on my machine the Rails version takes about 3.25 seconds and the non-Rails version takes about 0.5. That's not a bad savings, especially considering that the load time for the Rails version is only going to increase over time.

---

11. http://articles.coreyhaines.com/posts/active-record-spec-helper/
12. https://github.com/DatabaseCleaner/database_cleaner

One warning: if you separate rails and non-Rails tests you need to run your non-Rails tests separately. Otherwise Rails will load anyway and you'll lose the speed advantage and get some extra flakiness based on Rails being loaded at an arbitrary point in the suite. Also, SQLite seems to really, really not like combining regular Rails connections with this kind of ad hoc ActiveRecord connection.

active_record_test_helper in Minitest

The same Rails-bypassing test technique works in Minitest, but there are some minor differences based on the way the RSpec executable works versus the way Minitest works.

In Minitest, the active_record_test_helper looks like this:

```
environment/01/gatherer/test/active_record_test_helper.rb
require "minitest/autorun"
require "mocha/mini_test"
require 'active_record'
require 'active_support/test_case'
require 'minitest/reporters'

reporter_options = { color: true }
Minitest::Reporters.use!(
  [Minitest::Reporters::DefaultReporter.new(reporter_options)])

connection_info = YAML.load_file("config/database.yml")["test"]
ActiveRecord::Base.establish_connection(connection_info)

module ActiveSupport
  class TestCase
    teardown do
      ActiveRecord::Base.subclasses.each(&:delete_all)
    end
  end
end
```

This is based on a MiniTest version I got from Robert Evans on GitHub.[13]

The basic setup is similar. We load Minitest and ActiveRecord, and then some files that will help us in testing: minitest/autorun, which lets us run test files as standalone scripts; Mocha for mocks; active_support/test_case so we don't have to rewrite all our tests that use it; and minitest/reporters, which gives us color output at the terminal. We also have a couple of lines setting up the reporter.

---

13. https://gist.github.com/revans/4196367

By default, Minitest doesn't have the around behavior we used in RSpec. For the moment, we're doing a very simple and blunt thing, which is adding into our ActiveSupport::TestCase a teardown block that will be called after every test. It tells all known subclasses of ActiveRecord::Base to delete_all, cleaning up the database.

In practice this will likely be slower than the RSpec behavior, though for some reason SQLite seems to like it more. (If you want the around behavior in Minitest, you can get it with the minitest-around gem.)[14] And you can still use DatabaseCleaner if you want something fancier.

We then need to change the header of our test files as well. Here is a sample for our project_test:

environment/01/gatherer/test/models/project_test.rb
```
require_relative '../active_record_test_helper'
require_relative '../../app/models/project'
require_relative '../../app/models/task'
```

If you're trying to bypass Rails, don't use the Rails-provided rake testing tasks. All of them load the environment as a dependency even if you don't explicitly do so in your test helper.

> **Prescription 47** The only way to know the boundaries of a new coding tool is to go past them. Try things.

Action Tests without Rails

Limiting model tests to use only ActiveRecord doesn't seem like that big a win overall since almost by definition a model test doesn't explore anything beyond the model.

Ideally, we'd be able to also isolate our action object since those are specifically created to be plain Ruby objects. Also, if you aren't careful, testing these actions can be particularly slow because we potentially create and save a lot of model objects.

Our existing CreatesProject tests can be isolated without much trouble, although there are rather a lot of dependencies. The header looks like this:

environment/01/gatherer/spec/actions/creates_project_spec.rb
```
require_relative '../active_record_spec_helper'
require 'devise'
require 'devise/orm/active_record'
```

---

14. https://github.com/splattael/minitest-around>

```
require_relative '../../app/models/project'
require_relative '../../app/models/task'
require_relative '../../app/models/role'
require_relative '../../app/models/user'
require_relative '../../app/actions/creates_project'
```

About that list of dependencies: it seems kind of long. Especially since four of those require statements—the two devise lines, the role, and the user—are there only to support the User class. We need to import the User class in part because we have a line in the action that assigns the incoming user objects to project.users. That line causes Rails to autoload the User class, which brings in Role and indirectly brings in Devise because the user class calls the devise method to set up authentication.

That seems like a lot of dependency being brought in for a single line. When we were using Rails in this test, Rails autoload prevented us from having to care about dependencies. Now that we are specifying them explicitly, we can see how interconnected this test is.

We can remove this dependency from the action and the test by putting the dependency back in the Project method, which is already tied to users, and adding in some judicious test doubles to block the user from being called.

The new test looks like this:

`environment/02/gatherer/spec/actions/creates_project_spec.rb`
```
it "adds users to the project" do
  project = Project.new
  user = double
  expect(project).to receive(:add_users).with([user])
  allow(Project).to receive(:new).and_return(project)
  creator = CreatesProject.new(name: "Project Runway", users: [user])
  creator.build
end
```

We start the test with four lines setting up test doubles. There's a common pattern here, where we create a blank object of a certain type—in this case, Project—then stub Project.new to return that instance. This allows us to set further stubs on the specific project instance being used, secure in the knowledge that the code being tested will be using the same instance. Without stubbing Project.new, the new instance created in the action code would not have the stub assigned to the project instance in this test.

There are at least two other ways to handle this situation. We could use the RSpec framework's any_instance feature:

```
allow_any_instance_of(Project).to receive(:add_users).with([user])
```

This would save us a line in the setup. I try to avoid any_instance these days on the grounds that it's too big and broad a weapon for the job, I prefer being more specific about what I want the code to do. Alternatively, we could move the Project.new call to its own method inside the action object and stub that method, which I would be more likely to do.

For the preceding code to work, we need to move the project.users = call inside the Project class:

environment/02/gatherer/app/models/project.rb
```ruby
def add_users(users)
  self.users << users
end
```

And then we update CreatesProject to use that new method:

environment/02/gatherer/app/actions/creates_project.rb
```ruby
def build
  self.project = Project.new(name: name)
  project.tasks = convert_string_to_tasks
  project.add_users(users)
  project
end
```

And the tests pass again. We can now remove the four user-related require statements and the tests still pass.

What have we gained by writing our test this way and what have we lost?

This is tricky because the loss is up front and clear at the moment while the potential gain is further down the road. We've lost a small piece of Rails convenience by bypassing the Rails users association in favor of a method specifically designed to be part of the public API.

We've gained the ability to think about creating projects without dealing with the complexity of users. (Many Rails conveniences work against separation of concerns in a complex program, which is a good summary of the community's argument over this kind of code.)

This particular case is too small for that to seem like much of a win—an occupational hazard of trying to show object-oriented techniques to manage complexity is that they all look like crazy overkill when applied to your typical book-example-sized problem. In a more complicated problem, separating one wildly complex piece from another wildly complex piece can make it easier to deal with each part separately.

> **Prescription 48** You can use test doubles to remove test dependencies.

Removing dependencies starts to get more challenging as the underlying logic becomes more complex. For example, we might need some information about the user to create projects, most likely for access-control purposes. We might want to prevent a user from having created two projects with the same name, scoped to only the projects that particular user has created.

We have a few options for managing that complexity:

- We could just give up, add User back to the CreatesProject, and just deal with the dependency. I don't want to underestimate this option. Sometimes it's the correct option, or at least the minimally complex one.
- We can create a dummy User class inside the test and require that version of User rather than the ActiveRecord version. I don't recommend this, as it's really tricky to manage the namespaces and also hard to keep the dummy and the real user in sync.
- We can have some other object in the system filter the necessary information to CreatesProject. In the case of access information, the controller is a logical place for that; it's arguably the controller's role to police access to other services. In other cases, whoever invokes the CreatesProject action might be responsible for sending the necessary data as simple Ruby data, like a hash or even a simple struct.
- Similarly, we can create a wrapper object—ProjectCreatingUser or something—that wraps a user and provides an API for CreatesProject. In tests, the ProjectCreatingUser can easily stub information, making the dependency a single plain Ruby object rather than a complex tree of ActiveRecord objects.

The last two options may seem like way, way too much structure to you. (Maybe you came to Rails to avoid the kind of hyper-indirect object models that characterize, say, enterprise Java projects.) And sometimes I'd agree. In most cases I wouldn't start with this level of complexity and indirection. But I would refactor to it when things start to get complex—this kind of refactoring is much easier to do if you catch it early.

The point is that writing application tests that bypass Rails requires you to be more thoughtful about your dependencies (or, looked at from the other direction, writing tests that use Rails autoloading allows you to be sloppy about dependencies). However you choose to manage the dependencies, being aware of them is the first step in keeping your program easy to change over time.

> **Prescription 49** You don't need to start with elaborate object indirection, but it's useful when logic gets complicated.

Running Rails-Free Tests

If you're going to have some tests that run without loading the Rails environment, you need to be careful to run those tests separately from the slower Rails-loading tests. You lose the benefit of not loading Rails if some of your tests *load Rails*. Also, if you're doing any namespace munging in your fast tests, mixing and matching fast and slow tests is guaranteed to give weird errors.

The easiest way to manage running fast tests is to keep them in their own directory or directories and just pass those directories as arguments to ruby. In RSpec this is easy, as the rspec command will take directories or globs as arguments:

```
$ rspec spec/models spec/actions
```

In Minitest this is a little more complicated since we're loading ruby directly, and ruby doesn't handle file globs. We could create a rake task like this:

```
require 'rake/testtask'

Rake::TestTask.new(:fast) do |t|
  t.pattern = "test/{models,actions,values}/**/*_test.rb"
end
```

Or this way:

```
task :fast_tests do
  Dir.glob("test/{models,actions,values}/**/*_test.rb").each { |file| require file }
end
```

You can also do this directly from your shell if you think the rake tasks are too slow:

```
$ for file in test/{models,actions,values}/**/*_test.rb; do ruby $file; done
```

The side effect of the last approach is that each file will run and report separately, which may not be desirable.

Whatever you do, you probably want to make it a system alias, assign it a key shortcut, or do something else that is dependent on your own workflow. You want to be able to run these tests with as little effort as possible.

Recommendations for Faster Tests

The topic of Rails code structure and the attendant ability to write tests always winds up in a mixture of things everyone should try once, things I do regularly, things I wish I could do regularly, things I don't do but generally regret not doing, and so on.

In that spirit, a few recommendations:

- My current practice is to move complex transaction logic out of controllers into action objects, complex creation logic out of models and into factory objects, and view logic into presenters—all of those are plain, non-Rails Ruby objects. David Heinemeier Hansson thinks all of these lead to overly complicated code. That has not been my experience. You should try for yourself.

- I like to use SimpleDelegator to create a new object that has functionality that applies to an ActiveRecord object only some of the time—for example, logic about whether a user has access to a resource. Or logic for purchasing an item, which is needed only during the purchase process itself.

- Where I can, I like to use immutable value objects—for instance, taking a start and end date from an object and making a DateRange class or taking a name class from a first name, last name, etc. The value objects are super-fast to test, and tend to attract logic.

- In tests, I try to create as few objects as possible, touch the database as little as possible, and be aware of dependencies and places to mock that can limit the amount of setup a test needs.

- RSpec has a —profile option that shows you the slowest tests in a test run. You need to be careful with it (often the slow test will be the one that had the garbage collector run during it), but it's a good thing to run now and then and try to speed up your slowest tests.

- All that said, don't despair if you can't make this all work immediately. I've never quite been able to make an entire project work using the ActiveRecord-specific test helper. My main problem is not making an individual test run, and it's not keeping track of dependencies manually. Rather, my main problem has typically been integrating the separate sets of tests into the entire ecosystem of the project—that includes my ability to run the entire spec suite, other developers' ability to run the suite, extra continuous-integration setup, and the like. Being aware of dependencies (and using Spring) provides most of the benefit with a fraction of the fuss. Still, it's probably something I could be more aggressive on; most of my codebases wind up with tests suites that are slower than I'd like.

A lot of this advice is particularly difficult to apply to legacy codebases that have not been built to support these ideas. The next chapter talks about strategies for dealing with the particular issues of legacy code.

## CHAPTER 16

Testing Legacy Code

You won't always get to start from scratch.

There's a strong possibility that you'll need to bring your testing skills to bear on a codebase that already exists. A codebase that—gasp—may not have a complete or accurate test suite to guide you.

Not all that long ago, there were no Rails legacy projects. Now there are Rails codebases that are old enough to attend kindergarten and beyond. These codebases tend to be large, and almost by definition they aren't using the latest tools. All the advice in this book so far is well and good, but what if you're not starting your TDD experience with a new application? How does testing change when you're dealing with a legacy codebase?

Entire books have been written on working with legacy codebases. In this chapter we'll focus on techniques for getting legacy code under test. There are many other issues you'll need to deal with in a legacy codebase. Getting the legacy system up and running can be a chore, and there's a variety of techniques for safely adding features to or refactoring existing code. We'll discuss those topics here only as they intersect with testing. For a more detailed look at managing a legacy project, check out Michael Feathers's excellent *Working Effectively with Legacy Code [Fea04]*.

What's a Legacy?

The phrase "legacy code" is often used as a synonym for "bad code." While the two categories clearly overlap, assuming the legacy code is always awful isn't the most helpful way to think about a legacy.

What makes code "legacy" is not the quality, but the extent to which you have access to the context in which it was created and the reasons previous developers made the choices they made.

> **Prescription 50** When dealing with legacy code, respect code that works. You don't know what constraints the previous coders worked under.

Legacy code is scary—not because it's bad, but because you don't know what parts of the design are incidental and what parts are critical. When two different actions are backed by the same method but one of them has a bug, you don't know whether the other action is intended to have the current behavior.

When dealing with legacy code we use testing to do the following:

- Describe the current behavior of the code
- Make sure our code changes have no unintended consequences
- Promote isolation of new features

Set Expectations

You aren't going to convert this beast of an old project into a marvel of elegant, test-driven code overnight. And trying to do so is probably not a good idea. When you're exposed to a new codebase, you should do the following:

- If it makes you feel better, for 15 minutes shake your fists and curse the previous programmer's name (doubly effective if the previous programmer was you).

- Then move on and start working with the codebase. It's yours now.

If you're like me, the temptation to immediately fix everything and/or add tests to everything is pretty strong. Lie down until the feeling passes.

There are two reasons it's a bad idea to do nothing but add test coverage to a legacy project first thing. From a purely logistical standpoint, when you take over a legacy project you're often expected to do something with it immediately. Your new client may not perceive going off in the corner and doing nothing but writing tests for weeks at a time as forward motion. Every situation is different, but it's rare to find a client that considers test coverage a "quick win."

The second problem has to do with the often-noted paradox of legacy development. Legacy code, by its nature, is often too interdependent or poorly understood to make it easy to unit-test without substantial refactoring. However, substantial refactoring without unit tests is a great way to introduce bugs into the codebase—especially when working with new code that you may not fully understand. This is also unlikely to be considered a "quick win."

Working code that does not need to be changed explicitly needs *not* to be changed. If it's working and the requirements haven't changed, waking up the sleeping bear is not your highest priority.

What will work is to proceed incrementally, making small steps that you can verify. You need to tweak the existing code as little as possible to get it to a state you can live with. Then you can ensure that the new code you write is as good, and as tested, as possible. Over time, continually making small improvements to existing code while writing new code as best you can will make the overall codebase better.

Getting Started with Legacy Code

When you're presented with a new codebase for the first time, your first job is to figure out exactly what the heck is going on. Toward that end, there are three things you should do immediately.

Get It in Source Control

These days it probably is already under source control, but you can't be too careful. Make sure you have all the access to the repository that you need. While starting on a new legacy codebase is not the time to get fancy with new tools, you will be much better served by using Git or some other source-control system that lets you easily create and manipulate branches. This will enable you to easily explore changes to the codebase using branches as scratch pads that can be kept or discarded as needed.

Get It Running

If the legacy project was conceived without much knowledge of Rails community practices (evidenced by the lack of tests), it won't be a surprise if the production environment is also a little sketchy. Conventional wisdom suggests that your development, staging, and production environments should be as similar as possible to prevent environment-specific errors. And although this is true in general, if your legacy project is being run by some random goofy server setup, it may be difficult or impossible to replicate that setup on your staging server, let alone your development machine.

If the exact production environment isn't an option, the staging and development environments should be as generic as possible. If you can, push to migrate the production environment to a less fragile and more standard environment as soon as possible.

Get the Test Suite Running

At first glance this may strike you as a totally useless piece of advice. If the legacy team has been ignoring tests, nothing is there, right? Of course everything will run.

Well, not necessarily. There are at least two things you need to look out for. Even if the previous coders totally ignored tests, Rails may still have autogenerated test code. The most likely problem you'll run into is that fixtures, generated when the initial model was created, have moved out of date. If columns were deleted or renamed, the fixtures won't load and you'll get errors galore. It's only slightly less likely that the generated controller tests for a generated scaffold have drifted out of date with the code; if authentication and roles were added later, for example, you'll need to match that authentication in the tests.

In some ways your job is harder if the previous team flirted with writing tests and then gave it up because they had not yet read this book (I'm assuming). In that case, you're likely to have all kinds of tests that may or may not have passed at one point and have since been broken by later code—combined with inattention. You have to assume for the moment that the code is right and the tests are wrong—the exact opposite of a standard TDD scenario. (Mike Gunderloy presents a simple rule for initial triage of legacy tests in his *Rails Rescue Handbook*; if you can't figure out what a test is doing in five minutes, delete it.)

Take this opportunity to learn how the legacy code works, but do not change the code to match the tests at this point. If you can't figure out how to make a test pass, comment it out or delete it, add a note, and come back to it when you have a more thorough test scaffold in place. As we've discussed, test coverage is not the priority at this stage. The priority is a green test run that you can use as a base for future work.

Test-Driven Exploration

Testing a legacy codebase starts in earnest when there is a change to make. Often the first order of business on a new project is to deal with a critical bug left by the previous team—something that must be accomplished while preserving existing behavior and that does not demand a dramatic refactoring of the application.

In this case, there are two goals to getting the code under test. You want to be able to tell when the bug has been fixed. This step involves a more or less standard TDD bug-fixing session with one or more failing tests isolating the bug. The tests should pass when the bug is fixed. Also, you must confirm that any existing correct behavior hasn't been compromised. In a project that was TDD from the beginning you'd already have this ability, but in a testless legacy project you need to build up that coverage.

Generally speaking, tests against an existing system come in two flavors: black-box and white-box testing—the phrases far predate software testing and apply to any kind of test process. A black-box test is so called because it ignores the internal structure of the application and tests only top-level input into the system and the output that is returned. Conversely, a white-box test uses knowledge about system internals to explicitly test specific paths through the code.

Black-Box Testing

We've already talked about black-box testing of Rails applications in this book, back in Chapter 10, *Integration Testing with Capybara and Cucumber*, on page 177. According to our definition, a black-box test of a Rails application works only at the level of user input and system output, typically HTML. That sounds a lot like a Cucumber or Capybara integration test. Since integration testing works from outside the normal Rails code, it's ideal for interaction with legacy code.

The integration tests interact with the system as a user would. Since there is no interaction with the code's internal structure, it's possible to write integration tests no matter how gunky the code is.

Integration testing can be useful in a bug situation because bugs are often specified in terms of the users' actions and responses. These actions and responses are often reasonably straightforward to translate to Cucumber or Capybara, and it's easy to recognize if you've changed the behavior. In addition, it's not unheard of for a codebase with few tests also to lack written requirements; the acceptance tests act as baseline requirements as you move forward.

The general plan here is to use integration testing to quickly write high-level tests surrounding both the bug and the correct behavior it is related to—not to try and cover the entire application, but to cover the entire feature to be able to discover regressions.

Acceptance-level tests are relatively easy to write for a legacy application but have somewhat limited utility. An integration test won't tell you where in the application you need to make the change that fixes the bug or adds the feature. Also, integration tests tend to run slowly, so you don't want them to be the only part of your test arsenal.

White-Box Testing

Eventually, there's no way around writing real unit tests. Two distinct kinds of user tests are helpful when dealing with legacy applications. We'll talk about the standard TDD tests in a moment; first let's examine the unit test equivalent of the integration tests discussed in the previous section. These tests are used to figure out what is going on in the application—a process we might call test-driven exploration (TDE) if we didn't have enough three-letter acronyms already.

The basic process is straightforward: the difficulty of implementation depends on just how tangled the code is. First, select a method to test. Ideally the method should be related to a change you're planning to make in the app, although this process also works for "what is going on here?" exploration.

For this method, let's write a test we know will fail. We don't need to go deep into the internals for this. We're sonar—sending a test into the depths of the code and hoping to get a signal back:

```
it "calculates sales tax" do
  user = User.create(state: :il)
  order = user.orders.create
  order.line_items.create(:price => 250)
  order.line_items.create(:price => 300)
  expect(order.sales_tax).to eq(-300_000)
end
```

We have a simple, straightforward test, right up until the last line. (Insert cheesy DJ scratch-record sound effect.) We don't really expect the sales tax to be –300,000 dollars. But we don't want to guess what it is; we'll let the app tell us. Run the test. At this point, one of two things will happen. (Well, three things, if you include the remote possibility that the sales tax really is –300,000 dollars, in which case we might have bigger problems.)

Most of the time the test will error out because there is some object dependency we didn't know about, some value is not as expected, or we have otherwise disturbed the delicate balance that our legacy app needs to function. We'll need to figure out how to smooth things over. Often we'll have to create more objects. In this example, we might explicitly create product objects. The object chain can get unwieldy, which is okay at this point: the goal is to understand what's happening. If the code itself is unwieldy, let the test stand as a monument to things that need to be changed.

Eventually we run out of errors, the application spits out the sales tax, and the test has a normal validation failure—since, again, the answer probably isn't –300,000. At this point we insert the actual value into the test and declare victory. We have some test coverage and a greater understanding of how the application fits together. It's time to move on to the next test, most likely trying the existing method in some other test case, such as one designed to trigger a bad response.

We don't care if the value for the sales tax is correct. Well, we care in the sense that calculating sales tax is important from a business perspective; however, from a test perspective we must assume that the code is correct so we have a stable base when we start making changes because of all the bugs.

> **Prescription 51** When writing initial unit tests for legacy code, use the test to explore the code's behavior. Try to write a passing test without changing code.

Pry can be our friend and ally during this exploration process. The console is a great way to try some of these object interactions quickly. Once we figure things out in the console, we transfer the commands to the test so they can be run repeatedly.

What Tool Should I Use? (Legacy Edition)

Taking over a legacy codebase has the side effect of clarifying tool decisions we might otherwise agonize over—meaning if the previous coder used a tool and there's anything salvageable, use that tool. We don't want to be in the position of adding code coverage while juggling our RSpec tests with a batch of existing Minitest tests. I recommend adding a factory tool if there isn't one already in the mix. It's likely that writing tests for the legacy app will require creating complete chains of related objects. Setting up a factory tool to create the associations all at once saves a lot of time.

There are, of course, exceptions to this rule. Two that spring to mind are when the original developer has chosen a tool that's unsuitable for supporting the kind of testing weight we want to put on it. More often, the existing tests are useless and it's best to delete them quickly and start over, at which point we can pick whatever tools we want.

Dependency Removal

Dependencies are the single most challenging issue in legacy testing. Perhaps the greatest virtue of well-done TDD code is that the tests force individual pieces of the code to be maximally independent of each other.

Without tests, legacy code tends to be highly interdependent. This makes adding tests difficult in several ways: multiple objects might need to be created to test a single method, or it might be hard to limit a test to a true functional unit if that unit is hard to reach or encased in some massive 300-line method. There are ways to have the code we need to test be separate enough to enable the tests we must write.

Keep Things Separate

Perhaps the easiest way to keep our new code from being dependent on legacy code is to separate it ourselves. Where possible, write new code in new methods or new classes, and merely call those from the existing legacy mess. In theory this leaves our new code unencumbered enough to be written via TDD.

Let's try a brief example. Consider a kind of messy method from a social-networking site called Flitter:

```ruby
class Flit
  def process_flit
    if text =~ /##/
      flit.text = "testing: remove this code after 3/10/10"
    end
    if text.ends_with?("%fb%")
      send_to_facebook
    else if user.flits_in_last_day > 423
      return
    end
    flit_server.check_for_mentions(self)
    flit_server.follower_list(user)
    user.update_attributes(:flit_count => user.flit_count + 1)
    # and so it goes…
  end
end
```

Within this tangled mess, we must add a new feature: if a flit contains text of the form $username, the user in question must be informed of the message. We could just add another if statement in the long line of if statements already in the method, but then it would be very hard to test the new behavior without testing all the process_flit apparatus, which brings in all kinds of other stuff. (In real life this method could be 300 lines, and for all we know it could invoke PayPal.)

Instead we add a method check_for_dollar_sign, and then call that method in the appropriate place inside process_flit, writing the new method using regular TDD.

If we're feeling adventurous and it seems plausible, a mock test to confirm that process_flit calls check_for_dollar_sign might also be appropriate.

If we're adding or extracting a lot of functionality, we might consider creating our own separate class rather than just a method. One sign that a new class is warranted is if it passes the same set of instance variables to multiple methods. I'm a big fan of classes that represent processes and replace long complex methods. For testing purposes, moving new code to a new class can make testing the new code easier because the new code is less dependent on the existing application.

Although this technique helps us make a clean break from the legacy code, it has the short-term effect of making the code more opaque. In the words of Michael Feathers, "When you break dependencies in legacy code, you often have to suspend your sense of aesthetics a bit." To put it another way, you know how when you're cleaning off your desk, you have an intermediate stage in which the room is covered in piles of paper and it looks like an even bigger mess? Or is that just me? In any case, we're in an intermediate state here, between the undifferentiated mass of the original and the nicely factored and organized new version. Building up the test suite one broken dependency at a time moves us steadily toward cleaner code.

Legacy Databases, Testing, and You

If our legacy application has only a nodding relationship with Rails common standards, chances are the database is also a mess. Many issues that plague a legacy database can be frustrating (such as odd naming conventions or unusual use of ActiveRecord features), but they don't affect our ability to test the features.

We do need to be careful if the database has added constraints that are not evident in the code. Typically this involves column constraints that go beyond any validations specified in the ActiveRecord model or foreign key constraints that are not specified anywhere in the Rails code. Foreign key constraints are hardest to deal with. Rails has no native mechanism for specifying them, but they are beloved by database admins the world over.

From a testing perspective, the problem is twofold. First there is business logic outside the Rails code and in the database, where it is hard to find, test, and change. Even worse, foreign key constraints add dependencies that require certain objects to be created together. In a test environment, that kind of dependency leads to mysterious bugs: the database doesn't let you create test data, and there are objects that need to be created that have nothing to do with the test but are there only to make the database happy. Keep a close eye on this in a legacy application created by a database-heavy development team that didn't trust ActiveRecord.

Using Mock Objects to Remove Dependencies

If you don't want to start off at 20,000 feet with acceptance tests, mock-object testing is another way to get tests started without disrupting the untested code.

In a legacy context, the advantage to using mock objects is their ability to isolate a single class and method from the rest of the application. When working with a legacy application, this allows us to temporarily put aside the issue of how shaky the rest of the application may be and focus on the single part we're trying to figure out at that very moment.

In practice this is very similar to the test-double behavior-centric tests we saw in Chapter 7, *Using Test Doubles as Mocks and Stubs*, on page 117, except that the code already exists so we don't have the element of designing the API.

Let's look at an example. Take the following legacy method (which we can assume is part of some kind of nebulous order model):

```ruby
def calculate_order_status
  self.total = 0
  line_items.each do |item|
    if item.quantity.blank?
      LineItem.delete(item.id)
      next
    end
    if item.cost.nil? then item.cost = 0 end
    if credit_card_is_valid? && item.ready_to_ship?
      self.total += item.cost * item.quantity
    end
  end
  self.to_be_paid = self.total - self.amount_paid
  if self.to_be_paid == 0
    self.paid_in_full = true
  end
end
```

This code is a bit of a mess. (It is a special and weird kind of fun to write deliberately awful example code.) It's doing things that should be part of the LineItem class, and it probably could stand to be split. Of course, this example barely scratches the surface of how tangled a poorly written legacy system might be. (You really want to beware the ones with 300-plus-line controller methods.)

This code uses a number of things that are probably attributes that could be set with data, such as amount_paid or item.quantity, but it also calls a few things that could be complex methods in their own right, such as credit_card_is_valid? or item.ready_to_ship.

A possible test for this code would mock those methods and might look like this (assume we're using factory_girl):

```
Line 1   it "calculates order status" do
           order = FactoryGirl.create(:order, amount_paid: 2.50)
           expect(order).to receive(:credit_card_is_valid?).at_least(:once).and_return(true)
           item1 = FactoryGirl.create(:line_item, quantity: 1, cost: 3.50)
     5     expect(item1).to receive(:ready_to_ship?).and_return(true)
           item2 = FactoryGirl.create(:line_item, quantity: 2, cost: 5)
           expect(item2).to receive(:ready_to_ship?).and_return(false)
           order.line_items << [item1, item2]
           order.calculate_order_status
    10     assert_equal 3.50, order.total
           assert !order.paid_in_full
         end
```

Lines 2 and 3 set up the order and a mock for the credit_card_is_valid? method. (We're using factory_girl's create method even though it saves to the database, because it's the least likely to disrupt a fragile method.) This can be switched to build_stubbed after the test passes. Lines 4–8 set up individual items, with the actual action of the test taking place in line 9 and the last lines performing the validation.

In a full test suite we'd test a couple of other combinations of values, so some of the mock setup would probably be extracted to a repeatable method—either an explicit setup block or a method that is called by each test.

The strength of this process is that it allows us to unit-test without further tangling the existing code logic: it's possible that credit_card_is_valid? depends on another three different attributes of the order, the user, or the payment system, and that's a mess we don't want to get into at this moment. The mock test lets us isolate logic issues. This style of mock-object testing also limits test coverage to the method under test, making the coverage report more accurate.

However, there are some problems to watch out for. It can become time-consuming to set up the external mocks for a complex method, and we run the same risk as with any mock-object testing—namely, that our test becomes a tautology because it's just parroting the input to the mock objects. We can avoid that problem by trying not to mock the data of the exact object under test.

Find the Seam

Mock objects are a specific version of a more general technique for working with legacy code, which involves finding *seams* in the code and exploiting them to make testing the legacy functionality possible

A seam is a place where we can change our application's behavior without changing the actual code. A mock object acts as a seam because adding the mock object, which happens in the test, changes the behavior of the code by mandating a specific response to a method call without executing the method. Again, the behavior of the method under test changes in the test environment without affecting behavior in production and without changing the existing development code.

It sounds magical, but the basic idea is simple and Ruby makes it easy to execute. We redirect a method call from its intended target to some other code that we want to run during tests. A mock object does this by replacing the entire method call with a return value, but the generic form lets us do anything we want instead of the method call.

We might create our own object if we wanted a side effect that a mock package wouldn't normally provide, such as diagnostic logging. (Feathers calls this a *pebble*: a fake object that logs its own path through the code.) Alternatively, we might want a more elaborate processing of arguments or state than a mock can easily provide—to re-create the output of a web service our application depends on, for example. (Even if the mock library allows us to pass an arbitrary block as the result of the stubbed call, it's often more readable to just create our own object.)

Let's take some sample Ruby code that we want to test. In this sample, flit_server is an object in our system representing an internal server, and those innocent-looking calls are actually genuine external service calls to a real server that exists in production but not in the test:

```ruby
def process_flit
  # a bunch of messy stuff
  flit_server.check_for_mentions(self)
  # more messy stuff
  flit_server.follower_list(user)
  # more messy stuff
end
```

Now we need to get the process_flit method under test. The test might look like this:

```
it "processes a flit correctly if it has followers" do
  user = User.create(screen_name: "zot")
  follower = user.followers.create(screen_name: "jennyw")
  flit = Flit.new(user, "Hello to $jennyw, How are things on earth?")
  flit.process_flit
  expect(follower.timeline.size).to eq(1)
end
```

For this test to work, we need to prevent the flit_server object in the original code from calling the production server that will not exist in the test environment. For the sake of argument, we'll assume there's a compelling reason a normal mock package can't be used here—possibly because the flit_server object is too tightly intertwined with the rest of the code. We have two problems to solve. We need to create a flit_server object that will perform test-safe activities when called, and we need to inject that object into the test so it is the object used when the method is run under test.

Luckily, Ruby is extremely flexible when it comes to redirecting code execution. (Of course, this is exactly the kind of flexibility that drives security-minded programmers from other languages crazy. But here we're using for it good, not evil.) In a compiled object-oriented language, we might have to create a new subclass of the expected object and override the methods in question. We can do that in Ruby, too:

```
class TestFlitServer < FlitServer
  def check_for_mentions(flit)
    # test code
  end

  def follower_list(user)
    # test code
  end
end
```

Depending on the details of the FlitServer class, we may have to override other methods, such as the constructor.

There are a couple of other Ruby ways to do something similar. Rather than create a subclass, we can create an instance for testing and add overriding methods to that instance's singleton class.

That class might be defined like this:

```ruby
test_server = FlitServer.new
class << test_server
  def check_for_mentions(flit)
    # test code
  end
  def follower_list(user)
    # test code
  end
end
```

Alternatively, we could create a complete dummy class that covers the calls made by our method under test. Since Ruby doesn't do any type checking beyond seeing whether the object responds to methods, that's perfectly fine.

```ruby
class FakeServer
  def check_for_mentions(flit)
    # test code
  end
  def follower_list(user)
    # test code
  end
end
```

Now we need to inject our new object into the test code. In some sense we're reimplementing what a mock-object package would be doing. We can try to inject in the test itself by doing the same thing to the flit object that we did for the flit_server object. Here's an example:

```ruby
Class TestFlit < Flit
  def flit_server
    TestFlitServer.new
  end
end
```

```ruby
it "processes a flit correctly if it has followers" do
  user = User.create(screen_name: "zot")
  follower = user.followers.create(screen_name: "jennyw")
  flit = TestFlit.new(user, "Hello to $jennyw, How are things on earth?")
  flit.process_flit
  expect(follower.timeline.size).to eq(1)
end
```

In this case we're mimicking the first option by subclassing Flit. The two options shown earlier also have analogous usages inside the test.

If we're willing to allow a little bit of manipulation of the original code, we can use Ruby's default arguments to get an almost-seam:

```ruby
def process_flit(flit_server = nil)
  flit_server ||= self.flit_server
  # a bunch of messy stuff
  flit_server.check_for_mentions(self)
  # more messy stuff
  flit_server.follower_list(user)
  # more messy stuff
end
```

In the new method, flit_server is a local, which, if not passed as an argument, is given the value of the object's instance method. Thanks to the magic of Ruby's ||= operator, if the argument is passed a value, the passed value is used for the rest of the method. The existing legacy code, which does not use this argument, behaves as is. But it gives us a lever to insert our own server in the test by calling process_flit with the test server as an argument:

```ruby
it "processes a flit correctly if it has followers" do
  user = User.create(screen_name: "zot")
  follower = user.followers.create(screen_name: "jennyw")
  flit = Flit.new(user, "Hello to $jennyw, How are things on earth?")
  flit.process_flit(TestFlitServer.new)
  expect(follower.timeline.size).to eq(1)
end
```

Although this mechanism is slightly intrusive to the original code, you'll probably find you use this pattern often, not just for testing code but also as you add new features to existing code. The default argument lets new code have new behavior while leaving old code behavior untouched.

Each legacy program you work on is going to have its own quirks and require its own kind of creativity, using these methods or others to bring the code the kind of test coverage needed to confidently move forward with bug fixes and new features. As you tackle new problems, remember that reducing dependencies makes it easier to test your code, makes the code cleaner, and makes future work that much easier.

Don't Look Back

It's almost certainly not worth your time and effort to cover an entire complex legacy application before writing any code. I love tests, but the risks involved in doing that much coverage work at once are high, especially if the customer is expecting you to start working on new functionality.

You draw a line in the sand and start working in a test-driven mode moving forward. One critical element of moving forward is to ensure that every bug fix starts by writing a failing test somewhere—whether unit, functional, or integration. This is a good way to ramp up tests on your project and it allows you to organically build test coverage over time with relatively small risk to your deadlines and fairly little chance of breaking existing functionality.

Similarly, new features must be added using a TDD process. In the beginning this often requires the heightened use of mock objects, but over time the codebase and the test coverage both improve.

If you're like me, the temptation to clean up the entire codebase at once can be almost overwhelming. In this situation, lie down until the feeling passes or you're so close to your deadline that fixing everything is no longer a viable option.

Finally, *do one thing at a time, to the extent possible*. Don't extend test coverage while you're adding new functionality. And don't try to clean the code up while you're extending test coverage (occasionally this will be unavoidable, but keep it to a minimum). The fewer things you have moving at any one time, the easier it will be to identify the culprit when things go wrong.

Bibliography

[FBBO99] Martin Fowler, Kent Beck, John Brant, William Opdyke, and Don Roberts. *Refactoring: Improving the Design of Existing Code*. Addison-Wesley, Reading, MA, 1999.

[Fea04] Michael Feathers. *Working Effectively with Legacy Code*. Prentice Hall, Englewood Cliffs, NJ, 2004.

[Hen13] Elisabeth Hendrickson. *Explore It!: Reduce Risk and Increase Confidence with Exploratory Testing*. The Pragmatic Bookshelf, Raleigh, NC and Dallas, TX, 2013.

[Mes07] Gerard Meszaros. *xUnit Test Patterns*. Addison-Wesley, Reading, MA, 2007.

[RTH13] Sam Ruby, Dave Thomas, and David Heinemeier Hansson. *Agile Web Development with Rails 4*. The Pragmatic Bookshelf, Raleigh, NC and Dallas, TX, 2013.

[Wie03] Karl Wiegers. *Software Requirements, 2nd Edition*. Microsoft Press, Redmond, WA, 2003.

Index

Explore Testing and Cucumber

Explore the uncharted waters of exploratory testing and beef up your automated testing with more Cucumber—now for Java, too.

Explore It!

Uncover surprises, risks, and potentially serious bugs with exploratory testing. Rather than designing all tests in advance, explorers design and execute small, rapid experiments, using what they learned from the last little experiment to inform the next. Learn essential skills of a master explorer, including how to analyze software to discover key points of vulnerability, how to design experiments on the fly, how to hone your observation skills, and how to focus your efforts.

Elisabeth Hendrickson
(160 pages) ISBN: 9781937785024. $29
https://pragprog.com/book/ehxta

The Cucumber for Java Book

Teams working on the JVM can now say goodbye forever to misunderstood requirements, tedious manual acceptance tests, and out-of-date documentation. Cucumber—the popular, open-source tool that helps teams communicate more effectively with their customers—now has a Java version, and our bestselling *Cucumber Book* has been updated to match. *The Cucumber for Java Book* has the same great advice about how to deliver rock-solid applications collaboratively, but with all code completely rewritten in Java. New chapters cover features unique to the Java version of Cucumber, and reflect insights from the Cucumber team since the original book was published.

Seb Rose, Matt Wynne & Aslak Hellesoy
(250 pages) ISBN: 9781941222294. $36
https://pragprog.com/book/srjcuc

Advanced Ruby and Rails

What used to be the realm of experts is fast becoming the stuff of day-to-day development—jump to the head of the class today.

Crafting Rails 4 Applications

Get ready to see Rails as you've never seen it before. Learn how to extend the framework, change its behavior, and replace whole components to bend it to your will. Eight different test-driven tutorials will help you understand Rails' inner workings and prepare you to tackle complicated projects with solutions that are well-tested, modular, and easy to maintain.

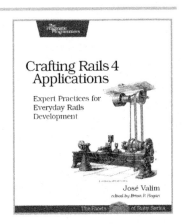

This second edition of the bestselling *Crafting Rails Applications* has been updated to Rails 4 and discusses new topics such as streaming, mountable engines, and thread safety.

José Valim
(200 pages) ISBN: 9781937785550. $36
https://pragprog.com/book/jvrails2

Metaprogramming Ruby 2

Write powerful Ruby code that is easy to maintain and change. With metaprogramming, you can produce elegant, clean, and beautiful programs. Once the domain of expert Rubyists, metaprogramming is now accessible to programmers of all levels. This thoroughly revised and updated second edition of the bestselling *Metaprogramming Ruby* explains metaprogramming in a down-to-earth style and arms you with a practical toolbox that will help you write your best Ruby code ever.

Paolo Perrotta
(250 pages) ISBN: 9781941222126. $38
https://pragprog.com/book/ppmetr2

Seven in Seven

From Web Frameworks to Concurrency Models, see what the rest of the world is doing with this introduction to seven different approaches.

Seven Web Frameworks in Seven Weeks

Whether you need a new tool or just inspiration, *Seven Web Frameworks in Seven Weeks* explores modern options, giving you a taste of each with ideas that will help you create better apps. You'll see frameworks that leverage modern programming languages, employ unique architectures, live client-side instead of server-side, or embrace type systems. You'll see everything from familiar Ruby and JavaScript to the more exotic Erlang, Haskell, and Clojure.

Jack Moffitt, Fred Daoud
(302 pages) ISBN: 9781937785635. $38
https://pragprog.com/book/7web

Seven Concurrency Models in Seven Weeks

Your software needs to leverage multiple cores, handle thousands of users and terabytes of data, and continue working in the face of both hardware and software failure. Concurrency and parallelism are the keys, and *Seven Concurrency Models in Seven Weeks* equips you for this new world. See how emerging technologies such as actors and functional programming address issues with traditional threads and locks development. Learn how to exploit the parallelism in your computer's GPU and leverage clusters of machines with MapReduce and Stream Processing. And do it all with the confidence that comes from using tools that help you write crystal clear, high-quality code.

Paul Butcher
(296 pages) ISBN: 9781937785659. $38
https://pragprog.com/book/pb7con

The Pragmatic Bookshelf

The Pragmatic Bookshelf features books written by developers for developers. The titles continue the well-known Pragmatic Programmer style and continue to garner awards and rave reviews. As development gets more and more difficult, the Pragmatic Programmers will be there with more titles and products to help you stay on top of your game.

Visit Us Online

This Book's Home Page
https://pragprog.com/book/nrtest2
Source code from this book, errata, and other resources. Come give us feedback, too!

Register for Updates
https://pragprog.com/updates
Be notified when updates and new books become available.

Join the Community
https://pragprog.com/community
Read our weblogs, join our online discussions, participate in our mailing list, interact with our wiki, and benefit from the experience of other Pragmatic Programmers.

New and Noteworthy
https://pragprog.com/news
Check out the latest pragmatic developments, new titles and other offerings.

Save on the eBook

Save on the eBook versions of this title. Owning the paper version of this book entitles you to purchase the electronic versions at a terrific discount.

PDFs are great for carrying around on your laptop—they are hyperlinked, have color, and are fully searchable. Most titles are also available for the iPhone and iPod touch, Amazon Kindle, and other popular e-book readers.

Buy now at *https://pragprog.com/coupon*

Contact Us

Online Orders:	*https://pragprog.com/catalog*
Customer Service:	*support@pragprog.com*
International Rights:	*translations@pragprog.com*
Academic Use:	*academic@pragprog.com*
Write for Us:	*http://write-for-us.pragprog.com*
Or Call:	+1 800-699-7764

CPSIA information can be obtained at www.ICGtesting.com
Printed in the USA
BVOW08s0851050115

381960BV00017B/236/P